LAWYER'S DESK BOOK

TENTH EDITION

by Dana Shilling

1997 SUPPLEMENT

PRENTICE HALL

Library of Congress Cataloging-in-Publication Data

Lawyer's desk book / by Dana Shilling. — 10th ed., 1997 Supplement
   p.   cm.
  Includes bibliographical references and index.
  ISBN 0-13-266248-5
    1. Law—United States.   2. Practice of Law—United States.
I. Shilling, Dana.
KF386.L39   1996
349.73—dc20
[347.3]
                                         95-13736
                                            CIP

This publication is designed to provide accurate and authoritative information in regard to the subject matter covered. It is sold with the understanding that the publisher is not engaged in rendering legal, accounting, or other professional service. If legal advice or other expert assistance is required, the services of a competent professional person should be sought.

—From a Declaration of Principles jointly adopted by a Committee of the American Bar Association and a Committee of Publishers and Associations.

Printed in the United States of America

10 9 8 7 6 5 4 3 2 1

ISBN 0-13-226248-5

ATTENTION: CORPORATIONS AND SCHOOLS

Prentice Hall books are available at quantity discounts with bulk purchase for educational, business, or sales promotional use. For information, please write to: Prentice Hall Career & Personal Development Special Sales, 113 Sylvan Avenue, Englewood Cliffs, NJ 07632. Please supply: title of book, ISBN number, quantity, how the book will be used, date needed.

PRENTICE HALL
Career & Personal Development
Englewood Cliffs, New Jersey 07632
A Simon & Schuster Company

On the World Wide Web at http://www.phdirect.com

Prentice-Hall International (UK) Limited, London
Prentice-Hall of Australia Pty. Limited, Sydney
Prentice-Hall Canada, Inc., Toronto
Prentice-Hall Hispanoamericana, S.A., Mexico
Prentice-Hall of India Private Limited, New Delhi
Prentice-Hall of Japan, Inc., Tokyo
Simon & Schuster Asia Pte. Ltd., Singapore
Editora Prentice-Hall do Brasil, Ltda., Rio de Janeiro

INTRODUCTION

This is the first Supplement to the revised Tenth Edition published in 1995. As such, it deals predominantly with the legal events of 1995. However, some developments from late 1994, not included in the Tenth Edition, are discussed here, as are some "late-breaking developments" in the first quarter of 1996, up to press time.

In addition to discussion of statutes and cases supplementing the Tenth Edition, this Supplement includes discussion of some new material added, specifically:

➤ Law office computing (including the Internet)

➤ Health insurance and managed care

➤ Long-term care insurance

➤ Adoption

➤ Premises liability

➤ Securities litigation reform.

The next Supplement will carry the story forward, covering events of 1996–7.

Dana Shilling

How to Use This Supplement

This first Supplement provides additional information on important developments that have occurred since publication of the Tenth Edition.

The section titles and paragraph numbers used in the Tenth Edition are retained in the Supplement to facilitate its use. To illustrate: the subject Arbitration is Paragraph 401 in the Tenth Edition; it is updated concerning Labor Arbitration by the inclusion of Paragraph 401.2 in this Supplement. In addition, part of this Supplement is a cumulative index, including entries for the Tenth Edition as well as the Supplement entries. The latter entries are preceded by the prefix "S." The cumulative index should be used in place of the index in the Tenth Edition. To look up a topic, the reader need only check the cumulative index to find the major topic and any recent additions to it.

TABLE OF CONTENTS

ANTITRUST PROBLEMS: PRICES AND UNFAIR COMPETITION

[¶201] Antitrust consent decrees can be modified or terminated—provided that the defendant can show that the basic purposes of the decree (e.g., safeguarding competition within the market; preventing market power) have been achieved.[1]

The statute of limitations in an antitrust case can be tolled for fraudulent concealment. The defendant must commit affirmative acts of concealment, but they need not be identifiable separate and apart from the underlying antitrust conspiracy.[2]

In the view of the Eleventh Circuit, international antitrust disputes are arbitrable—but domestic ones are not.[3] However, the Tenth Circuit takes the view that antitrust claims are arbitrable provided that they have a reasonable factual connection with a contract containing an arbitration clause. Thus, antitrust claims of a conspiracy to divide the U.S. beer market were properly litigated rather than arbitrated, because the claims are not covered by the arbitration clause in a brewery licensing agreement predating the allegedly anticompetitive deal between the defendant and a third brewer.[4]

[¶202] MONOPOLIZATION

Early in 1995, the District Court for the District of Columbia rejected a proposed consent decree involving the Department of Justice's allegation that Microsoft had monopolized the market for computer operating systems. The applicable statute, the Tunney Act (15 U.S.C. §16(e)) requires that the court certify that a proposed decree is in the public interest. The District Court felt unable to do so because the government did not provide enough information for the court to assess the public interest impact. Furthermore, the decree was characterized as too narrow in scope and lacking adequate compliance mechanisms.[5]

When the case next appeared in court mid-year, the D.C.Circuit held that the District Court's rejection was improper. The court considered the possibility of anticompetitive use of "vaporware" (announcement of fictitious products in an attempt to dissuade purchasers from buying competitive products that already existed or that might be developed), even though the Department of Justice did not make this allegation. The D.C. Circuit interprets the court's job under the Tunney Act as determining whether the proposed consent decree is in the public interest—not raising new issues or possible areas of contention.[6]

[¶203] THE RELEVANT MARKET

In a recent Seventh Circuit case,[7] one HMO charged another with signing up so many doctors that the plaintiff HMO could not enlist enough doctors to furnish a competing service. However, the court denied that HMOs are a separate market where competition can be analyzed. Instead, all HMOs compete with other methods (especially Preferred Provider Organizations) of delivering health care services. Furthermore, doctors have high mobility between HMOs, or between HMOs and the fee-for-service sector.

[¶206] HORIZONTAL RESTRAINTS

The partners of a law firm in the course of dissolution signed an agreement not to advertise in one another's territories. Because the lawyers were personal injury attorneys heavily dependent on advertising, the Seventh Circuit treated the action as a horizontal allocation of markets among competitors and a per se violation of Sherman Act §1.[8] However, the plaintiffs in the action were co-signatories who were equally responsible for the restraint and had no antitrust injury, so Clayton Act treble damages were not available to them.

[¶216] PATENTS AND THE ANTITRUST LAWS

An antitrust claim that a patent was obtained fraudulently and used to destroy competition is not a compulsory counterclaim in an infringement suit involving that patent.[9]

— ENDNOTES —

1. *U.S. v. Eastman Kodak*, 63 F.3d 95 (2nd Cir. 8/4/95).

2. *Supermarket of Marlinton, Inc. v Meadow Gold Dairies Inc.*, 71 F.3d 119 (4th Cir. 12/1/95).

3. *Kotam Electronics Inc. v. JBL Consumer Products Inc.*, 59 F.3d 1155 (11th Cir. 7/28/95).

4. *Coors Brewing Co. v. Molson Breweries*, 51 F.3d 1511 (10th Cir. 3/30/95), *on remand*, 889 F.Supp. 1394.

5. *U.S. v. Microsoft Corp.*, 159 F.R.D.318 (D.D.C. 2/14/95).

6. *U.S. v. Microsoft Co.*, 56 F.3d 1448 (D.C.Cir. 6/16/95).

7. *Blue Cross and Blue Shield of Wisconsin v. Marshfield Clinic*, 63 F.3d 1406 (7th Cir. 9/18/95).

8. *Blackburn v. Sweeney*, 53 F.3d 825 (7th Cir. 5/3/95).

9. *Hydranautics v. FilmTec Corp.*, 70 F.3d 533 (9th Cir. 11/15/95).

— FOR FURTHER REFERENCE —

Hamilton, Arthur, Judy Tansley and Peter A. Veglahn, "Wage Surveys and Anti-Trust Law," 46 *Labor Law J.* 763 (December '95).

Kobak, James B. Jr., "Running the Gauntlet: Antitrust and Intellectual Property Pitfalls on the Two Sides of the Atlantic," 64 *Antitrust L.J.* 341 (Winter '96).

Monroe, Murray S. and William J. Seitz, "Health Care Under the Antitrust Guidelines," 64 *U. of Cincinnati L.Rev.* 71 (Fall '95).

Paredes, Troy, "Turning the Failing Firm Defense Into a Success," 13 *Yale J. on Regulation* 347 (Winter '96).

Pomerantz, Stewart A., "Recent Antitrust Developments and a Selective Antitrust Perspective of the Information Superhighway," 64 *Fordham L.Rev.* 808 (December '95).

Soobert, Allan M., "Antitrust Implications of Bundling Software and Support Services," 21 *U. of Dayton L.Rev.* 63 (Fall '95).

Travers, Arthur B., "Commercial Bribery and the Antitrust Laws," 40 *Antitrust Bulletin* 779 (Winter '95).

APPEALS

[¶302] It is interesting to note several Supreme Court cases on appellate issues during the supplement period; given the extremely small number of cases decided by the Court each term, even four or five cases constitute a significant portion of the workload.

[¶302.1]   Timing of Appeals

Attorney negligence may constitute "excusable neglect" under the Federal Rules of Appellate Procedure, sufficient to justify a late filing.[1]

[¶302.2]   Interlocutory and Immediate Appeals

If the basis for a summary judgment motion is qualified immunity, denial of that motion is a final decision that is entitled to immediate appeal under 28 U.S.C. §1291—even if the defendant has already lost an interlocutory appeal on denial of his motion to dismiss based on the same grounds.[2]

[¶303]   SCOPE OF APPELLATE REVIEW

In a late-1995 Supreme Court case, a creditor sued a debtor in state court to collect rent and enforce a guaranty of performance. A successor in interest to the guarantor used 28 U.S.C. §1452(a), and the general removal statute, §1441(a), to bring the action into federal court. The holding is that if there is a timely objection to the removal procedure or to the court's subject-matter jurisdiction, and the case is remanded to a state court, that remand is not reviewable. The Court of Appeals has no jurisdiction under §1447(d) in that situation.[3]

When a District Court confirms or does not vacate an arbitration award, that ordinarily is subject to ordinary standards of review. In other words, questions of law are reviewed de novo, not merely to see if an abuse of discretion has occurred. Questions of fact are reviewed to see if the court's determination was clearly erroneous.[4]

If an arbitration agreement states that "errors of law are subject to appeal," the Fifth Circuit says that the appellate court is supposed to review questions of law in the arbitration award de novo, even though the FAA does not allow an award to be vacated unless there was fraud, partiality, corruption, or action by the arbitrators exceeding their appropriate powers.[5]

If a case is settled after an appeal was filed or certiorari applied for (and thus becomes moot), the federal appellate court is not justified in vacating the underlying judgment unless exceptional circumstances are present.[6]

4

A bankruptcy court's denial of a motion to disqualify counsel cannot be challenged; it is neither a collateral order nor a final order appealable under 28 U.S.C. §158(d).[7]

— ENDNOTES —

1. *Reynolds v. Wagner*, 55 F.3d 1426 (9th Cir. 5/26/95). See *Pioneer Investment Services Co. v. Brunswick Assoc. LP*, 113 S.Ct. 1489, 123 L.Ed.2d 74 (Sup.Ct. 1993) treating attorney negligence as excusing a late filing of an appeal under Bankruptcy Rule 9006(b)(1).

2. *Behrens v. Pelletier*, #94-1244, 116 S.Ct. 834 (Sup.Ct. 2/21/96).

3. *Things Remembered Inc. v. Petrarca*, #94-1530, 116 S.Ct. 494 (Sup.Ct. 12/5/95).

4. *First Options of Chicago Inc. v. Kaplan*, #94-560, 115 S.Ct. 1920, 131 L.Ed.2d 985 (Sup.Ct. 5/22/95).

5. *Gateway Technologies Inc. v. MCI Telecommunications Corp.*, 64 F.3d 993 (5th Cir. 9/27/95).

6. *U.S. Bancorp Mortgage Co. v. Bonner Mall Partnership*, #93-714, 115 S.Ct. 386, 130 L.Ed.2d 233 (Sup.Ct. 11/8/94).

7. *Brouwer v. Ancel & Dunlap*, 46 F.3d 653 (7th Cir. 1/31/95).

— FOR FURTHER REFERENCE —

Davidson, Michael J., "A Modest Proposal: Permit Interlocutory Appeals of Summary Judgment Denials," *Military L.Rev.* 145 [no issue number] (Winter '95).

Elligett, Robert T. Jr. and John M. Scheb, "Appellate Standards of Review—How Important Are They?" 70 *Florida Bar J.* 33 (February '96).

Hanes, Connie, "The Riddle of the Early, Late Notice of Appeal," 43 *The Federal Lawyer* 34 (February '96).

Kenety, William H., "Observations on Teaching Appellate Advocacy," 45 *J. of Legal Education* 582 (December '95).

Koch, William C. Jr., "Intermediate Appellate Court Consolidation," 31 *Tennessee Bar J.* 10 (November-December '95).

Ulrich, Paul G., "Creating Appellate Handbooks for Fun and Profit," 36 *Law Office Economics & Management* 455 (Winter '96).

ARBITRATION

[¶401.1]   Securities Arbitration

The U.S. Supreme Court permits an award of punitive damages if the arbitration agreement incorporates a Self-Regulatory Organization's rules by reference, and those rules permit punitive damages. This is true even if the arbitration agreement also has a choice of law provision calling for interpretation under the laws of a state in which punitive damages can only be ordered by a court.[1]

If the underlying agreement (here, one dealing with commodities trading) does not specifically provide for class arbitration, the court cannot order it, because Federal Arbitration Act §4 requires enforcement of arbitration agreements in accordance with their terms.[2] Nor can a court compel expedition unless the arbitration agreement specified expedited arbitration.[3]

[¶401.2]   Labor Arbitration

The EEOC got a preliminary injunction preventing an employer from requiring its employees to sign and abide by an "ADR policy" instead of suing for alleged violations of Title VII. The employer was further enjoined from forcing employees to agree to pay ADR costs, and from interfering with the EEOC charge or any ensuing Title VII action.[4]

The U-4—the standard employment agreement within the securities industry—requires arbitration of whatever disputes are made arbitrable by a Self-Regulatory Organization, and the NASD manual says that any dispute arising out of members' business is arbitrable. The Ninth Circuit found that, although employees can certainly agree to submit their ADEA and Title VII claims to arbitration, they can be compelled to arbitrate only if they knowingly waive the right to litigate such claims. The U-4 does not explicitly deny the possibility of a Title VII suit, so U-4 signatories retain the right to sue when they allege discrimination.[5]

An employee can bring a Fair Labor Standards Act suit in federal court without first arbitrating the wage claim under his or her collective bargaining agreement.[6] However, where the collective bargaining agreement specifically submits sex discrimination and disability discrimination claims to arbitration, a union member is not permitted to litigate such claims under Title VII or the ADA.[7]

According to the Third Circuit, an arbitrator was justified in suspending rather than discharging a bus driver who caused a rear-end collision. The underlying contract merely permitted discharge for "proper cause," so the arbitrator could appropriately interpret this to mean that a system of progressive discipline was intended.[8]

[¶404]   HOW TO PROVIDE FOR ARBITRATION

The Court of Federal Claims decided in late 1995 that there is no Constitutional barrier preventing federal agencies from forming agreements that contain binding arbitration clauses.[9]

[¶405]   ARBITRABLE ISSUES

Early in 1995 the U.S. Supreme Court applied Federal Arbitration Act §2 (arbitration provisions are enforceable in contracts "evidencing a transaction involving commerce") to any contract that in fact involves interstate commerce— whether or not the contracting parties contemplated substantial interstate activity. Therefore, state anti-arbitration laws were preempted by the FAA.[10]

Later that year, the Supreme Court held that the arbitrator decides whether the dispute is arbitrable under the FAA if the parties have agreed to submit this threshold issue to arbitration.[11] Otherwise, the judge must make an independent determination of the issue. The usual standards of review apply to a District Court's order confirming or not vacating an arbitration award (i.e., questions of law are reviewed de novo and not merely to test abuse of discretion). Questions of fact are reviewed to see if the District Court's decision was clearly erroneous.

FAA §1 excludes the contracts of "seamen, railroad employees, or any other class of workers engaged in foreign or interstate commerce" from arbitrability, but the Sixth Circuit read this narrowly to workers who actively move goods between states, not all employment affecting commerce.[12]

Even though, in general, the FAA assigns questions of timeliness to the arbitrator, the FAA does not preempt a New York arbitration law that places statute of limitations questions within the domain of the judge.[13]

However, according to the Fifth Circuit, the arbitrator and not the federal court is responsible for determining the timeliness of an investor's claims against a securities brokerage, because this is a question of "procedural arbitrability" and not a substantive eligibility requirement to be established by a federal court prior to the brokerage's obligation to submit to arbitration.[14]

FAA §4, allowing a petition to compel arbitration in any district (with the arbitration to be held there) does not override the forum selection clause of the underlying agreement. Nor can the District Court in which the petition was filed enjoin arbitration in the location that is proper under the forum selection clause.[15]

The statute of limitations for an FAA action does not begin until there has been an unequivocal refusal to arbitrate. Non-compliance with an arbitration demand, or other unambiguous manifestation of unwillingness to arbitrate, would qualify.[16]

The Coors and Molson brewing companies entered into a licensing agreement. Later, Molson entered into an allegedly anticompetitive deal with the Miller brewery. Coors brought suit, charging a conspiracy to divide the United States beer market. The Tenth Circuit held[17] that Coors was entitled to litigate the antitrust claims instead of arbitrating them, because the claims fall outside the licensing agreement's arbitration clause. Antitrust claims are arbitrable,[18] but only if they have a reasonable factual connection to the contract that contains the arbitration clause.

In contrast, a mid-1995 Eleventh Circuit case finds international antitrust disputes are arbitrable, but domestic ones are not.[19]

Alleged misappropriation of trade secrets is a separate tort and does not "arise out of" breach of a licensing agreement, and thus is not covered by the arbitration clause within the licensing agreement.[20]

[¶413]   ENFORCEMENT OF THE ARBITRATION AWARD

Florida's statute, requiring 35% of the punitive damages in any "civil action" to be paid to the state applies only to litigation, not to arbitration proceedings.[21]

[¶414]   VACATING ARBITRATION AWARD

If the arbitration agreement provides that "errors of law are subject to appeal," the appellate court is supposed to provide de novo review of questions of law in the arbitration award—even though the FAA does not allow an award to be vacated absent fraud, partiality, corruption, or action by the arbitrators exceeding their powers.[22]

— ENDNOTES —

1. *Mastrobuono v. Shearson Lehman Hutton Inc.*, #94-18, 115 S.Ct. 1212, 131 L.Ed.2d 76 (Sup.Ct. 3/6/95), *reversing* 20 F.3d 713; *on remand*, 54 F.3d 779.

2. *Champ v. Siegel Trading Co.*, 55 F.3d 269 (7th Cir. 5/18/95).

3. *Salvano v. Merrill Lynch*, 647 N.E.2d 1298 (N.Y.App. 2/21/95).

4. *EEOC v. River Oaks Imaging and Diagnostic*, 63 LW 2733 (S.D.Tex. 4/19/95).

5. *Prudential Insurance Co. v. Lai*, 42 F.3d 1299 (9th Cir. 12/20/94).

6. *Tran v. Tran*, 54 F.3d 115 (2nd Cir. 5/5/95).

7. *Austin v. Owens-Brockway Glass Container, Inc.*, 64 LW 2586 (4th Cir. 3/12/96).

8. *Transportation Union Local 1589 v. Suburban Transit Corp.*, 51 F.3d 376 (3d Cir. 3/16/95).

9. *Tenaska Washington Partners II LP v. U.S.*, 34 Fed.Cl. 434 (Ct Fed.Cl. 11/9/95).

10. *Allied-Bruce Terminix Cos. v. Dobson,* #93-1001, 115 S.Ct. 834, 130 L.Ed.2d 753 (Sup.Ct. 1/18/95). However, see *Casarotto v. Lombardi,* 901 P.2d 596 (Mont.Sup. 8/31/95), holding that the state adoption of the Uniform Arbitration Act, which requires notice on the frant page of a contract that arbitration is required, is not FAA-preempted. *Casarotto* reads *Allied-Bruce Terminix* as limited to cases involving true interstate commerce. The Montana court saw the objective of the state statute as informing contracting parties of potential consequences, an aim that does not violate Congress' pro-arbitration policy in enacting the FAA.

11. *First Options of Chicago Inc. v. Kaplan,* #94-560, 115 S.Ct. 1920, 131 L.Ed.2d 985 (Sup.Ct. 5/22/95).

12. *Asplundh Tree Expert Co. v. Bates,* 57 F.3d 592 (6th Cir. 12/14/95).

13. *Smith Barney v. Luckie,* 647 N.E.2d 1308 (N.Y.App. 2/21/95).

14. *Smith Barney v. Boone,* 47 F.3d 750 (5th Cir. 3/20/95).

15. *Merrill Lynch v. Lauer,* 49 F.3d 323 (7th Cir. 3/1/95).

16. *PaineWebber Inc. v. Faragalli,* 61 F.3d 1063 (3rd Cir. 8/4/95).

17. *Coors Brewing Co. v. Molson Breweries,* 51 F.3d 1511 (10th Cir. 3/30/95); *on remand,* 889 F.Supp. 1394.

18. See *Mitsubishi Motors v. Soler Chrysler-Plymouth,* 473 U.S. 614 (1985).

19. *Kotam Electronics Inc. v. JBL Consumer Products Inc.,* 59 F.3d 1155 (11th Cir. 7/28/95).

20. *Tracer Research Corp. v. National Env. Services Co.,* 42 F.3d 1292 (9th Cir. 12/19/94).

21. *Miele v. Prudential-Bache Securities Inc.,* 656 So.2d 470 (Fla.Sup. 6/8/95).

22. *Gateway Technologies Inc. v. MCI Telecommunications Corp.,* 64 F.3d 993 (5th Cir. 9/27/95).

— **FOR FURTHER REFERENCE** —

Benson, Robert E., "The Power of Arbitrators and Courts to Order Discovery in Arbitration," 25 *Colorado Lawyer* 35 (March '96).

Gorman, Robert A., "The Gilmer Decision and the Private Arbitration of Public Disputes," 1995 *U. of Illinois L.Rev.* 635 (Summer '95).

Hill, Richard, "Non-Adversarial Mediation," 12 *J. of International Arbitration* 135 (December '95).

Krislov, Joseph, "The Consent Award in Labor Arbitration," 46 *Labor Law J.* 685 (November '95).

Naranjo, Dan A., "Alternative Dispute Resolution of International Private Commercial Disputes Under the NAFTA," 59 *Texas Bar J.* 116 (February '96).

Schickman, Mark I., "New Ground Rules for Discrimination Disputes," 13 *Compleat Lawyer* 57 (Winter '96).

Wigner, Preston Douglas, "The United States Supreme Court's Expansive Approach to the Federal Arbitration Act," 29 *U. of Richmond L.Rev.* 1499 (December '95).

Williams, Victor, "Punitive Damages in Arbitration," 100 *Commercial L.J.* 281 (Fall '95).

ATTORNEYS' FEES

[¶501] Attorneys' fees are not only an expense that litigants must pay, but property belonging to attorneys. According to the West Virginia Supreme Court, an attorney who is in the process of getting a divorce has separate property in the part of a contingent fee that relates to work done of a case after separation. It is not necessary to construct a legal fiction that the attorney resigned from his law firm on the date of the separation.[1]

Attorneys can be compelled to testify about fee arrangements when the federal government tries to seize assets from convicted money launderers. The District Court for the District of Rhode Island says that in this situation, the lawyers are not being compelled to incriminate themselves; nor are discussions about fees legal advice qualifying for attorney-client privilege.[2]

Unpaid attorneys' fees left over from earlier unsuccessful attempts at Chapter 11 and 12 reorganizations do not get administrative expense priority when the debtor tries again in Chapter 7—only the expenses of the current proceeding qualify.[3]

A Chapter 7 debtor's pre-petition agreement to pay attorney's fees in installment after the petition has been held[4] to be dischargeable. The court acknowledged that this might impair debtors' ability to secure legal counsel, but believed the solution to be a legislative rather than a judicial matter.

[¶502] FEDERAL STATUTES RE ATTORNEYS' FEES

According to the District Court for the Central District of California, ERISA preempts a state domestic relations law that requires pension plans to pay attorneys' fees incurred in connection with Qualified Domestic Relations Orders (QDROs).[5]

In ERISA cases, the prevailing parties are not presumed entitled to a fee award. Entitlement depends on factors such as the loser's culpability and ability to pay fees; if a fee award would serve to deter improper conduct; the value of the victory to plan participants; and the relative strength of the arguments adduced by each side.[6]

In a Clean Water Act citizen suit, all plaintiffs who want a fee award must satisfy the pre-suit notice requirement; it is not permitted for one plaintiff to provide notice for the plaintiffs as a group.[7]

A creditor of a forfeiture defendant who brings a claim under 21 U.S.C. §853(n), as a third party with a legal interest in the forfeited property, is deemed to have brought a "civil action" for EAJA purposes (even though the forfeiture is based on criminal charges). Thus, a fee award can be made to a creditor who prevails in the challenge.[8]

[¶503]   DEFINITION OF PREVAILING PARTIES

The Southern District of New York tackled EAJA issues in early 1995,[9] finding that determination of the substantial justification of the government position need not be made at each procedural stage of a case. However, once the case is concluded, it is appropriate to examine each distinct claim to test the justification of the government position, and whether an EAJA fee is appropriate with respect to that claim.

Cumulative refunds due to retired federal employees who prevailed in a challenge to state taxation of retiree benefits do not constitute a common fund from which an attorney's fee can be paid. Instead of a pool of money created by attorney efforts, there are only individual amounts owed to individual retirees based on their incomes.[10]

In contrast, a common fund was found to exist when refunds were granted after a challenge to Florida's motor vehicle impact fee—but nevertheless the attorney's fee was based on the lodestar rather than a percentage of the fund.[11]

In the view of the Second Circuit, shareholders have created a common benefit, and thus can be awarded attorneys' fees, if they win an action under securities law Rule 14a-8 and mandate the inclusion of a shareholder proposal in a corporate proxy statement.[12] This is true even if the proposal is soundly defeated when the vote is held. To the Second Circuit, corporate voters at least got to consider the proposal, so they were benefited by the ability to exercise a broader corporate franchise.

Code §7430 permits the award of fees against the IRS and to a prevailing party, subject to the EAJA's net-worth limits ($2 million for an individual, $7 million and 500 employees for a corporation) at the time the civil action was filed. However, the Seventh Circuit points out that the net worth of an estate always declines over time and vanishes when the distribution is complete. Thus, an estate's ability to litigate without help from the EAJA depends on the net value of the entire estate, adding back in assets already distributed when the suit was filed.[13]

A defendant who is awarded attorneys' fees after defending against a frivolous civil rights suit is also entitled to be reimbursed for the necessary expenses of collecting the award.[14]

[¶504]   COMPUTATION OF FEES

In Social Security Act §406(b) SSI disability cases, the lodestar remains the primary determinant of the fee—although the lodestar may be adjusted in accordance with the contingent fee agreement.[15]

Where an attorney prevails on one of multiple claims, the fee should be based on the hours reasonably expended to secure the result; there should not be an automatic reduction based on the lack of success of the other claims.[16]

An attorney was awarded $150/hour in a complex bankruptcy case, because it was below her prevailing rates, and her special expertise justified an increase from the ordinary $75 rate. However, she was awarded only $100 for each hour spent on the fee application, because there was no complex legal analysis involved in pursuing the award.[17]

In a Florida case, it was held that the true value of services rendered to the client before the discharge, not the lodestar, should be used to set the quantum merit fee of a contingent-fee attorney who was discharged without cause before the contingency occurred.[18]

[¶505]   DEDUCTIBILITY OF LEGAL FEES

In law-firm "gross fee" contracts, firms get a percentage of settlement or judgment proceeds, but nothing—including expenses—if the case is lost. A law-firm partner has been permitted to deduct (under Code §162) litigation costs that the firm paid[19]—even though local ethical rules forbid the firm to do anything except advance costs for later repayment. The holding depends on the fact that there was no state statute making it unlawful for law firms to assume responsibility for expenses; "unethical" expenses can be deducted, although "unlawful" ones cannot.

—   ENDNOTES   —

1. *White v. Williamson*, 453 S.E.2d 666 (W.Va.Sup. 12/21/94).

2. *U.S. v. Saccoccia*, 898 F.Supp. 53 (D.R.I. 8/28/95).

3. *Stuart v. Carter (In re Larsen)*, 59 F.3d 783 (8th Cir. 7/14/95).

4. *Hessinger & Associates v. Voglio*, 64 LW 2431 (D.Ariz. 12/12/95).

5. *AT&T Management Pension Plan v. Tucker*, 64 LW 2224 (C.D.Cal. 8/17/95).

6. *Eddy v. Colonial Life Co.*, 59 F.3d 201 (D.C.Cir. 7/7/95).

7. *New Mexico Citizens for Clean Air and Water v. Espanola Mercantile Co.*, 72 F.3d 830 (10th Cir. 1/2/96).

8. *U.S. v. Douglas (Lussier)*, 55 F.3d 584 (11th Cir. 6/21/95); *U.S. v. Bachner*, 877 F.Supp. 625 (S.D.Fla. 1/20/95).

9. *SEC v. Morelli*, 143 F.R.D. 42 (S.D.N.Y. 1/11/95).

10. *Hagge v. Iowa Department of Revenue*, 539 N.W.2d 148 (Ia.Sup. 10/25/95).

11. *Kuhnlein v. Department of Revenue*, 662 So.2d 309 (Fla.Sup. 10/12/95).

12. *Amalgamated Clothing and Textile Workers Union v. Wal-Mart Stores*, 63 LW 2666 (2nd Cir. 4/20/95).

13. *Estate of Woll v. U.S.*, 44 F.3d 464 (7th Cir. 12/30/94).

14. *Vukadinovich v. McCarthy*, 59 F.3d 58 (7th Cir. 7/5/95).

15. *Allen v. Shalala*, 48 F.3d 456 (9th Cir. 2/24/95).

16. *Goos v. National Association of Realtors*, 68 F.3d 1380 (D.C.Cir. 10/31/95).

17. *In re Brickell Investment Corp.*, 75 AFTR2d 2032 (D.Fla. 1995). Also see the 42 U.S.C. §1988 civil rights case, *Thompson v. Gomez*, 45 F.3d 1365 (9th Cir. 1/25/95), which holds that if the attorneys' fee requested on the merits is reduced, it is not a judicial abuse of power for the "fees on fees" application for the cost of recovering the fees to be reduced proportionately.

18. *Searcy, Denney, et al. v. Poletz*, 652 So.2d 366 (Fla.Sup. 3/16/95). Also see *Klein v. Eubank*, 64 LW 2434 (N.Y.App. 1/9/96): the attorney maintains a charging lien if he or she voluntarily withdraws from representation for just cause; the lien is not limited to the counsel of record at the time of judgment or settlement of the case. The charging lien is lost only if the attorney refuses or neglects to pursue a case without just cause.

19. *Boccardo v. C.I.R.*, 56 F.3d 1016 (9th Cir. 5/26/95).

— FOR FURTHER REFERENCE —

Brown, Toby and Michelle Roberts, "Pricing Your Legal Products," 8 *Utah Bar J.* 16 (December '95).

Musselman, Francis H., "Abandon the Billable Hour!" 36 *Law Office Economics and Management* 296 (Fall '95).

Raby, William L. and Burgess J.W. Raby, "Legal Fees and Expenses from the IRS When the Taxpayer Wins," 70 *Tax Notes* 1383 (March 4, 1996).

Shepard, Kevin L., "Adding Certainty to Fixed Fee Quotes," 12 *The Practical Real Estate Lawyer* 13 (January '96).

Sherwood, Arthur M., "A Tax Perspective on Recent Legislation Affecting Compensation of an Attorney-Executor," 68 *New York State Bar J.* 54 (February '96).

Siegel, Eric L., "Ethical Obligations and Billing Practices," 10 *Washington Lawyer* 38 (January-February '96).

Susco, Albertina D., "Recovery of Attorneys' Fees in Private Cost-Recovery Actions Under CERCLA," 6 *Villanova Environmental Law J.* 405 (Summer '95).

ATTORNEYS' RULES OF PROFESSIONAL CONDUCT

[¶601] An attorney who helps the police perform an unconstitutional search can be subject to liability under *Bivens v. Six Agents of the Federal Bureau of Narcotics*, 403 U.S. 388 (1971), because the attorney is deemed to be a federal agent under these circumstances. Nor is the qualified *Bivens* immunity given to government employees available to the attorney—although a good-faith defense may be.[1]

The D.C. Circuit has allowed a client who seeks return of legal fees (and not compensatory damages) to sue for attorney malpractice without establishing causation and damages.[2] If an attorney permits the statute of limitations to expire, thus depriving the client of the ability to be awarded a judgment, the uncollectability of the judgment must be used to adjust the malpractice damages.[3]

An attorney formerly employed as house counsel can sue for wrongful discharge if it is alleged that discharge was a penalty for complying with a statutory or ethical duty—provided that the attorney doesn't have to violate client confidences to prove the case.[4]

Alcoholism, manic depression, and bipolar disorder have been held not to be mitigating factors that would prevent disbarment of an attorney who has misappropriated client funds or engaged in other very severe misconduct. The need to protect clients outweighs compassion for impaired attorneys. Although mental illnesses are disabilities as defined by the Americans with Disability Act, it is impossible to modify working conditions to prevent further attorney misconduct.[5]

Fortunately for clients, attorney negligence is sometimes treated as "excusable neglect" under the Federal Rules of Appellate Procedure that would justify late filing of a bankruptcy appeal.[6]

[¶601.1]   Sanctions Under FRCP 11

Sanctions cannot be imposed on an attorney for filing a grounded complaint in a proper forum—even if the forum is not the most convenient one for the defendant, and even if the plaintiff's lawyer tried to get the defendant to settle by threatening to create bad publicity for the State of Israel. In this reading,[7] if there is a valid legal grievance, the impropriety of the motives of those who pursue it does not support sanctions.

The First Amendment protected a variety of unflattering statements that a lawyer made about a judge to a reporter ("ignorant," "anti-Semitic," "drunk on the bench")—and thus the attorney could not properly be sanctioned by a suspension. Statements about a judge's integrity are protectable under the First Amendment unless they are susceptible of factual proof (e.g., alleging that a particular judge is a bigamist or did not pass the bar exam).[8]

As long as an attorney has exercised his or her best efforts to get the client to comply, the attorney should not be sanctioned for the client's failure to comply with a court order (in this case, ordering the client to appear at a settlement conference).[9] Similarly, the Third Circuit says that the lawyer can be sanctioned only if the court can show how the attorney (as distinct from the client) has violated the rule or statute cited to support the sanctions.[10]

[¶602]　CLIENT-LAWYER RELATIONSHIP

Sexual relations with a divorce client are not per se a breach of professional responsibility [in a jurisdiction with no explicit rule on this point]. However, if other ethical rules, such as those involving conflict of interest, are violated, the West Virginia Supreme Court says that the attorney can be disqualified from further representation of the client.[11]

Where the lawyer, rather than the client, is the target of an IRS investigation, the IRS can serve the lawyer with a summons requiring the disclosure of names of clients that were not reported on Form 8300. The IRS does not have to follow its John Doe summons procedure (which requires court authorization). In general, client identity and the nature of fee arrangements are not privileged—particularly where the IRS isn't after the clients anyway.[12]

Attorney-client privilege is not available for in-house counsel's work in negotiating contracts and reporting to management on negotiations. The Southern District of New York deemed this work to be business advice, not the traditional, confidential functions of an attorney.[13]

Neither tort nor contract law (in California) make lawyers liable if they violate a private agreement with opposing counsel not to disclose confidential documents that were uncovered during the discovery process.[14] This is true even if the agreement was incorporated into a protective order from the court.

Although the upshot of the disclosure of the documents was substantial litigation against the corporation that sought to keep the documents confidential, the California Court of Appeals ruled that it is not tortious to induce a third party to pursue a meritorious claim. Although sanctions are available for violation of the protective order, the underlying contract was extinguished by the protective order, so damages for breach of contract were not available.

Under California law, an attorney has no duty to advise an ex-client to get a new lawyer before the statute of limitations runs out, where the lawyer must stop representing that client because of that client's potential claims against a current client of the lawyer. Giving such advice would violate the duty of loyalty to the current client by making it easier to subject that client to liability.[15]

Under Idaho law, there is a continuing duty to ex-clients, so it constitutes malpractice to represent another party who is adverse to the ex-client in a substantially related matter—even if the former client's confidences are not violated during the subsequent representation.[16] A recent Arkansas case finds a conflict of interest if one of a firm's lawyers represents the plaintiff in a malpractice suit against a hospital where another lawyer from the same firm recently served on the hospital's Board of Governors.[17]

[¶603] COUNSELOR

A divorce lawyer can be sued for malpractice for failing to give proper advice about well-established legal principles (e.g., the substantive law governing termination of the alimony obligation upon remarriage of the former spouse).[18]

[¶604] ADVOCATE

Given the attorney's duty to be truthful and trustworthy, an adversary can sue a defendant's attorney for deliberate misrepresentation of the amount of the defendant's insurance, where the representation induced the plaintiff to settle the case.[19] Ohio has a rule imposing per se suspension in disciplinary cases where the attorney has misrepresented a material fact or point of law to a tribunal.[20]

Damages for malicious defense of a tort action (involving false evidence and testimony fabricated by the defense counsel) are available on the same terms as for malicious prosecution, on the theory that a litigant is not made whole by mere reimbursement of attorneys' fees.[21]

[¶605] TRANSACTIONS WITH PERSONS OTHER THAN CLIENTS

The New Jersey Supreme Court found a duty of attorneys to third parties whom the attorney knows will rely on the attorney's representations (here, the condition of real estate vis-a-vis its septic system)—unless the third party is too remote from the representation to be entitled to protection.[22]

In a Florida case, adoptive parents falsified Florida residence, with the result that a child was taken away from the grandmother who cared for the child, who was then unlawfully adopted out-of-state. The child was held to have standing to sue the adoptive parents' lawyers (one of whom acted as intermediary with the birth mother). A limited exception was read into the privity requirement for attorney malpractice where the plaintiff was the intended beneficiary of the attorney's actions.

Furthermore, attorneys who act as adoption intermediaries have a duty to act in the best interests of the child. The child was also permitted to sue the attorneys for malicious prosecution, because the gravamen of that tort is the misuse of legal machinery for an unlawful purpose. However, the claim for intentional infliction of emotional distress was dismissed, because interstate transport of a child by a mother who had legal custody at that time did not constitute conduct that is "reckless and utterly outrageous in a civilized community."[23]

Attorneys have been held liable to non-clients for negligent misrepresentations in opinion letters, where the opinion letter either is addressed to the third party or expressly authorizes reliance by the third party (e.g., as here, where there was a material misstatement of fact as to a bank's purchase of bonds issued by a municipality represented by the attorney).[24] However, this case says that a malpractice claim requires privity.

In contrast, absolute judicial privilege has been deemed to protect allegedly defamatory statements about potential defendants made in solicitation letters sent (at a client's request) to fellow corporate shareholders at a time when litigation was contemplated in good faith.[25]

[¶606]   LAW FIRMS AND ASSOCIATIONS

According to the New Jersey Superior Court, it is inappropriate for a law firm employment agreement to restrict the amount a lawyer can earn from clients who move with him when the firm fires him. In this analysis, no matter how much a firm may invest in a contingent case, it's just one of the risks of doing business.[26]

In contrast, the New York Court of Appeals upheld an arbitrator who in turn upheld a provision in a law firm partnership agreement that limited compensation paid to withdrawing partners based on their income from other sources. The court viewed the provision as "competition neutral" because it did not single out partners who leave to join competing law firms.[27]

[¶607]   INFORMATION ABOUT LEGAL SERVICES

Both a Florida statute and a Texas bar rule that forbid direct-mail solicitation of accident victims within 30 days of an accident have survived First Amendment challenges brought by lawyers wishing to send such solicitations.[28] In both cases, the state was permitted to protect the privacy of victims and their families, even if perhaps the restriction on commercial speech could have been more narrowly tailored.

Florida's state bar had the obligation of proving the validity of the limitations it imposed on the use of testimonials, illustrations, and dramatizations in attorney advertisements. The Eleventh Circuit ruled that lawyers did not have the burden of proof, because they were challenging the application of the rules, not their facial validity.[29]

— ENDNOTES —

1. *Victor Research Inc. v. Howard & Howard*, 64 LW 2514 (6th Cir. 2/14/96).

2. *Hendry v. Pelland*, 64 LW 2543 (D.C.Cir. 1/19/96).

3. *Klump v. Duffus*, 71 F.3d 1368 (7th Cir. 12/18/95).

4. *GTE Products Corp. v. Stewart*, 653 N.E.2d 161 (Mass.Sup.Jud.Ct. 8/1/95).

5. *Attorney Grievance Commission v. Kenney*, 339 Md. 578 (Md.App. 9/11/95) [alcoholism]; *Florida Bar v. Clement*, 662 So.2d 690 (Fla.Sup. 11/2/95) [manic depression/bipolar disorder].

6. *Pioneer Investment Services Co. v. Brunswick Association LP*, 504 U.S. 956 (Sup.Ct. 1993); *Reynolds v. Wagner*, 55 F.3d 1426 (9th Cir. 5/26/95).

7. *Sussman v. Bank of Israel*, 56 F.3d 450 (2d Cir. 6/2/95).

8. *Standing Committee on Discipline v. Yagman*, 55 F.3d 1430 (9th Cir. 5/30/95).

9. *Universal Cooperative Inc. v. Trial Cooperative Marketing Development Federation of India*, 45 F.3d 1194 (8th Cir. 1/23/95).

10. *Martin v. Brown*, 63 F.3d 1252 (3d Cir. 8/23/95).

11. *Musick v. Musick*, 453 S.E.2d 361 (W.Va.Sup. 1/25/95).

12. *U.S. v. Blackman*, 72 F.3d 1418 (9th Cir. 12/29/95).

13. *Georgia-Pacific Corp. v. GAF Roofing Mfg. Corp.*, 64 LW 2497 (S.D.N.Y. 1/24/96).

14. *Westinghouse Electric Corp. v. Newman & Holtzinger PC*, 39 Cal.App. 4th 1194, 46 Cal.Rptr.2d 151 (Cal.App. 10/30/95).

15. *Flatt v. Superior Court (Daniel)*, 885 P.2d 950 (Cal.Sup. 12/28/94).

16. *Damron v. Herzog*, 67 F.3d 211 (9th Cir. 9/26/95).

17. *Berry v. Saline Memorial Hospital*, 70 F.3d 981 (Ark.Sup. 10/23/95).

18. *McMahon v. Shea*, 657 A.2d 938 (Pa.Super. 2/23/95).

19. *Fire Insurance Exchange v. Bell*, 643 N.E.2d 310 (Ind.Sup. 11/28/94).

20. *Office of Disciplinary Counsel v. Greene*, 655 N.E.2d 1299 (Ohio Sup. 11/1/95).

21. *Aranson v. Schroeder*, 64 LW 2347 (N.H.Sup. 10/31/95).

22. *Petrillo v. Bachenberg*, 655 A.2d 1354 (N.J.Sup. 3/29/95).

23. *Rushing v. Bosse*, 652 So.2d 869 (Fla.App. 3/8/95).

24. *Mehaffy, Rider, Windholz & Wilson v. Central Bank Denver N.A.*, 829 P.2d 230 (Colo.Sup. 1/30/95).

25. *Kittler v. Eckberg, Lammers, Briggs, Wolff & Vierling*, 535 N.W.2d 653 (Minn.App. 8/8/95).

26. *Leonard & Butler PC v. Harris*, 653 A.2d 1193 (N.J.Super. 2/27/95).

27. *Hackett v. Milbank Tweed*, 654 N.E.2d 95 (N.Y.App. 7/5/95).

28. *Florida Bar v. Went For It Inc.*, 115 S.Ct. 2371 (Sup.Ct.6/21/95); *Moore v. Morales*, 65 F.3d 358 (5th Cir. 8/23/95); *Moore* was remanded to test the effect of the solicitation statute on other professions, such as the medical profession.

29. *Jacobs v. Florida Bar*, 50 F.3d 901 (11th Cir. 4/10/95).

— FOR FURTHER REFERENCE —

Aiello, Lucy, "What a Law Firm Should Consider When Purchasing Malpractice Insurance," 49 *Washington State Bar News* 21 (December '95).

Appel, David M., "Attorney Disbarment Proceedings and the Standard of Proof," 24 *Hofstra L.Rev.* 275 (Fall '95).

Fortney, Susan Saab, " 'Am I My Partner's Keeper?' Peer Review in Law Firms," 44 *Defense L.J.* 547 (Winter '95).

Levi, Jennifer, "Preventing Insider Trading at Law Firms," 14 *Preventive Law Reporter* 24 (Winter '95).

Martin, Robert W., "Affiliated Firm Arrangements Raise Ethical Issues," 39 *Advocate* 16 (January '96).

Moses, Jonathan M., "Legal Spin Control: Ethics and Advocacy in the Court of Public Opinion," 95 *Columbia L.Rev.* 1811 (November '95).

O'Roark, Dell, "Negligence Liability to Nonclients," 59 *Kentucky Bench and Bar* 32 (Fall '95).

Peck, Bridget Robb, "It's Splitsville: The Ethics and Realities of Leaving a Law Firm in the 90's," 3 *Nevada Lawyer* 19 (December '95).

Seale, John T. and David Gruning, "Lawyer Advertising: Past and Present," 43 *Louisiana Bar J.* 380 (December '95).

Silver, Charles and Kent Syverud, "The Professional Responsibilities of Insurance Defense Lawyers," 45 *Duke L.J.* 255 (November '95).

Sloane, Richard, "When Ineptness Becomes Frivolous Conduct," *N.Y.L.J.* 5 (Feb. 20 '96).

Thar, Anne E., "How Long Should You Retain Client Files?" 83 *Ill. Bar J.* 649 (December '95).

Trazenfeld, Warren R., "Legal Malpractice: A Framework for Assessing Potential Claims," 70 *Florida Bar J.* 38 (January '96).

Wharton, Joseph A., "Lawyer Advertising: Solicitation Waiting Period Upheld," 82 *A.B.A.J.* 48 (January '96).

BANKRUPTCY

[¶701] See the Bankruptcy Reform Act of 1994, P.L. 103-394 (10/22/94) for provisions designed to improve the administration of bankruptcy cases. In the commercial context, the procedures for electing trustees were changed; the trustee's avoiding power was subjected to new limits; and there are enhanced creditor's rights provisions for demanding return of goods. Consumer bankruptcy fraud was criminalized; more exceptions to dischargeability were enacted; and child support and alimony were given additional protection from discharge.

False statements in unsworn papers filed in Bankruptcy Court cannot give rise to an indictment under 18 U.S.C. §1001 (false statements in any matter within the jurisdiction of any "department or agency of the United States") because the U.S. Supreme Court says that a federal court is neither a department nor an agency.[1]

The mere fact that a personal injury defendant or co-defendant is bankrupt (utilizing the federal bankruptcy statute) will not justify removal of what is inherently a state personal injury action to the federal court system.[2] However, state tort claims alleging improper filing of an involuntary bankruptcy petition are impliedly preempted by the Bankruptcy Code's own (§303(i)) penalties for wrongful filing.[3]

Note: in most legal contexts, it's clear that a reference to "the Code" means the Internal Revenue Code. However, there is also a Bankruptcy Code and, because of the relevance of tax issues to bankruptcy planning and practice, it's important to be sure which "Code" is being referenced in any given citation.

[¶704]   VOLUNTARY BANKRUPTCY

Joint bankruptcy filing is available only for legally married couples—not, e.g., for a same-sex couple who have undergone a religious marriage ceremony.[4]

[¶704.1]   Operation of the Automatic Stay

Imposing Code §6672 tax penalties that violate the automatic stay is merely voidable, not void. Thus, a taxpayer is not necessarily able to void the assessment in bankruptcy, as long as the assessment does not frustrate the purpose of the automatic stay.[5]

The automatic stay does not apply to benefit the partners, guarantors, sureties, or insurers of the bankruptcy debtor.[6] However, IRC §6503(h) which suspends the tax statute of limitations during the taxpayer's bankruptcy also suspends the running of the statute of limitations against derivatively liable parties such as partners of a bankrupt partnership.[7] The theory is that if derivatively liable parties can take advantage of the statute of limitations which time-bars a main suit, they are back on the hook if the main suit can be revived.

Bankruptcy courts have discretion to lift the automatic stay so that an equitable distribution action against the debtor can proceed in state court.[8]

In a matrimonial case, the Bankruptcy Court for the Eastern District of California ruled that a District Attorney's office, enforcing a wage assignment against a delinquent child support obligor, should either have filed for relief from the automatic stay or stopped accepting payments once it became aware of the obligor's Chapter 13 filing. However, the non-dischargeable nature of the child support obligation means that the office had no obligation to return amounts already collected.[9]

In another matrimonial case, the automatic stay was held not to prevent distribution of 50% of a pension, based on a decree granted before the filing of the Chapter 13 petition. However, because spousal support payments come from current income, which becomes property of the estate, the trustee cannot make the payments without getting relief from the automatic stay.[10]

The automatic stay is not violated if the creditor sends a non-threatening, non-coercive letter to the debtor's attorney (with a copy to the debtor), requesting reaffirmation of the debt. The Seventh Circuit said[11] that the stay protects the debtor against lawsuits, but not necessarily against communications (at least non-abusive communications).

Where a plaintiff does not have notice of the transfer of the Chapter 11 debtor's assets (including a disclaimer of liability for certain personal injury claims), the bankruptcy court cannot enjoin a personal injury suit against the purchaser of all the debtor's assets. Retailers and wholesalers of the firearms produced by the debtor did not have notification and had no chance to comment on the reorganization plan.[12]

[¶707]   PROPERTY OF THE ESTATE

Despite the debtor's power to withdraw pension assets, the Ninth Circuit found that the pension assets did not become part of the bankruptcy estate because of Bankruptcy Code §541(c)(2).[13]

A 62-year-old Chapter 13 debtor's IRA funds were not "disposable income" as long as they remained in the IRA. The amount of such funds affects confirmation of the plan (by affecting whether the plan satisfies the best interests of the creditors), but state law makes these funds exempt as retirement plans.[14]

[¶710]   THE TRUSTEE'S AVOIDING POWER

Bankruptcy Code §113, which limits the trustee's power to avoid a collective bargaining agreement, applies only to Chapter 11 and not Chapter 7. The Ninth Circuit decided[15] that the statutory language reflects the Chapter 11 reorganization process rather than liquidation.

Only a pension plan administrator or the PBGC can terminate a pension plan—the trustee can't do it unilaterally, and can't be ordered to do so by the bankruptcy court.[16]

[¶715]   MAKING CLAIMS AGAINST A BANKRUPT

A Due Process challenge to Bankruptcy Code §523(a)(3)(B), dealing with objections to dischargeability, was unsuccessful in the Second Circuit.[17] The provision requires creditors to take action to protect their claims when they have actual knowledge but not formal notice of a petition. According to the Second Circuit, mere knowledge that a petition has been filed does not inform creditors of the bar date—but creditors can make an estimate based on the petition's filing date.

It is not "reasonably ascertainable" who counts as a former resident of, or visitor to, an environmentally contaminated site, so such persons cannot be considered "known creditors" entitled to notice of bankruptcy proceedings involving the site's owner.[18]

[¶717]   ALLOWANCE OF CLAIMS

The Tenth Circuit refused to apply res judicata to prevent the IRS from making additional claims for taxes in a year in which the bankruptcy court has already determined an amount of taxes—notwithstanding the argument that this prevents the debtor from achieving a fresh start.[19] Under this analysis, a reasonable debtor would expect the IRS to seek all non-dischargeable taxes, so the IRS was not guilty of misconduct in failing to inform the debtor that further claims might be made. The IRS was not guilty of misrepresentation or concealment of material fact, so equitable estoppel was not available—assuming arguendo that the IRS can be estopped; the Tenth Circuit did not regard this as a settled issue.

IRS' Form 872-A (extension of time to assess tax) operates as a waiver of the statute of limitations, not a contract that automatically terminates 60 days after the taxpayer's bankruptcy filing.[20]

[¶719]   HOW ASSETS OF THE BANKRUPT ARE DISTRIBUTED: PRIORITIES OF CLAIMS

Federal taxes on the debtor's income earned or accrued before the bankruptcy petition, but payable after the petition, are not treated as first-priority administrative expenses. Instead, they are unsecured claims, entitled to seventh priority.[21]

According to the Sixth Circuit, in Chapter 13 even IRS priority claims must be timely filed to be allowed.[22] The Second and Ninth Circuits have allowed untimely IRS claims in Chapter 7 cases,[23] but Chapter 7 is liquidating bankruptcy, unlike Chapter 13 where the debtor retains assets and makes periodic payments to creditors.

Unpaid attorney's fees remaining from earlier, unsuccessful attempts at Chapter 11 and Chapter 12 reorganization do not get administrative expense priority when the debtor takes another swing at it in Chapter 7. Only the expenses of the current proceeding qualify for the administrative expense priority.[24]

[¶720]   DISCHARGE OF THE DEBTOR FROM HIS DEBTS

A prepetition agreement by a debtor to pay attorneys' fees in installments after the petition, is dischargeable in bankruptcy. The District Court for the District of Arizona noted that this result might make it difficult for debtors to secure representation, but felt that the problem had to be corrected by Congress, not the courts.[25]

[¶721]   EXCEPTIONS TO DISCHARGE

Certain broad classes of transaction are often involved in litigation (e.g., fraudulent or allegedly fraudulent ones; federal tax enforcement; support of the ex-spouse or children of a dissolved marriage).

The personal property of a Chapter 13 debtor is exempt from the IRC §6334 administrative levy. Nevertheless, the property is not exempt from a federal tax lien under §6321 (neglect or refusal to pay a tax after an IRS demand).[26]

The taxpayer's knowledge that taxes were not paid is not sufficient to prove a willful attempt to evade or defeat the tax (see Bankruptcy Code §523(a)(1)(C)) that would prevent discharge of the tax liabilities; evasion has been deemed by the Eleventh Circuit to be worse than simple non-payment.[27] However, hiding income or assets or failing to file returns is likely to be interpreted as a willful attempt to evade or defeat liability, notwithstanding the fact that simple non-payment of taxes is not a felony.[28] Filing a sham bankruptcy petition with the objective of releasing an IRS levy on wages has been held, by the Ninth Circuit, to constitute a willful attempt to evade tax.[29]

A debtor's obligation to pay part of his military pension to his ex-wife, created by a decree entered nine days before filing of the bankruptcy petition, is not dischargeable. The wife's pension share becomes her separate property, and never enters the bankruptcy estate; the debtor becomes a constructive trustee of the separate share.[30]

Compare this with the Eighth Circuit's determination[31] that the obligation to pay a set amount to the former spouse to settle the pension interest, embodied in a pre-petition divorce decree, is dischargeable, even if installment payments were supposed to continue after the filing of the petition. The divorce decree was neither a Qualified Domestic Relations Order (QDRO) nor linked to amounts actually received by the employee spouse. The Eighth Circuit saw the obligation as an amount certain that the debtor had to pay from whatever assets he had—in other words, a pre-petition debt, not in the nature of maintenance or support, and thus dischargeable.

In an ongoing marriage, one spouse is reasonably entitled to rely on the other spouse's record-keeping (if they have agreed that one of the spouses is responsible for family record-keeping). Therefore, the Ninth Circuit determined that the trial court erred in refusing a discharge to the spouse who delegated the duties because of the other spouse's poor record-keeping. The debtor spouse had no affirmative duty to question the record-keeper unless there was reason to suspect some error or irregularity.[32]

The discharge exception for spousal and child support has been interpreted quite broadly. For instance, the fees that a divorce court orders one spouse to pay to the other spouse's lawyer in a divorce and custody proceeding have been denied discharge, even though they are paid to the attorney rather than the spouse or child. In the Tenth Circuit's reading, coping with support issues is a higher priority of the legal system than giving the debtor a fresh start.[33] Nor can an ex-husband discharge child support **arrears** that his ex-wife assigned to a non-governmental collection agency, on the grounds that the ex-wife did not make a true assignment (which would have been dischargeable), but only an assignment for collection.[34]

Although an obligation to make restitution in a criminal case is not dischargeable, the Sixth Circuit has ruled that criminal fines (and costs imposed in state criminal proceedings) are merely debts and therefore can be discharged.[35]

Promissory notes for the obligation to make installment payments to settle federal False Claims Act civil claims and common-law fraud claims are non-dischargeable. The D.C. Circuit said[36] that these notes fall under the Bankruptcy Code §523(a)(2)(A) ban on discharge of debts involving money or property obtained by fraud.

If a debt was incurred because of fraud, false pretenses, or false representations by the debtor, the Eleventh Circuit says that the debt is non-dischargeable as long as the creditor's reliance would have been justified. Neither actual nor reasonable reliance is required.[37]

[¶723] BANKRUPTCY APPEALS

The Seventh Circuit says that there is no way to get review of a bankruptcy court's denial of a motion to disqualify counsel—because this is neither a collateral order nor a final order that is appealable under 28 U.S.C. §158(d).[38]

— ENDNOTES —

1. *Hubbard v. U.S.*, #94-172, 115 S.Ct. 1754, 131 L.Ed.2nd 779 (Sup.Ct. 5/15/95).

2. *McCratic v. Bristol-Myers Squibb & Co.*, 183 Bank. 113 (N.D.Tex. 6/14/95).

3. *Mason v. Smith*, 64 LW 2568 (N.H.Sup. 3/7/96).

4. *Bone v. Allen*, 186 Bank. 769 (Bank. N.D.Ga. 10/3/95).

5. *Bronson v. U.S.*, 46 F.3d 1573 (Fed.Cir. 1/26/95).

6. *National Tax Credit Partners v. Havlik*, 20 F.3d 705 (7th Cir. 1994).

7. *U.S. v. Wright*, 57 F.3d 561 (7th Cir. 6/14/95).

8. *Roberge v. Roberge*, 188 Bank. 366 (E.D.Va. 11/7/95).

9. *In re Price*, 179 Bank. 209 (Bank. E.D.Cal. 3/14/95).

10. *Debolt v. Comerica Bank*, 177 Bank. 31 (Bank. W.D.Pa. 12/23/94).

11. *In re Duke,* 64 LW 2583 (7th Cir. 3/15/96).

12. *Western Auto Supply Co. v. Savage Arms Inc.,* 43 F.3d 714 (1st Cir. 12/14/94).

13. *Barkley v. Conner,* 64 LW 2511 (9th Cir. 1/11/96).

14. *Solomon v. Cosby,* 67 F.3d 1128 (4th Cir. 10/23/95).

15. *Carpenters Health & Welfare Trust Funds v. Robertson,* 53 F.3d 1064 (9th Cir. 5/8/95).

16. *PBGC v. Pritchard,* 33 F.3d 509 (5th Cir. 4/5/95).

17. *GAC Enterprises Inc. v. Medaglia,* 52 F.3d 451 (2nd Cir. 4/14/95).

18. *Chemetron Corp. v. Jones,* 72 F.3d 341 (3rd Cir. 12/18/95).

19. *De Paolo v. U.S.,* 45 F.3d 373 (10th Cir. 1/9/95).

20. *Bilski v. C.I.R.,* 69 F.3d 64 (5th Cir. 11/20/95).

21. *Towers v. IRS,* 64 F.3d 1292 (9th Cir. 8/23/95). The same thing is true of state taxes:*Missouri Department of Revenue v. L.J. O'Neill Shoe Co.,* 64 F.3d 1146 (8th Cir. 8/30/95).

22. *U.S. v. Chavis,* 47 F.3d 818 (6th Cir. 2/23/95).

23. *In re Vecchio,* 20 F.3d 555 (2nd Cir. 1994); *In re Pacific Atlantic Trading Co.,* 33 F.3d 1064 (9th Cir. 1994).

24. *Stuart v. Carter (In re Larsen),* 59 F.3d 783 (8th Cir. 7/14/95).

25. *Hessinger & Associates v. Voglio,* 64 LW 2431 (D.Ariz. 12/12/95).

26. *In re Voelker,* 42 F.3d 1050 (7th Cir. 12/12/94).

27. *Haas v. IRS,* 48 F.3d 1153 (11th Cir. 3/30/95).

28. *Bruner v. U.S.,* 55 F.3d 195 (5th Cir. 6/21/95).

29. *U.S. v. Huebner,* 48 F.3d 376 (9th Cir. 12/16/94).

30. *McGraw v. McGraw,* 176 Bank. 149 (Bank. S.D. Ohio 12/23/94). However, *In re Omegas Group Inc.,* 16 F.3d 1443 (6th Cir. 1994) reaches the opposite conclusion. *Debolt v. Comerica Bank,* cited above, also takes the position that the divided pension interest immediately becomes separate property of the recipient spouse and does not enter the bankruptcy estate.

31. *In re Ellis,* 72 F.3d 628 (8th Cir. 2/18/95).

32. *Cox v. Lansdowne,* 41 F.3d 1294 (9th Cir. 12/2/94).

33. *Miller v. Gentry,* 55 F.3d 1487 (10th Cir. 5/19/95). Also see the similar cases of *Brown v. Brown,* 21 Fam.L.Rep. 1148 (Bank M.D. Fla. 11/22/94) and *Holliday v. Kline,* 65 F.3d 749 (8th Cir. 9/12/95). However, *In re Perlin,* 30 F.3d 39 (6th Cir. 1994) does permit discharge of the fees.

34. *Smith v. Child Support Enforcement,* 21 Fam.L.Rep. 1287 (D.Utah 4/13/95).

35. *Hardenberg v. Virginia,* 42 F.3d 986 (6th Cir. 12/9/94).

36. *U.S. v. Spicer,* 57 F.3d 1152 (D.C.Cir. 6/30/95).

37. *City Bank & Trust Co. v. Vann*, 67 F.3d 277 (11th Cir. 10/19/95).

38. *Brouwer v. Ancel & Dunlap*, 46 F.3d 653 (7th Cir. 1/31/95).

— FOR FURTHER REFERENCE —

Allred, Steven F., "Protect a Claim in Bankruptcy," 8 *Utah Bar J.* 22 (December '95).

Blackman, Josh and Sean Jenkins, "Finding Good Bankruptcy Data Online and Off," 5 *Law Office Computing* 50 (December '95).

Carlson, David Gray, "Commingled Bank Accounts in Bankruptcy," 28 *Uniform Commercial Code Law J.* 238 (Winter '96).

Howard, Margaret, "Avoiding Powers and the 1994 Amendments to the Bankruptcy Code," 69 *American Bankruptcy L.J.* 259 (Summer '95).

Katz, Owen W., "Valuation of Secured Claims in a Bankruptcy Reorganization," 100 *Commercial L.J.* 320 (Fall '95).

McClain, Bruce W. and Donald C. Haley, "Should the Judgment Debtor File for Bankruptcy?" 42 *Practical Lawyer* 59 (January '96).

Scott, Robert J., "When a Claim Arises Under the Bankruptcy Code," 24 *Hofstra L.Rev.* 253 (Fall '95).

Sheppard, Lee A., "Bankruptcy Tax Policy: How Far Should Equitable Subordination Go?" 69 *Tax Notes* 1317 (December 11, 1995).

White, Michaela M., "Divorce After the Bankruptcy Reform Act of 1994," 29 *Creighton L.Rev.* 617 (March '96).

Vician, Glenn S., "The Legal Effect of a Bankruptcy Discharge on State Court Judgments," 39 *Res Gestae* 14 (December '95).

COMPENSATION AND FRINGE BENEFITS

[¶1201] An early 1995 Supreme Court case clarifies ERISA §402(b)93), which requires plans to maintain a procedure for amending the plan, including the identity of the person(s) with authority to amend. According to the Supreme Court, this requirement is satisfied by reserving the right of "the company" to amend, without greater specificity.[1]

In the spring of 1996, the Supreme Court ruled that the employer acted as an ERISA fiduciary when, in its role as plan administrator, it informed employees that they would retain their benefits if they transferred employment and benefit plan participation to a reorganized corporate entity. In fact, the reorganized entity was insolvent, and the employees lost benefit entitlement. The employees were permitted to sue for breach of fiduciary duty based on the employer's deceptive scheme. Individual beneficiaries can sue for breach of fiduciary duty; the cause of action is not limited to relief for the plan as an entirety.[2]

The Pension Annuitants Protection Act of 1994, P.L. 103-401 (10/22/94) amends 29 U.S.C. §1132(a). The Department of Labor, a plan participant or beneficiary, or a plan fiduciary can sue to make sure that a participant or beneficiary actually receives the amounts that are supposed to be provided under an insurance contract or annuity purchased in connection with the termination of the beneficiary's status as a plan participant. In other words, if the insurer or annuity fails, the deprived beneficiary or persons acting on his or her behalf will have legal redress.

The State Income Taxation of Pension Income Act, P.L. 104-95 (1/10/96) amends 4 U.S.C. §114. It is impermissible for a state to impose income tax on retirement income paid to anyone who is neither a resident or domiciliary of the would-be taxing state (as determined by the would-be taxing state's own laws). The ban applies to income from qualified plans, IRAs, SEPs, and 403(a) and (b) annuity plans, as long as the income is provided in substantially equal periodic payments, at least annually, for a period of at least 10 years, or for the life of the participant or the joint lives of participant and beneficiary.

[¶1202] PENSION AND PROFIT-SHARING PLANS

One of the first questions that arises in the pension context is whether there is a "plan" at all. To the First Circuit, for instance, a series of four early retirement offers made in connection with Reductions in Force did not constitute an ERISA plan, because the offers were unrelated and did not impose a continuing obligation on the company.[3]

The actuarial assumptions of a defined benefit plan are tested to see if they are reasonable in the aggregate—not whether they are "substantially unreasonable"; but they are not presumed to be reasonable. The plan's actuary must satisfy a procedural test of making the best estimate of the funds needed to satisfy the obligations. The actuary can properly make conservative assumptions, but the Sixth Circuit found that the actual assumptions behind a law firm's plan were unreasonable (e.g., assuming partners would retire at age 60, although enhanced benefits were not available unless they deferred retirement to age 63).[4]

Even where the employer has the option of reducing or terminating non-vested benefits (in this case, early retirement benefits), ERISA's anti-retaliation provision forbids firing employees as a means of avoiding making the payments.[5]

It is fairly common for employers to promise their workers that health benefits will be maintained at the existing level (often 100% paid for by the employer) for the lifetime of those who retire early—and then to attempt to terminate the benefits or increase the payments expected of the employees. An early 1996 Sixth Circuit case grants an injunction forcing the employer to reinstate the benefits to their original level, premised on the likelihood that the employees will prevail on their LMRA §301 claim.[6]

However, in this reading, the employees are not entitled to a jury trial because their claim for damages (health costs incurred because of the employer's inappropriate termination of benefits) is merely incidental to the equitable remedy of injunction. A little later, the Eleventh Circuit decided that employees do have a Seventh Amendment right to jury trial of their LMRA §301 claim that the employer breached its collective bargaining agreement obligations with respect to retirement benefits.[7] In this interpretation, the right to a jury trial is not lost by joining the LMRA claim and an ERISA claim for the same monetary relief.

The IRS has ruled that defined benefit plans with 100 or more participants must maintain liquid plan assets approximately equal to three times the total disbursements made from the plan trust in the 12-month period preceding each quarter in which a quarterly contribution must be made to the plan.[8]

When a plan is terminated, the 1987 ERISA amendments affecting 29 U.S.C. §1362 (employer's liability to the PBGC for unfunded benefits) preempt LMRA §301, so neither employees nor the union can bring a claim to recover non-guaranteed pension benefits.[9]

In a Tax Court case from mid-1995, a wife filed for divorce in February, 1985. In March of 1986, the husband's corporation voted to terminate its profit-sharing plan. He withdrew his balance (about $200,000 in community property and $100,000 in separate property) and gave it to his wife, who distributed the balance in accounts in her sole name designated as rollover IRAs.

The couple entered into a separation agreement in October, 1988. This agreement, later incorporated into the divorce decree, awarded the profit-sharing plan to the wife. The husband was in the unfortunate position of being held liable for early distribution of the lump sum (he was only 49 when the amount was distributed) and the tax on excess plan distributions. The wife was liable for the excise tax on excess contributions to a plan because the amount was far greater than one year's permissible IRA contribution, and did not qualify as a rollover because the Tax Court says it is impermissible for one person to roll over a balance to another person's IRA. The QDRO rules do not apply, because the transfer was made before the separation agreement and therefore could not have implemented the agreement.[10]

On a simpler QDRO question, the Central District of California has held that ERISA preempts a state domestic relations law that requires pension plans to pay attorneys' fees in connection with QDROs.[11] According to the Eighth Circuit, no QDRO was present in a case in which a bankruptcy debtor was obligated to pay a set amount to his spouse to settle her interest in his pension. The obligation was created by a pre-petition divorce decree. The Eighth Circuit permitted discharge of this obligation in bankruptcy, seeing the obligation as a simple pre-petition debt (even though installment payments were due after filing), and not liability for family support or maintenance that would be non-dischargeable.[12]

With respect to other bankruptcy issues, the Ninth Circuit ruled that Bankruptcy Code §541(c)(2) kept the debtor's pension assets out of his bankruptcy estate, despite his power to withdraw them.[13] The Fifth Circuit held that only a plan administrator or the PBGC can terminate a pension plan—a bankruptcy trustee can neither do so on his own motion nor be ordered to do so by a bankruptcy court.[14]

Prevailing parties in ERISA cases (unlike those in civil rights cases) are not presumed entitled to attorneys' fees—it depends on factors such as the loser's degree of culpability, ability to pay fees, deterrent effect of fee awards, the relative strength of each side's arguments, and the value of the victory to plan participants.[15]

ERISA's anti-alienation provision does not prevent garnishment of a vested plan interest to satisfy an IRS judgment. The Sixth Circuit says that the anti-alienation provision contains an explicit exemption of federal tax levies and judgments; given the strength of the federal interest in collecting taxes, this cannot be called an arbitrary or capricious regulation.[16]

Amounts received in settlement of an ERISA suit are not sufficiently like tortious personal injuries to be excluded from the recipient's gross income—at least according to the Southern District of Texas.[17] On another tax issue, the Ninth Circuit held that pass-through income from an S Corporation does not constitute net earnings from self-employment that can be used to calculate the Keogh plan deduction.[18]

[¶1216] GROUP HEALTH INSURANCE

By and large, employers draft their plans reserving the right to alter or even terminate the benefits, and such provisions are valid and enforceable. However, employers may subject themselves to liability if they make independent promises that benefits will be continued—and especially if the employees surrender something (such as current compensation or continued employment) in return for the promise. An employer may also be liable if it misleads its employees and ex-employees, even though it would not be liable if it had communicated truthfully to them and informed them that benefits would be unavailable.

An employer was enjoined against violating its promise of lifetime retiree health benefits, at no cost to the employees, by the Sixth Circuit.[19] However, the plaintiff employees could not get a jury trial in their quest for damages (health care costs they encountered because the employer broke its promise), on the grounds that the damages are only incidental to the equitable remedy of the injunction.

Another, similar case holds that it would be a breach of fiduciary duty if, in fact, the employer did repeatedly lie about whether retiree benefits would continue for life; equitable relief is available under ERISA §502(a)(3) if falsehoods can be proved. In this reading, it is wrongful for an employer to give a vague or incorrect answer to a specific employee inquiry—particularly on a "repeated or pervasive basis."[20] However, given the equitable nature of the claim, employees cannot get money damages for the breach of fiduciary duty—only equitable, restitutionary measures such as back benefits and restoration of the status quo.

The Ninth Circuit permitted a plan's fiduciaries to sue the fiduciaries of a predecessor plan for harm caused to the second plan by the errors of the earlier fiduciaries—because mergers or spinoffs should not be used to protect fiduciaries against the consequences of their own mistakes.[21]

— ENDNOTES —

1. *Curtiss-Wright Corp. v. Schoonejongen*, #93-1935, 115 S.Ct. 1223, 131 L.Ed.2d 94 (Sup.Ct. 3/6/95).

2. *Varity Corp. v. Howe*, #94-1471, 64 LW 4138 (Sup.Ct. 3/19/96), *affirming* 36 F.3d 746 and 41 F.3d 1263, both 8th Cir. 1994.

3. *Belanger v. Wyman-Gordon Co.*, 71 F.3d 451 (1st Cir. 12/14/95).

4. *Rhoades, McKee & Baer v. U.S.*, 43 F.3d 1071 (6th Cir. 1/10/95). Compare with *Citrus Valley Estates Inc. v. C.I.R.*, 49 F.3d 1410 (9th Cir. 3/8/95) permitting conservative actuarial assumptions in a defined benefit plan (which have the effect of increasing both the employer's contributions to the plan and its tax deductions) because the actuary's responsibility includes prevention of underfunding in addition to preventing inappropriate contributions and tax deductions.

5. *Heath v Varity Corp.*, 71 F.3d 256 (7th Cir. 11/30/95).

6. *Golden v. Kelsey-Hayes Co.*, 64 LW 2458 (6th Cir. 1/18/96).

7. *Steward v. KHO Deutz of America Corp.*, 64 LW 2574 (11th Cir. 2/28/96).

8. Rev.Rul. 95-31, 1995-1 C.B. 76.

9. *United Steelworkers of America v. United Engineering Inc.*, 63 LW 2699 (6th Cir. 5/2/95).

10. *Rodoni v. C.I.R.*, 105 T.C. No. 3 (7/24/95).

11. *AT&T Management Pension Plan v. Tucker*, 64 LW 2224 (C.D.Cal. 8/17/95).

12. *In re Ellis*, 72 F.3d 628 (8th Cir. 2/18/95).

13. *Barkley v. Conner*, 64 LW 2511 (9th Cir. 1/11/96).

14. *PBGC v. Pritchard*, 33 F.3d 509 (5th Cir. 4/5/95).

15. *Eddy v. Colonial Life Co.*, 59 F.3d 201 (D.C.Cir. 7/7/95).

16. *U.S. v. Sawaf*, 64 LW 2475 (6th Cir. 1/26/96).

17. *Dotson v. U.S.*, 876 F.Supp. 911 (S.D.Tex. 2/15/95).

18. *Durando v. U.S.*, 70 F.3d 548 (9th Cir. 11/16/95).

19. *Golden v. Kelsey-Hayes Co.*, 64 LW 2458 (6th Cir. 1/18/96).

20. *In re UNISYS Corp. Retiree Medical Benefits ERISA Litigation*, 58 F.3d 896 (3rd Cir. 6/28/95).

21. *Pilkington PLC v. Perelman*, 72 F.3d 1396 (9th Cir. 12/27/95).

— FOR FURTHER REFERENCE —

Basi, Bart A. and Ed Rodnam, "Retirement Plan Rules Supersede Premarital Contract," 24 *Taxation for Lawyers* 226 (January-February 1996).

Behling, Paul L., "Not All Domestic Relations Orders Satisfy QDRO Rules," 24 *Taxation for Lawyers* 212 (January-February '96).

Frankel, George, "Planning Strategies for Inherited IRA Withdrawals," 24 *Taxation for Lawyers* 231 (January-February '96).

Fredman, James, "COBRA Continuation Coverage," 28 *J. of Health and Hospital Law* 264 (November-December '95).

Golub, Ira M., "Multiemployer Group Health Plans and COBRA," *21 J. Pension Planning and Compliance* 1 (Winter '96).

Kautter, David J. and Jennifer L. Wells, "Rollover of Qualified Plan Benefits—The Importance of Form," 27 *Tax Adviser* 9 (January '96).

Navin, Patrick T., "401(k) Wraparound Arrangements," 23 *J. of Corporate Taxation* 70 (Spring '96).

Rickel, Alice, "Extending Employee Benefits to Domestic Partners," 16 *Whittier L.Rev.* 737 (Fall '95).

Wharton, Joseph, "Employee Benefits: Misrepresentations Violate Duty," 82 *A.B.A.J.* 48 (January '96).

COMPUTER LAW

[¶1301] The Telecommunications Act of 1996, P.L. 104-104 (enacted 2/8/96) includes §509, "Online Family Empowerment." This section, which adds a new section, 47 USC §230, is nicknamed the Communications Decency Act. The Congressional findings for the enactment are that, although Internet and other interactive computer services have immense educational and information potential, families need control over what materials are transmitted to their homes.

To this end, on-line services and Internet service providers are encouraged to screen the materials appearing on their services, to eliminate offensive materials. (See ¶1305, below, for court cases that create the problem Congress was trying to eliminate.) Furthermore, a provider or user of an on-line or Internet service is not treated as the "publisher" or "speaker" of information that derives from another information content provider. There is a "good Samaritan" rule which absolves on-line and Internet services from liability if they undertake the burden of restricting access to obscene, violent, harassing, or other objectionable material.

As the discussion below shows, court rulings discourage computer services from exercising editorial control; Congress wants to "remove disincentives for the development and utilization of blocking and filtering technologies that empower parents to restrict their children's access to objectionable or inappropriate online material."[1]

Another Congressional objective is "vigorous enforcement of Federal criminal laws to deter and punish trafficking in obscenity, stalking, and harassment by means of computer."[2] The Communications Decency Act is often discussed as adding new criminal penalties, but in fact all the statute says is that it has no effect to impair the enforcement of existing federal criminal statutes, including those dealing with obscenity and sexual exploitation of children.

A coalition of civil liberties and computer users' organizations has challenged the statute's conformity to the First Amendment. The first case to be heard is in the District Court for the District of Pennsylvania; a similar case was heard in the Southern District of New York.[3] Both struck down the CDA.

On the issue of transmission of obscene material, the Sixth Circuit decided early in 1996 that 18 U.S.C.§1465, knowing transport in interstate commerce of obscene materials, applies to transmission of pornographic images on a BBS (computer bulletin board system).[4] The defendants said that the computer image files were intangible and therefore not covered by the legislation. However, the court found the means of transmission to be irrelevant if the illicit result occurs. To protect themselves, BBSs can limit downloading of images to areas where the images are not in violation of community standards.

The Department of Justice engaged in a prolonged investigation as to whether Microsoft had monopolized the market for operating systems. A consent decree was agreed to. The District Court for the District of Columbia initially refused to grant the required approval of the consent decree, finding that the scope of the decree was too narrow; the government had not furnished enough information to test the impact on the public; and the decree did not have adequate enforcement mechanisms. The D.C. Circuit reversed the District Court, however, finding that the trial court improperly extended its inquiry to subjects that were outside the scope of the DOJ's investigation.[5]

Spare parts used to repair computers under service contracts have been held not to be inventory by the Federal Circuit. The parts are not held primarily for sale to customers, so they can be treated as a depreciable capital asset.[6]

This supplement adds a discussion of law office computing and the Internet.

[¶1304] COMPUTERS AND COPYRIGHT ISSUES

The case of *Lotus Development Corp. v. Borland* has had an adventurous history in the courts. The case arose when Borland's Quattro Pro spreadsheet program copied Lotus' "menu tree" (the arrangement of about 500 computer commands into over 50 menus and submenus) in order to make Quattro Pro files compatible with Lotus files. The District Court deemed this to be an infringement of Lotus' copyright on its software. However, in early 1995, the First Circuit reversed the District Court, finding the menu tree to be a "method of operation" rather than copyrightable subject matter. Certiorari was granted. However, at the beginning of 1996, the Supreme Court merely affirmed the First Circuit, 4-4 (Justice Stevens did not participate) without opinion.[7]

A company that invested heavily in compiling a CD-ROM telephone directory was defeated in the Western District of Wisconsin when it sued for copyright infringement when a competitor put the contents of the proprietary CD-ROMs on the Internet.[8] In the court's judgment, the competitor proceeded by copying the CDs on the hard drive of its own computer, then added its own search engine for Internet use. The copying to the competitor's hard drive was deemed "personal use," so there was no copyright infringement; furthermore, the telephone directories were not copyrightable subject matter because they were purely factual listings. The CD-ROM disks were sold with the conventional "shrink-wrap license" that forbids copying, but the District Court refused to enforce the shrink-wrap license, deeming it to be a contract of adhesion contrary to the Uniform Commercial Code.

The federal wire fraud statute cannot be used to pursue criminal copyright infringement charges under 17 U.S.C. §506(a) against the operator of a BBS who allowed users to download pirated copies of copyrighted software. This result was reached because the BBS operator did not profit financially from software piracy, and the criminal copyright infringement statute (unlike the wire fraud statute) requires proof of personal financial advantage to the infringer.[9]

[¶1305] DEVELOPMENTS RELATING TO COMMERCIAL ON-LINE SERVICES

In mid-1995, the New York Supreme Court decided that the on-line service Prodigy was a "publisher" that could be sued for libel because the allegedly libellous communication appeared on a "forum" that had a moderator, and Prodigy held itself out as pre-screening posted material and exercising editorial control over material appearing on the service.[10]

A number of confidential, and copyrighted, Scientology documents were posted to the Internet by disaffected former Scientologists. Two District Courts reached opposite conclusions about the status of such activities. One court denied a preliminary injunction, finding the posting to be fair use because it was non-commercial, did not harm the church financially, and because it occurred in the context of discussion and criticism of the church.[11] Two months later, however, another court decided that a BBS or Internet Service Provider can be contributorily liable for copyright infringement if it is on actual notice—or should have known—that the posts were infringing yet failed to remove them once their copyright status became known.[12]

[¶1307] LAW OFFICE COMPUTING

Once an exotic device found only in the largest, most prosperous, and most technologically daring firm, the computer is now a device that (in desktop or laptop form) is becoming universal in all kinds of law practice settings. Law office computing can perform many functions:

➤ Simple word processing

➤ Document assembly

➤ Time keeping, calendaring, scheduling

➤ Billing

➤ Litigation support

➤ Preparation of exhibits and presentation materials

➤ Document transmission (fax, e-mail, file transfers)

➤ Communications among lawyers, between lawyers and clients, etc. (groupware)

➤ Management of databases (such as names and addresses of clients, past clients, potential clients). There are also powerful databases of corporate information, patent applications, trademarks, and many other areas available as software or on-line.

➤ Legal research

➤ Law firm marketing

➤ Obtaining referrals; referring matters

➤ Training attorneys (e.g., in courtroom skills).

In order to use these powerful functions effectively, the attorney or law firm must choose the right balance of hardware and software. Depending on individual needs and technological sophistication, the choice might be made by practicing lawyers; delegated to Management Information Systems (MIS) personnel within a firm; or premised on advice from an outside consultant.

The equation is complicated by the rapid pace of change in computer technology. Many firms have confidently invested large sums of money in what was then advanced technology, only to find that their equipment is soon wildly outdated, incompatible with other firms' and court system equipment, and hard to use in the bargain.

A consensus has emerged: the vast majority of law office computing now uses IBM or IBM clone computers (PCs), and most of those use some version of the Windows operating system, with an increasing trend toward adopting Windows '95. Some lawyers still prefer Apple computers, a few prefer the more technically elaborate Unix system, but overall DOS, and especially Windows on a PC "platform," are favored.

Computers are described in terms of their operating system (OS), such as Windows '95 or Unix; in terms of the kind of processor running the computer (the most common kinds on the market today are 486, Pentium, and Pentium Pro); how fast they operate (specified in megahertz, or mHz; speeds over 100 mHz are typical); how much Random Access Memory—RAM—they have available (4 MB is an absolute minimum for running Windows, and 8 MB or 16 MB is better); and how much storage space they have on their hard drives. Law office computers need at least 200 megabytes of hard disk storage for each machine; it's easy to buy computers that store more than 1 gigabyte (a gigabyte is 1,000 megabytes). Most law offices use laser printers to print their work. Two or more computers can share a single printer. Printer speed is measured in terms of pages per minute; an 8 ppm printer is conventional for law office use.

[¶1307.1] Law Office Hardware

At its most basic, a law office computing system requires at least a Central Processing Unit (CPU) for handling data, devices for inputting data (keyboard and mouse are the most common), a monitor for viewing data, and a printer for producing output on paper. A sole practitioner, or an individual lawyer within a firm, may choose to supplement (or even replace) a desktop computer unit with a laptop—a portable computer that has a flat screen in the lid instead of a separate monitor.

A laptop computer can be transported on a business trip, to a law library, to court, to the location of a deposition, and functions such as word processing and data transmission can be carried out from these remote locations. Clearly, then, the laptop computer offers many advantages over the traditional yellow legal pad. However, it also has several disadvantages: the laptop weighs several pounds instead of several ounces; nothing too bad happens if you drop a yellow legal pad; and legal pads are not particularly attractive to thieves.

A more sophisticated law office system will include anywhere from a handful of computers to hundreds of them. Where there are multiple computers, it makes sense to connect them into a network so software, files, and printers can be shared. Two conventional ways of doing this are Ethernet and LAN (Local Area Networking). Networking requires additional hardware, software, and expertise. A LAN with more than two or three computers requires the firm to have a "server" (a special computer dedicated to directing information over the network).

Networking also has its own problems and risks: a problem on one computer could crash the whole system; data could inadvertently be made available to someone who isn't supposed to see it. (Any information on any computer is at risk of being "hacked" by an inquisitive or hostile person, or by someone with an interest in industrial espionage; networks are especially vulnerable because they are designed to share information.)

Computers and computer systems can also include other options for capturing and transmitting information. For instance, scanners—which capture a drawing, photograph, or other image and transmit it into computer-usable form—can be used to add documents to a database or word processing system without having to retype text.

The traditional medium for storing data is either the hard disk (within the computer) or the floppy disk. Newer options include CD-ROM drives, which play small, silvery platters that look like music CDs. Originally, CDs were a "read-only" mechanism—that is, users could read them but could not make their own recordings. Today, it is fairly easy and fairly inexpensive to create CDs with desktop equipment, so this may become an option for backing up large amounts of data (e.g., litigation documents).

A research session may require the use of multiple CDs: for instance, one CD containing cases from your state's trial courts, another CD with state appellate cases, a third with federal cases, and a fourth containing a treatise on practice in your state. Devices called "towers" or "jukeboxes" are useful so you can access multiple CDs quickly. These devices are also useful for a law firm library, where many lawyers share single copies of CD publications.

There are other options for back-up, including tape drives, portable hard disks, and "floptical" drives and magnetic media that are something like a hybrid between floppy disk and a hard drive. Backing up data is vitally important for all users, and especially so for law firms—a computer or system malfunction could easily wipe out thousands of hours of work. However, computer and back-up technology evolve continually, so a one-time perfect solution may become obsolete. It doesn't do much good to have years of data stored on 8½″ floppy disks using proprietary software if you don't own and can't buy any equipment that uses 8½″ disks, and no one remembers how to use the software! Every law firm must have policies for backing up data, and it's a useful discipline for solo practitioners to develop personal routines for ensuring regular back-ups.

In addition to fax machines (which are really a specialized type of computer printer), law offices can have fax modems. A modem—which stands for MODulator/DEModulator—transmits computer signals over a telephone wire. A modem is used to transmit information between two computers. They can be four feet apart, in the same office, or several continents apart. Modems are also used to connect to on-line services, the Internet, and the World Wide Web. Modems are measured by the speed at which they can transmit data. Standard modems are rated at 9600 kB (thousand bytes transmitted per second; a byte is a unit of data approximately equal to one character) or 14.4 kB (14,400 bytes per second). The fastest modems available usually have a speed of 28.8 kB.

However, there are many factors that reduce the actual speed of a modem way below the maximum speed that its manufacturer advertises. A modem can't work any faster than the other modem it's communicating with, and problems with the telephone line over which the communication takes place can also slow things down considerably.

Law office computing also has implications for the firm's phone system. Voice mail is a useful service that complements electronic mail (e-mail) and written communications. Furthermore, if a law firm spends a lot of time connected to the Internet, it may make sense to replace its conventional telephone service with special ISDN or T-1 lines. These lines make it possible to speed up electronic communications very significantly, but they also require heavy investment in non-standard equipment.

E-mail is an extremely useful technology, and one which can be utilized by anyone with a computer (even an old computer with little memory) and a modem. E-mail service is provided by on-line services and Internet services providers, or is also available by purchasing specialized communications software.

Messages and computer files can be transmitted directly to anyone who has an e-mail address. Lawyers find it particularly useful because it avoids "telephone tag" (when one party attempts to return a phone call from an original caller who is now unavailable, and leaves a message which in turn is returned when the caller is unavailable) and makes it possible to transmit factual information in writing without having to dictate the information to a clerical worker or leave a voice mail message. However, it must always be remembered that e-mail is not entirely private, so confidential matters should not be transmitted because there is a risk that unauthorized people will gain access.

[¶1307.2] Electronic Legal Research

Anyone with a modem can connect to distant computers. For more than a decade, huge repositories of legal information have been available on for-profit computer systems such as LEXIS and Westlaw. To use these research resources, the attorney gets an account with the service provider, learns how to search the databank, and agrees to pay fees for the time connected to the service. Each service (and sometimes, each part of a service) has its own methods for setting up "queries" (directions to the system to perform a computer search). Complaints from users have borne fruit—services are making it easier to do "natural language" searches that approach closer to the ideal of just telling the computer what you want.

Electronic legal research can also be done by buying CD-ROMs from legal publishers. CD-ROMs can store the equivalent of dozens or even hundreds of books; CD technology makes it easy to search through the material on the CD for a particular case, or for information on a particular topic. "Hybrids" are common (i.e., the publisher sells a CD-ROM that contains an archive of cases, regulations, or other materials, and also gives the customer on-line access to the latest update material to supplement the disks).

[¶1308] THE INTERNET

The much-hyped Internet began as a U.S. military project for devising a computer system that would survive a nuclear war so government operations could resume after the smoke cleared. A "protocol" (communications standard) was developed so computers at great distances could communicate over ordinary telephone lines. The Internet, then, consists of all the computers that can use this basic protocol or a related protocol.

Although the military is no longer involved in Internet operations, originally the Internet was very much a sophisticated scientific tool. There was no interest in making it "user-friendly." However, as more and more people became interested in Internet access, more programmers designed "front ends" (interfaces that make it easier to connect to the Internet, and to communicate with other Internet users).

Sites on the Internet are identified by "domain names." A domain name has many resemblance to a trademark. A domain name is acquired by registration, but in this case with the voluntary organization InterNic rather than with a government agency. Domains are divided into several types: .com, for commercial domains, .edu for educational organization domains (typically universities), .gov for government agencies, and .org for organizations (usually non-profit organizations). There are some significant intellectual property and antitrust issues in selecting a domain name—for instance, InterNic had to act to prevent "grabbing" of a competitor's domain name for the specific purpose of denying the competitor access to its own name.[13]

[¶1308.1] On-Line Services

In addition to specialized legal on-line services, law firms may use more general on-line services such as Compuserve or America OnLine. They have databanks of information (e.g., continually updated stock quotes). Subscribers to the service can also join "forums" or "chat rooms" where they can communicate with other subscribers by typing into their own computers and reading typed messages from others. In general, on-line services provide their subscribers with free software for connecting to the service. The users pay a monthly fee, and often have to pay an additional fee based on the amount of time they spend connected to the service. There may also be additional charges (e.g., for access to specialized forums or copying documents from those forums).

On-line services offer several benefits to the law firm whose staff has little technical sophistication. It's easy to set up the account, use the software, and establish communications. On-line service subscribers also get an e-mail (electronic mail) address. E-mail is the extremely useful ability to type a message into one's own desktop computer, have it conveyed to the on-line service's central computer, and have that computer convey the message in a form that can be accessed by the intended recipient or recipients of the message. (The same message can easily be sent to multiple parties—e.g., a request to reschedule a deposition.)

A few years ago, there was a clear distinction between the proprietary nature of on-line services, where fees were charged for access to a database, and the free materials available from the Internet. However, today the distinction is blurred. Most on-line services make it possible for their users to connect to the Internet and World Wide Web. Furthermore, there is an increasing trend to require subscriptions or other fees for access to materials on the Internet.

[¶1308.2] The World Wide Web

Originally, the Internet was designed by computer scientists for computer scientists, so the ability to find (or program) complex software and use arcane Unix commands was necessary to use the Internet. As more and more people became interested in Internet access, a number of "front end" programs were created to facilitate this process.

At the same time, the concepts of Graphical User Interface (GUI) and hyperlinks were evolving. Instead of communicating with the computer by issuing commands or using menus, the GUI user communicates by using the computer mouse to point to and click on "icons"—pictures—representing the desired item or computer function. Hyperlinks are highlighted items within a computer document. Pointing to one of these items and clicking on it results in a "jump" to that item. For instance, if a cite within a court opinion is highlighted, it becomes possible to retrieve the cited case by pointing and clicking on the cite. Originally, this mechanism was called hypertext, but today links can be made to images, sounds, and even videos, so the broader term is used.

The World Wide Web is the portion of the Internet that uses GUIs and hyperlinks. To be usable by the Web, files have to be coded with HTML, the Hypertext Mark-Up Language, a simple system of identifying text, captions, headlines, and other features of a computer display.

An important—and fashionable—feature of the Web is the "home page." A person, agency, corporation, or organization that has a home page makes information available on the World Wide Web. Web users who reach the home page can learn about that person or institution, as well as linking to other information.

For example, a law firm can use a home page as an enhancement of its firm brochure and firm newsletter. The home page can give basic information about the firm; users can click on various areas in the home page to get more information about attorneys at the firm, their background and specialties, or about planning tips and new legal developments.

[¶1308.3]   Internet and Web Connections

The first requisites for using the Internet and World Wide Web are a computer, a modem, and a mouse. The broadest opportunities are available for those using Windows or Unix; Internet access is moderately available for Apple computer users, and very limited for DOS users.

Next, the user must have a way to connect. As noted above, most on-line services provide some degree of Internet access, and the companies supply their own software for reaching and using the Internet and Web. It is also possible to contract with an Internet Service Provider (ISP)—the equivalent of a telephone company—that offers a more direct connection to the Internet. As a general rule, ISPs charge a monthly fee; the fee may be a flat fee for unlimited usage, or there may be a basic entitlement with charges for additional hours or for connection to certain files. Very heavy Internet users can install special telephone lines for direct Internet connection without an ISP.

For the individual practitioner or firm, the choice comes down to whether an on-line service offers useful material in addition to Internet access, and whether the convenience and ease of use of an on-line service makes up for its higher cost as compared to establishing an account with an Internet Service Provider.

Using the various Internet tools, or connecting with the Web, requires special software. You may be able to get the software free, as part of your deal with an ISP or on-line service. A great deal of software can be borrowed or downloaded electronically because it is "freeware." Freeware is created by programmers who are willing to make their work available without charge. Another possibility is "shareware," which can be downloaded without an explicit charge. However, shareware uses an honor system: if you like the software, you are expected to pay a fee. The fee, in turn, entitles you to manuals, technical support, updates, and other advantages.

Sometimes freeware or shareware is a limited version of a commercial program; to get all the features of the program, you have to buy it. Huge quantities of software are available in computer stores and by mail order. There is an increasing trend to sell software directly over the Internet: as soon as payment is arranged, the software is transferred directly to your computer.

To search the Web, you will require two kinds of special software: a "socket" program (called a Winsock) and a "browser," such as Mosaic or Netscape Navigator, for actually looking at files and transferring their contents to your own computer.

[¶1308.4]   Internet/Web Tools

Immense quantities of information are available electronically, and more information is added each day. Of course, the mere fact that information comes to you from a computer does not make it any more reliable than information delivered verbally or in print. This obvious fact is often ignored, facilitating various kinds of errors and frauds.

The Internet isn't really run by anybody, and there are very few standards (other than some standards relating to obscenity, and ordinary legal principles of intellectual property and libel) for placing material on the Internet. In effect, the Internet is the equivalent of the Library of Congress if all the books were dumped on the floor, without call numbers and in no discernable order.

Materials on the Internet and World Wide Web don't have "call numbers," but they have Uniform Resource Locators, or URLs, which function as the equivalent of addresses or telephone numbers. The domain name (see above) is part of the URL; the rest of the URL identifies specific materials located within the domain. URLs for Websites usually (though not inevitably) begin with "http:/www." (HTTP is the hypertext transmission protocol, used for coding files so they can be displayed on the Web.) So the URL http:/www.BigMovieStudio.com would take you to the home page of Big Movie Studio, a commercial organization.

There are many ways to search for information on the Internet. You might see a potentially interesting URL in a book or article. If it's a Web site, viewing that site gives you the opportunity to link to other related sites simply by clicking on the relevant hyperlink. For instance, a site about real estate law might have links to related subjects such as real estate taxation and environmental law. Software for using the Internet gives users the opportunity to create "bookmarks," so it's easy for them to return to favorite sites during later sessions of computer research.

There are several "search engines" (Yahoo! and Lycos are among the most famous). Search engines are powerful programs that look at vast amounts of information and then create indexes, informing you of sites where relevant information may be located.

If you have a specific question to research, and need to learn the URLs of, or get access to, Internet and Web sites that contain relevant information, a search engine may offer the help you need. Most federal agencies, and an increasing number of state governments, courts, and agencies, have an Internet presence, so you may gain access to the relevant documents that way. There are also major research facilities maintained by universities and specialized organizations.

One of the earliest Internet tools still remaining in use is the gopher—a menu system that you consult when you want to "go for" information. You get gopher software (by purchase; from your on-line service or ISP; by downloading it) and then use it to make connections to files that are listed on the gopher system of a particular server (central Internet computer) or other gopher servers. Most legal information is found on large computers called "gopher servers," so expertise with the gopher tool is an important part of electronic legal research.

Another early Internet tool is "archie," the cumulative index of all the files on all Internet servers. There are variants and developments of archie called, of course, veronica and jughead. (No betty, though.)

Telnet is the process of "calling" a remote computer, so you need to know the relevant URL. You also must know the passwords needed to log on to that computer and access its files.

Once you know where to find a file you want to see, you can do just that (see it), or you can also transfer the file to your own computer. The most common way of doing this is "anonymous FTP" (using the File Transfer Protocol on an "anonymous" basis—you identify yourself as "anonymous" when you log in, and you use your e-mail address as a password). About half of all the traffic on the Internet consists of FTP. Using FTP requires mastering some UNIX commands. Many of the files are stored in compressed form, so you'll need decompression software to make them usable. Depending on the kind of Internet access you have, using FTP may transfer files to your server's computer instead of yours, so you'll need additional software and an extra step to get the files downloaded to your own computer.

[¶1308.5] Mailing Lists and Newsgroups

The Internet is not just a repository of existing information which can be viewed passively; it is also an important communications tool. People with common interests can create mailing lists and newsgroups so they can stay current on their favorite topics, or exchange information and opinions.

Listserv is a very basic technology under which individuals who have a computer and modem (whether or not they have Internet access) exchange information via e-mail. If you subscribe to a Listserv (which is done by sending e-mail to the Listserv's central administration), messages from the Listserv will be listed with your other e-mail messages. You can "post" (send) your own messages to the Listserv, or reply to messages posted by other participants.

A newsgroup is an electronic mailing list that is restricted to a predefined subject area. For instance, a legal newsgroup might deal with a specialized area such as breast implant products liability litigation. Some newsgroups limit the number of types of users who can participate. Many of them have a moderator to keep the discussion on-track. A defined time period may be set for a particular discussion.

A "thread" is a series of e-mail messages relating to the same topic. For instance, a Kansas attorney may post a query about the use of a particular type of trust in estate planning. Responses may be posted by two other Kansas attorneys, as well as lawyers in Ohio, New Jersey, and Florida. One important feature in choosing e-mail software is whether it only displays messages in chronological order, or whether it can arrange all the messages of a "thread" together. The messages make much more sense displayed together than scattered through all your other mail.

You subscribe to a mailing list or newsgroup by sending an e-mail message to the central administration e-mail address. Your request is usually granted automatically, but for moderated groups, you may need to ask permission. A similar routine is followed to "unsubscribe" if you don't like a list or newsgroup or have too much e-mail to read.

[¶1308.6] Law Firm Marketing on the Web

Several hundred law firms already have their own Web home pages. Some on-line services and ISPs provide the software for constructing simple home pages, and allow a simple home page to be displayed for free. At the high end of the market, it's possible to spend hundreds of thousands of dollars designing a site and thousands of dollars a month to display and maintain it. In between, it's easy to learn enough HTML (the Web language) to create a page that is somewhat more sophisticated than the basic model. It usually costs between $100 and $300 a month to display your page on a commercial Web server.

A law firm home page serves the same function as a firm brochure or client newsletter. However, merely putting those print materials into electronic form is not very appealing. It's better to offer clients and potential clients two-way interactive communication with the firm, and make sure that the information is constantly updated so clients will want to consult the home page (and think about your firm) frequently.

To give access to your home page to Web users, you can list it with the search engines. (So far, this is usually simple to do and free.) You can also contact law-related Web sites (such as Law Journal Extra or Lexis Counsel Connect) and see if they will list your firm's home page.

— ENDNOTES —

1. 47 U.S.C. §230(b)(4), as enacted by P.L. 104-104.

2. 47 USC §230(b)(5), as enacted by PL 104-104.

3. *Shea v. Reno,* 96 Civ0976 (S.D.N.Y. 7/29/96); see Pamela Mendels, "Judges Visit Cyberspace Sites in Suit Over an Indecency Law," *New York Times* 5/23/96 p. A12 and Harvey Berkman, "Medium is Message," *Nat L.J.* 8/19/96 p. AJ.

4. *U.S. v. Thomas,* 64 LW 2483 (6th Cir. 1/29/96).

5. *U.S. v. Microsoft Corp.,* 159 F.R.D. 318 (D.D.C. 2/14/95), *reversed* 56 F.2d 1448 (D.C.Cir. 6/16/95).

6. *Hewlett-Packard Co. v. U.S.,* 71 F.3d 398 (Fed.Cir. 12/7/95).

7. *Lotus Development Corp. v. Borland,* 831 F.Supp.223 (D.Mass. 1993), *reversed* 49 F.3d 807 (1st Cir. 3/9/95), *affirmed* #94-2003, 116 S.Ct. 1062 (Sup.Ct. 1/16/96).

8. *Pro CD Inc. v. Zeidenberg,* 908 F.Supp. 640 (W.D.Wis. 1/4/96).

9. *U.S. v. LaMacchia,* 871 F.Supp. 535 (D.Mass. 12/28/94).

10. *Stratton Oakmont v. Prodigy Services Co.,* 63 LW 2765 (N.Y.Sup. 5/30/95).

11. *Religious Technology Center v. FACTNET Inc.,* 901 F.Supp. 1519 (D.Colo. 9/15/95).

12. *Religious Technology Center v. Netcom,* 907 F.Supp. 1361 (N.D.Cal. 11/21/95).

13. See Ethan Horwitz and Robert S. Weisbein, "Claiming Internet Domain Names," Nat L.J. 3/18/96 p. S1.

— FOR FURTHER REFERENCE —

Articles

Alvarez, Guy, "New Legal Issues on the Net," 17 *American Lawyer* 518 (December '95).

Baird, Freddie, "Legal Issues and the Internet," 58 *Texas Bar J.* 1138 (December '95).

Black, Robert L., "Tips, Tricks and Traps of CD-ROM Tax Research," 27 *Tax Adviser* 23 (January '96).

Cavazos, Edward A. and G. Chin Chao, "System Operator Liability for a User's Copyright Infringement," 4 *Texas Intellectual Property L.J.* 13 (Fall '95).

Handelman, Eric, "Obscenity and the Internet," 59 *Albany L.Rev.* 709 (Winter '95).

Jaskunas, Paul, "Exploring the World of Groupware," 17 *American Lawyer* 115 (December '95).

Katsh, M. Ethan, "Is Cyberspace Lawyer-Friendly?" 31 *Trial* 34 (December '95).

Kornowski, "Learning the ABCs of Law Office Computing," 18 *Los Angeles Lawyer* 60 (January '96).

Lemann, Catherine, "Purchasing and Maintaining the Paperless Law Library," 43 *Louisiana Bar J.* 364 (December '95).

Losavio, Michael, "Taking Stock: What is Enough for the Automated Office?" 59 *Kentucky Bench & Bar* 40 (Fall '95).

Martin, Nina, "Megalitigation Tamed by Technology," 16 *California Lawyer* 51 (January '96).

Moignard, Stephen, "More PC Products for Lawyers," 69 *Law Institute J.* 1220 (December '95).

Morris, C. Frank Jr., "E-Mail Communications: The Next Employment Law Nightmare," 20 *ALI-ABA Course Materials J.* 49 (December '95).

O'Hanrahan, Prue, "The Software Shuffle: Choosing the Right Software Package," 69 *Law Institute J.* 1218 (December '95).

Panel Discussion, "The Do-It-Yourself Home Page," 18 *American Lawyer* 118 (January-February '96).

Robertson, Robert A., "Personal Investing in Cyberspace and the Federal Securities Laws," 23 *Securities Regulation L.J.* 347 (Winter '96).

Ryger, Barbara M., "Cyberporn: Contemplating the First Amendment in Cyberspace," 6 *Seton Hall Constitutional Law J.* 221 (Fall '95).

Skon, Linda, "Copyright Protection of Computer User Interfaces," 27 *Arizona State L.J.* 1063 (Fall '95).

Weber, Jeremy Stone, "Defining Cyberlibel," 46 *Case Western Reserve L.Rev.* 235 (Fall '95).

Listservs

Bankruptcy: bankrlaw@polecat.law.indiana.edu

Business law: bizlaw-l@umab.umd.edu

Contracts: contracts@austin.onu.edu; cjust@cunymvm.cuny.edu

Family law: familylaw-l@acc.wuacc.edu

Gophers

American Association of Law Libraries: telnet to lawlib.wuacc.edu; the login is aallnet

ACLU: aclu.org(port 6601)

Websites

Indiana University School of Law http://www.law.indiana.edu

Legal Information Institute (Cornell) http://www.law.cornell.edu

Center for Corporate Law (University of Cincinnati School of Law)· http://www.law.uc.edu

Criminal Justice (Vera Institute of Justice): http://broadway.vera.org

Law Links (Lexis Counsel Connect): http://www.counsel.com/lawlinks

Search Engines

Alta Vista: http://www.altavista.com

Yahoo!: http://www.yahoo.com

Lycos: http://lycos.cs.cmu.edu

WebCrawler: http://webcrawler.com

Excite!: http://www/excite.com

Savvy Search: http://www.sc.colostate.edu/~dreiling/smartform.html

CORPORATE MERGERS, ACQUISITIONS, AND REORGANIZATIONS

[¶1702] MERGERS

A Delaware corporation went through a short-form merger. Some of the shareholders did not tender their shares. The result was that they became creditors rather than stockholders, with a right to redeem their stock for cash. However, the merged corporation filed a Chapter 11 bankruptcy petition. According to the Seventh Circuit, the non-tendering shareholders were merely unsecured creditors of the corporation. Their claims could be subordinated equitably to the claims of other general unsecured creditors even if there is no proof that the shareholders acted wrongfully in any way.[1]

If a proxy statement includes a discussion of the history of the merger, the statement is incomplete if it fails to mention a rejected bid that was actually higher than the bid accepted by the merged company's Board of Directors.[2]

[¶1725] SEC REQUIREMENTS

In early 1995, the U.S. Supreme Court ruled that §12(2) of the Exchange Act, banning material misrepresentation or omission of fact in a prospectus or oral communication, is limited in its application to public offerings by an issuer or controlling shareholder. It does not apply to a private secondary sale of substantially all of the stock in a close corporation. Statements made in the contract of sale for such a transaction, whether true or not, do not constitute a prospectus.[3]

In early 1996, the Court ruled that federal courts must give full faith and credit to a state court release of class-action federal securities claims with respect to parties who failed to object or opt out,[4] even though the claims are subject to the exclusive jurisdiction of the federal court. The underlying Delaware suit involved a stockholder challenge to a takeover; the federal suit covered Exchange Act claims.

A lender who provides financing for a leveraged buy-out (LBO), but does not exercise control over the day-to-day management or policies of the borrower corporation, is not a "controlling person" as defined by Exchange Act §20(a), and therefore cannot be liable under Rule 10b-5 for fraud committed by the borrower in connection with the LBO.[5]

[¶1727.1] The Board's Duties and Adoption of Defensive Measures

In the fall of 1995, the Fourth Circuit upheld four Virginia anti-takeover statutes. The Court of Appeals did not find any Commerce Clause problems with the statutes, nor were they preempted by federal securities laws because of the state's role in regulating corporations within the state. In this reading, the Williams Act's investor protection function is not impaired by state statutes that give advantages to the retention of existing management.[6]

The Tax Court says that the costs of defending against a class action brought by minority shareholders who allege breach of fiduciary duty in a merger must be capitalized, not deducted currently.[7]

It also denied a current deduction for printing costs and investment banking fees incurred in response to a hostile takeover. (Eventually, the initial hostility was overcome and the target accepted the transaction.) In this analysis, such expenses are not "ordinary and necessary" because they do not relate to the production of current income or immediate corporate needs. The Tax Court theorized that a §165 loss deduction might have been available for the costs of an abandoned transaction (e.g., an unsuccessful attempt to find a white knight), but clearly this was unavailable in the case of a consummated transaction.[8]

— ENDNOTES —

1. *In re Envirodyne Industries Inc.*, 64 LW 2583 (7th Cir. 3/15/96).

2. *Arnold v. Society for Savings Bancorp Inc.*, 650 A.2d 1270 (Del.Sup. 12/28/94).

3. *Gustafson v. Alloyd Co.*, #93-404, 115 S.Ct. 1061, 131 L.Ed.2d 21 (Sup.Ct. 2/28/95); *on remand*, 53 F.3d 333.

4. *Matsushita Electric Industrial Co. v. Epstein*, 64 LW 4101 (Sup.Ct. 2/27/96).

5. *Paracor Finance Inc. v. G.E. Capital Corp.*, 64 LW 2593 (9th Cir. 3/13/96).

6. *WLR Foods Inc. v. Tyson Foods Inc.*, 64 F.3d 1172 (4th Cir. 9/22/95).

7. *Berry Petroleum Co.*, 104 T.C. No. 30 (5/22/95).

8. *A.E. Staley Mfg. Co.*, 105 T.C. No. 14 (9/11/95).

— FOR FURTHER REFERENCE —

Block, Dennis J., Richard L. Levine and Diane Harvey, "Selected Developments Concerning the Federal Securities Laws and in the Market for Corporate Control," 27 *Annual Inst. on Securities Regulation* 277 (Summer '95).

Brownstein, Andrew R. and Steven A. Cohen, "Shareholder Rights Plans Are Under Board Review," *National L.J.* 4/15/96 p.C6.

Clark, Jeffrey J., "A Major Step Toward Clarifying the Role of Independent Committees," 20 *Delaware J. of Corporate Law* 567 (Spring '95).

Henderson, Gordon D. and Stuart J. Goldring, "Berry Petroleum and Section 382," 70 *Tax Notes* 893 (February 12, 1996).

Lawlor, William G., "The Auction Process: Can It Ever Be Over?" 28 *Rev. of Securities & Commodities Regulation* 227 (December 20, 1995).

Lipton, Richard M., "Divided Tax Court Applies INDOPCO to Hostile Takeovers," 84 *J. of Taxation* 21 (January '96).

Ragasso, Robert A., "Unifying the Law of Hostile Takeovers," 32 *Houston L.Rev.* 945 (Winter '95).

Solomon, Eric, "Corporate Combining Transactions," 73 *Taxes: The Tax Magazine* 829 (December '95).

CREDIT AND COLLECTIONS, DISCLOSURE, AND CONSUMER PROTECTION

[¶1805] COLLECTION BY LAWSUIT

A creditor is permitted to send a non-threatening, non-coercive letter to a debtor's attorney (with a copy to the debtor), suggesting a reaffirmation of the underlying debt, without violating the bankruptcy automatic stay. The Seventh Circuit read the purpose of the automatic stay as protecting debtors from lawsuits, not from all communications (at least non-abusive communications) during the stay.[1]

[¶1813] APPLICABILITY OF CONSUMER PROTECTION LAWS

The Telemarketing and Consumer Fraud and Abuse Prevention Act, P.L. 103-297 (8/16/94) enacts a new 15 U.S.C. §6101. The FTC has the power to issue rules prohibiting deceptive or otherwise abusive telemarketing acts or practices. Unsolicited calls may not be made in a pattern that is coercive or violates recipients' privacy. Prompt disclosure must be made that the call is a sales call. States Attorneys General have the power to bring civil suits in federal District Court to enjoin or seek damages for abusive telemarketing.

According to the Third Circuit, the federal National Bank Act preempts state regulation of late fees and fees for exceeding the credit limit that national banks charge their credit customers—these fees are "interest" and therefore federally regulated.[2]

[¶1814] TRUTH-IN-LENDING

During the supplement period, Congress passed two Truth-in-Lending measures. P.L. 104-12, the Truth in Lending Class Action Relief Act of 1995 was enacted on May 18, 1995. From that date until October 1, 1995, no court was permitted to certify a class action with respect to a closed-end transaction (refinancing or consolidation secured by a first lien on a dwelling or other real property), if the premise of the suit is a failure to disclose the finance charge or provide due notice of rescission rights, and if the lender attempted to provide notice but chose the wrong model form for the purpose. Class actions during that period were permitted if based on an Annual Percentage Rate higher than the permitted level.

The Truth in Lending Amendments of 1995, P.L. 104-29, were enacted on September 30, 1995. The amendments provide that the finance charge does not include the fees of third party closing agents (attorneys, title companies, escrow companies, settlement agents) if the creditor neither requires that the services be performed or charges imposed, nor retains the charge for the services. However, the finance charge does include mortgage broker fees paid by the borrower and taxes on evidence of indebtedness (if payment of taxes is a condition of registering the mortgage). There is no right to rescind a transaction based on the form of notice if the creditor uses one of the official notices.

[¶1837] EQUAL CREDIT OPPORTUNITY

A spouse who is forced to sign a guarantee that violates the ECOA can use the ECOA defensively to defeat enforcement of the guarantee—even if the statute of limitations for recovering ECOA damages has expired.[3]

ECOA was not drafted with a federal immunity provision, so the federal government (e.g., the FHA) can be sued for rejecting an application on the basis of race.[4]

[¶1848] THE FAIR DEBT COLLECTION PRACTICES ACT

In April, 1995, the U.S. Supreme Court held that attorneys are "debt collectors" for FDCPA purposes if they regularly engage in litigation to collect consumer debts.[5]

— ENDNOTES —

1. *In re Duke*, 64 LW 2583 (7th Cir. 3/15/96).

2. *Spellman v. Meridian Bank (Delaware)*, 64 LW 2418 (3rd Cir. 12/29/95). However, *contra Sherman v. Citibank (South Dakota)*, 64 LW 2353 (New Jersey Sup. 11/28/95).

3. *Silverman v. Eastrich Multiple Investor Fund LP*, 51 F.3d 28 (3rd Cir. 3/28/95).

4. *Moore v. Department of Agriculture*, 55 F.3d 991 (5th Cir. 6/6/95).

5. *Heintz v. Jenkins*, #94-367, 115 S.Ct. 1489, 131 L.Ed.2d 395 (Sup.Ct. 4/18/95).

— FOR FURTHER REFERENCE —

Balto, David A., "The Next Antitrust Challenge for Payment Systems: Does Duality Harm Competition?" 49 *Consumer Finance Law Quarterly Rep.* 98 (Winter '95).

Beckelman, Steven A. and David J. Adler, "Forestalling Apocalypse: Counteracting Defenses to Foreclosure," 113 *Banking Law J.* 53 (January '96).

Ice, Laura L., "The Fair Debt Collection Practices Act: Attorneys Beware," 64 *J. of the Kansas Bar Ass'n* 32 (December '95).

Lippman, Steven N., "Proceedings Supplementary and the Uniform Fraudulent Transfer Act," 70 *Florida Bar J.* 22 (January '96).

Maurer, Michael T., "Using RESPA to Remedy Erroneous ARM Adjustments," 49 *Consumer Finance Law Quarterly Report* 115 (Winter '95).

Ortego, Joseph J., "When Advertising a Foreclosure Sale is Not Enough," 28 *Uniform Commercial Code L.J.* 290 (Winter '96).

Ramedin, David, "When the Database is Wrong..." 100 *Commercial Law J.* 390 (Fall '95).

Rongeau, Vincent D., "Rediscovering Usury: An Argument for Legal Controls on Credit Card Interest Rates," 67 *U. of Colorado L.Rev.* 1 (Winter '96).

Waldrep, Thomas W. Jr. and James D. Wall, "The Classification of Credit Card Receivables," 100 *Commercial L.J.* 355 (Fall '95).

CRIMINAL LAW AND PROCEDURE

[**¶1901**] In 1995, perhaps the "issue of the year" in criminal law was forfeiture—when is a forfeiture punitive, thus giving rise to a potential Double Jeopardy issue? What are the rights of third parties in seized property? However, as always, questions about the death penalty, search and seizure (especially brief on-street stops), and custodial interrogation occupied the courts.

Reference should also be made to the changes in the Federal Rules of Criminal Procedure, effective 12/1/95,[1] affecting Rules 5 (initial appearance before a magistrate judge), 40 (commitment to another district), 43 (presence of the defendant at trial), and 57 (rule-making by the District Courts). Rule 49's provisions for filing of a dangerous offender notice have been abrogated.

[¶1902] ELEMENTS OF OFFENSES

At the end of 1995, the Supreme Court decided that a conviction under 18 USC §924(c)(1)—the "use" of a firearm during or in relation to drug trafficking—requires proof of active employment of the firearm in connection with the predicate offense. Thus, a gun that was in the possession of the defendant—e.g., locked in a car trunk or in the defendant's apartment when the crime was committed somewhere else—will not support a §924(c)(1) conviction.[2]

Earlier in the year, the Supreme Court had found that false statements in unsworn papers filed in bankruptcy court cannot give rise to an indictment under 18 U.S.C. §1001 (false statements in any matter within the jurisdiction of any "department or agency of the United States"). The rationale is that a federal court is neither a department nor an agency.[3]

The Constitutionality of two rather dissimilar federal criminal statutes attracted significant attention during the supplement period. One criminalizes carjacking; the other, willful failure to pay support to a child who resides in another state. Of course, Commerce Clause issues were paramount in both cases.

In the Third Circuit, it has been held that 18 U.S.C. §2119, which makes it illegal to carjack a car that has been transported, shipped, or received in interstate commerce, is Constitutional, and does not violate Congress' Commerce Clause powers.[4]

The Child Support Recovery Act of 1992, 18 U.S.C. §228, has been assessed by many courts, to various possible outcomes. Constitutionality has been upheld by District Courts in Kansas and Connecticut.[5] However, other courts[6] ruled that Congress exceeded its powers under the Commerce Clause by legislating in an area that is not substantially related to interstate commerce, and where there are already Uniform Laws and state criminal statutes.

[¶1902.6] RICO

"Interstate commerce," for RICO purposes, includes taking money from drug transactions in Arizona and investing it in an Alaskan gold mine: equipment was purchased out of state, workers were hired from out of state, and about 15% of the mine's output was transported out of state.[7]

[¶1903] CRIMINAL LIABILITY OF PARTIES TO AN OFFENSE

In late 1994, the Supreme Court ruled that it is not necessary for the prosecution to prove an overt act in order to get a conviction under 21 U.S.C. §846, the drug conspiracy statute.[8] In early 1996, the high court deemed conspiracy to distribute controlled substances to be a lesser included offense of carrying on a continuing criminal enterprise with others (CCE; 21 U.S.C. §848). Therefore, the two counts are the "same offense" and it was improper to sentence the defendant to life imprisonment on each count—notwithstanding the fact that the sentences were concurrent rather than consecutive.[9]

[¶1905] STOPS AND ARRESTS

According to the California Supreme Court, merely running away from a police officer is not enough to create the suspicion that would justify an investigative stop.[10]

A Tenth Circuit case late in 1995 finds a traffic stop to be reasonable under the Fourth Amendment, not pretextual, if the police officer either saw a traffic violation or has a reasonable articulable suspicion of a traffic or equipment violation—and even if the officer had other motives for the stop (i.e., interest in detecting drugs or weapons).[11] Certiorari has been granted in a similar case, *Whren v. U.S.*, #95-5841[12] on the issue of whether the test is what the reasonable officer "could" do or "would" do when deciding whether to make a stop.

Once the stop occurs, Colorado treats as unreasonable (under the Fourth Amendment) continued detention or questioning of the motorist once the police have satisfied the purpose of a valid investigatory stop (i.e., once a valid license and registration have been displayed).[13] According to the Pennsylvania Supreme Court, items discarded by an individual fleeing a police officer who had neither probable cause for an arrest nor reasonable suspicion justifying a stop-and-frisk have been "seized." Therefore, the Pennsylvania Constitution requires exclusion of those items from evidence if they turn out to be contraband.[14]

If, in the course of a traffic stop, the police get the driver's consent to search a car for drugs, that does not give them the right to search a passenger's purse that was left in the car when the driver and passengers were ordered to leave the vehicle.[15] (That is, even if there had been a weapon in the purse, a passenger who was outside the car could not have used it to harm the police officers.)

Of course, it is difficult to draw a bright line between legal regulation of stops and legal regulation of searches, because it is common for a stop to result in at least a search, and often an arrest.

[¶1906] SEARCH AND SEIZURE

In mid-1995, the Supreme Court held that the common-law "knock and announce" principle is part of the Fourth Amendment inquiry into the reasonableness of police conduct. Nevertheless, there may be circumstances, such as danger to the officers, that make it reasonable to make an unannounced entry. The case was remanded for a factual determination of the reasonableness of police conduct in the case at bar.[16]

One of the most significant issues of 1995 continued to be police powers in cases of "plain sight" and "plain touch" of contraband. A Hawaii case tries to tackle the distinction between "open view" (sighting by the police before any intrusion on privacy occurs) and "plain view" (after the intrusion on privacy; involving materials that are not exposed to the public). In this reading,[17] police who have licit access to an area can seize plain-view evidence with no need to show exigent circumstances. However, exigency is required for warrantless seizure of objects that are located in a Constitutionally protected area to which the police have not gained access.

Illinois and Connecticut reached opposite conclusions on the "plain touch" question in two cases, both involving crack cocaine. It has been held that the Illinois Constitution permits warrantless seizure of such contraband when "plain touch" during a pat-down for weapons gives cause for suspicion. But Connecticut treats the power to make a *Terry* stop as the power to search for weapons to protect the safety of the officer. However illicit a vial of crack is, it does not menace the police officer who makes the stop.[18]

There are other potential situations in which it must be determined whether a search has occurred (e.g., the Tenth Circuit finds that using a thermal imager to detect "hot spots" indicative of marijuana cultivation on the premises does constitute a search for Fourth Amendment purposes).[19]

A warrantless search is legitimate if it occurs on consent, but whose consent is required? One recent case says that the police cannot permit the driver to consent to the search of a car if they are aware that the owner is present but not operating the vehicle;[20] another says that consent from one roommate permits search of an apartment even without consent of another roommate who happened to be present at the time of the search.[21]

With all that, it might seem as if searches pursuant to warrants never resulted in litigation; of course, that's not true. A Sixth Circuit case finds a search warrant invalid because it covered almost all of a business' records; it should have indicated what the alleged crime was, when the crime was alleged to have occurred, and the location of pertinent documents. The Sixth Circuit deemed the warrant so defective that no reasonable agent could have relied on its validity.[22]

California v. Glaser[23] permits police officers, executing a warrant to search for drugs, to briefly detain persons entering the premises. Occupants can be detained for the duration of the search; other persons must be released absent evidence either of a threat to the police or articulable suspicion of connection to the criminal activity for which the warrant was issued.

[¶1907] INTERROGATION AND SELF-INCRIMINATION

When a federal court performs habeas review of a state court judgment, the question of whether the suspect was "in custody" and thus entitled to a Miranda warning is a mixed question of law and fact. The U.S. Supreme Court decided in late 1995 that the federal court must resolve the question independently and cannot presume that the state court's judgment as to custody/non-custody was correct.[24]

The California Supreme Court ruled that an interrogatee, described as a "possible witness," who was asked—not ordered—to accompany the police to the police station and given a choice of going in either his own car or a police car, was not "in custody." Therefore, no Miranda warning was required for brief questioning that was not accusatory—even though the questioning occurred in the jail area of the police station.[25]

However, the California Court of Appeals held that the good-faith exception to the Fourth Amendment exclusionary rule does not cover evidence obtained contrary to the Fifth Amendment right to counsel: protection against self-incrimination is a "mainstay of our adversary system of criminal justice," requiring the police to cease interrogation of a person who has asked for counsel.[26] But what is an invocation of the right to counsel? According to the Virginia Supreme Court,[27] a suspect's statement "I'm scared to say anything without talking to a lawyer" is not a clear invocation of the right, and therefore further custodial interrogation is not barred by such a statement.

The District of Columbia decided two interesting cases in the latter half of 1995. In the first, a "safety" exception was found to the Miranda rule, permitting the police to ask about the location of weapons even after the right to remain silent has been evoked.[28] In the second, words of religious inspiration directed by a police officer to a suspect who he knew belonged to the same church are considered interrogation for Fifth Amendment purposes.[29]

[¶1907.1] Confiscation and Attorneys' Fees

In early 1996, the Supreme Court decided a somewhat atypical forfeiture case, *Bennis v. Michigan*,[30] in which the forfeited item was a family automobile that had been used by the husband for sexual activity with a prostitute. The court held that the wife was not entitled to an innocent owner defense against the forfeiture.

In the more typical case, items (real estate, cars, and particularly cash) used in drug trafficking are seized, and the question is whether the seizure violates the

Unlawful Fines clause of the Eighth Amendment, and especially whether an in rem civil forfeiture subjects an individual to double jeopardy if he or she is also prosecuted for the illegal conduct that justified the seizure of the property.

One strand of analysis is that civil forfeiture is not punitive in nature (perhaps unless it is irrational and grossly disproportionate to the alleged offense)—and, therefore, prosecution does not subject the individual to double jeopardy.[31] There are cases to the contrary, holding that the forfeiture itself is punitive, so the same conduct cannot give rise to a criminal prosecution.[32]

Some cases (e.g., in the District Courts of Massachusetts and Alabama) focus on whether the defendant concedes the forfeiture. It has been held that concession to civil forfeiture does not bar prosecution in a related criminal proceeding.[33]

Yet other cases turn on whether the forfeiture and criminal proceedings are a single, coordinated prosecution; several jurisdictions see no double jeopardy problem if the proceedings are coordinated and simultaneous or close in time,[34] but the Ninth Circuit has ruled to the contrary,[35] and certiorari has been granted to resolve the split.

The Eighth Amendment prohibition of excessive fines applies in the forfeiture context, so the scope of the forfeiture must be proportionate to the seriousness of the offense. According to the Eleventh Circuit, seizure of a lot worth $65,000 was not disproportionate: the property, close to a junior high school, was used in cocaine trafficking, and the owner was found with marijuana, a gun, ammunition, and large amounts of cash.[36]

Proportionality was also at issue in *U.S. v. Wild*,[37] albeit in the context of an in personam criminal forfeiture (21 U.S.C. §853(a)(2)) rather than an in rem civil forfeiture; the test is whether the value of the allegedly forfeitable property exceeds the seriousness of the offense. In this analysis, in rem forfeitures are never excessive in the Constitutional sense (because the property itself is tainted). In personam forfeitures—monetary punishment of a culpable individual—are more likely to be constitutionally defective, but even this is described by the court as unlikely.

A late-1995 Supreme Court ruling requires the court to make a determination (as required by Federal Rules of Criminal Procedure 11(f)) that there is a factual basis for a guilty plea. However, it is not necessary to inquire into the factual basis for a stipulated asset forfeiture that is a component of a plea agreement. The forfeiture is imposed after the guilty plea, and thus is not covered by Rule 11(f). Nor is it necessary for plea agreements to make a specific disclosure of F.R.Crim.P. 31's option of a jury determination of forfeitability. This option is an aspect of sentencing, and purely statutory in origin; it is not covered by the constitutional right to a jury determination of guilt or innocence of the charges.[38]

According to the Southern District of New York,[39] the Fourth Amendment exclusionary rule is applicable to civil forfeiture proceedings. The upshot was that the government could not retain cash improperly seized in a warrantless search. According to the Ninth Circuit,[40] 18 U.S.C. §984 [civil forfeiture of non-traceable funds found in a bank account used for money laundering] cannot be applied to seizures occurring before the statute's effective date.

As the title of this section suggests, the rights of third parties in forfeited property are a topic of continuing interest. An attorney who took the deed to real estate as his fee for representing accused cocaine traffickers, and who was aware of the potentially forfeitable acts occurring on the property, has been held by the Eleventh Circuit not to be an "innocent owner" who can block the forfeiture by asserting lack of consent to the criminal use of the property.[41] In this analysis, it is impossible to consent or fail to consent to crimes that have already occurred—the innocent owner defense is limited to those genuinely unaware of the transactions.

Bringing a claim under 21 U.S.C. §853(n) [claim by third party who has a legal interest in a forfeited property] counts as a "civil action" against the government, even though the actual forfeiture occurs in the course of a criminal proceeding. Therefore, in appropriate cases, the prevailing plaintiff can receive an Equal Access to Justice Act attorney's fee award.[42]

[¶1908] TRIAL ISSUES

It is clear that due process is violated if an incompetent defendant is tried. A state violates fundamental fairness if it presumes the defendant is competent unless he or she proves incompetence by clear and convincing evidence (the Oklahoma standard—46 other states merely require a preponderance of the evidence). In April, 1996, the Supreme Court agreed that competence can be presumed[43] but a standard is invalid if it may result in trying persons who, more likely than not, are incompetent to stand trial.

[¶1908.1] Jury Selection

Casarez v. Texas[44] permits the use of a peremptory challenge to remove Pentecostal worshippers from a jury. The Texas court permitted religious-based peremptory challenges because religion involves beliefs and attitudes that might affect the hearing of a case. Furthermore, co-religionists (unlike persons of the same race or gender) do not necessarily have anything in common other than their religious beliefs, so excluding them as a group does not involve judgments about a group. (The opinion could have, but did not, stress the voluntary nature of choice of religious affiliation, as opposed to the involuntary nature of racial or gender identity.)

The Ninth Circuit case of *U.S. v. Annigoni*[45] deals with several significant jury issues. The case involved a real estate fraud; an Asian juror was challenged, either because of his race or because he was evasive about his involvement in litigation about the real estate limited partnerships he owned. The Ninth Circuit found that this uncertainty would not support a challenge for cause, but did make the peremptory challenge race-neutral. Thus, the District Court should have permitted the juror to be struck from the panel.

However, the Ninth Circuit's position is that a defendant is merely entitled to a fair trial, not a perfect one. Reversal is mandatory only in the case of a structural error such as a biased judge or attorney incapable of rendering effective assistance. Good-faith denial of a peremptory challenge does not prevent jury impartiality; peremptory challenges have "neither constitutional nor structural status." Because the defendant lost only one peremptory, and not an impartial juror, his conviction must be affirmed.

The Third Circuit did not deem a defendant in the Virgin Islands to have received ineffective assistance of counsel when his lawyer did not alert the court that a juror had been seen with a newspaper that contained an article derogatory to the defendant. The lawyer said that he did not mention this factor because he wanted to avoid a mistrial.

The jury, in a homicide case where the defendant was white and the victim (like the majority of the Virgin Islands populace) black, contained three white jurors and nine blacks. The lawyer didn't think he could get another jury with that many white jurors. The court ruled that this was a reasonable legitimate strategic decision (although it didn't work; the case got the Third Circuit when the defendant appealed his conviction). In this reading, defendants must be given the right to discuss strategy with their lawyers, but lawyers are not obligated to take strategic direction from their clients.[46]

It is constitutionally permissible to deny a motion by an accused sexual abuser of children to be appointed as his own co-counsel. (The objective was to permit him to cross-examine the allegedly abused children personally.) According to the Fourth Circuit,[47] the state interest in preventing trauma to complaining witnesses outweighs the defendant's dignity interest in being able to control every facet of his defense.

[¶1909] EVIDENCE

In a capital case, the defendant's conviction was reversed and the Supreme Court remanded his case for a new trial[48] because *Brady* material was not supplied. In this reading, favorable evidence is material, and its suppression is a Constitutional issue, if there is a reasonable probability (not necessarily a preponderance of evidence) that the result of the case would have been different if the material had been disclosed. The prosecution's disclosure burden depends on the cumulative impact of all the material, not an item-by-item analysis of the impact of each.

Several evidence questions from past years continued to occupy the courts. The decisions were generally favorable to polygraphy. According to the Fifth Circuit, polygraph evidence cannot be considered presumptively inadmissible, both because of the shift in scientific standards from *Frye* to *Daubert*, and because polygraph technique has improved.

Similarly, the District of New Mexico permits admission of test results performed by a competent polygrapher (and submitted by the defendant, to show that he did not understate his income) because polygraphy has been researched enough to satisfy the *Daubert* test, and the District of Arizona permits the defendant to use passing the polygraph test to rebut attacks on his credibility. On the other hand, the Sixth Circuit did not permit another defendant to introduce polygraph evidence without prior agreement as to its admissibility, because of the perceived danger of prejudice outweighing the probative effect.[49]

A Southern District of New York case from July, 1995 adds some interesting components to the analysis: for admissibility, the manner of conducting polygraph testing must give the jury genuinely helpful evidence. Questions that merely test the defendant's belief in his own innocence are not sufficiently enlightening.[50]

1995 was a year in which the Supreme Court decided several cases on criminal evidence. Under *Arizona v. Evans*,[51] the exclusionary rule does not require suppression of evidence gained in the course of an arrest, where the arrest was due to an incorrect computer record caused by courthouse clerical errors. The test was who committed the errors: police officers or non-law-enforcement personnel?

F.R.Evidence 410 and F.R.Crim.Pro. 11 exclude statements made by the defendant in the course of plea negotiations that break down, and the rules have no explicit waiver provision. Nevertheless, *U.S. v. Mezzanatto*[52] permits such statements to be admitted if the defendant knowingly and voluntarily waived the protection of those rules.

F.R.Evidence 801(d)(1)(B) says that prior consistent statements are not hearsay if offered to rebut a charge of recent fabrication, improper evidence, or improper motive. Early in 1995, the Supreme Court held that the rule can only be used to introduce a witness' prior out-of-court statement made before the alleged impropriety arose.[53]

Another implication of out-of-court statements was explored by *N.Y. v. Geraci*.[54] Many people were present in a night club where a stabbing occurred; only one person claimed to have seen anything. This witness was later threatened and became uncooperative. The New York Court of Appeals permitted admission of his sworn Grand Jury statement, as an out-of-court statement, based on the prosecution's showing that this "practically unavailable" witness' non-appearance was caused by intimidation from the defendant.

Several recent cases deal with out-of-court statements in cases of alleged sexual abuse of children. The Ninth Circuit permitted admission of statements made by the child's mother to the child's doctor, relating to sex acts she had observed between the defendant and his stepson. The statements were admitted under F.R.Evidence 803, the hearsay exception for statements made for medical diagnosis and treatment. The California Court of Appeals affirmed the conviction of a father for lewd and lascivious conduct, based on accusatory out-of-court statements made by his children and repudiated at trial.[55]

Revived memories are often an important component of trials for sexual abuse of children. According to the Second Circuit, hypnotically produced testimony about buried memories of sexual trauma may or may not be admissible, depending on the circumstances (e.g., any corroboration of the revived memories; the reliability of the procedure; and the qualifications of the hypnotist). The Michigan Supreme Court denies the use of the discovery rule in cases of alleged revived memories; nor is the statute of limitations tolled for insanity in cases where adults allege recently revived memories of childhood sexual abuse.[56]

The Ninth Circuit has held that it does not violate the Fourth Amendment to require a convicted murderer or sex offender to submit a blood sample for the state's DNA database; the state's compelling interest in having this information (to close other cases) outweighs the minimal intrusion on the convicted person.[57]

[¶1910] POST-TRIAL ISSUES

The seven-day deadline (measured from the date the jury was discharged) for seeking an order of acquittal despite a federal conviction is absolute. The Supreme Court would not permit any extension, no matter how brief, and no matter who was responsible for the delay or why.[58]

[¶1910.1] Sentencing Guidelines

On May 1, 1995, the United States Sentencing Commission submitted amendments to Guidelines 5 and 18 for Congressional approval. Approval was denied (P.L. 104-38), so the amendments did not take effect. Congress ordered the Commission to submit new guidelines, this time providing higher sentences for offenses involving crack than for powdered cocaine, and for major traffickers than for minor traffickers.

According to the Eastern District of New York,[59] F.R.Crim.Pro. 11(e) permits a court to accept the sentence evolved under a plea bargain, even if it is lower than the Guideline sentence and even if no downward departure factors are present.

[¶1910.2] Death Penalty

Given the seriousness of the issues, it is understandable that death penalty cases continue to occupy the attention of the Supreme Court—this year, specifically with reference to habeas corpus petitions.

According to the Supreme Court, habeas can be used to pursue a claim of actual innocence if it can be shown that an innocent defendant was convicted and a Constitutional violation "probably occurred." The habeas petition is not required to show by clear and convincing evidence that, but for the error, no reasonable juror could have convicted him or her.[60]

An April, 1996 case involves a case in which state habeas petitions were filed and dismissed. Almost six years later, shortly before the scheduled execution date, the petitioner filed another state habeas petition. When it, too, was denied, the petitioner filed his first federal petition on an eleventh-hour basis. A somewhat exasperated Supreme Court decided that Federal Habeas Corpus Rules Rule 9 does not allow the dismissal of a first federal habeas petition merely because it was filed after an extensive delay; the state must show some prejudice from the delay. The District Court is obligated to issue a stay if it cannot dispose of the federal petition on its merits before the scheduled execution date.[61]

However, Congress as well as the Supreme Court weighed in on the issue of habeas. One of the provisions of the Anti-Terrorism and Effective Death Penalty Act of 1996, S. 735, enacted April 24, 1996 (P.L. 104-32) limits the number of habeas appeals that can be used to appeal any conviction and permits a federal court to overturn a state conviction if, and only if, an egregious mistake was made by the state court. Certiorari was granted on May 3, 1996 to challenge this statute.[62]

If a state's death penalty statute requires the judge to consider the advisory jury verdict on penalty level, the Eighth Amendment ban on cruel and unusual punishment does not specify how much weight the judge must give to the verdict.[63]

Cruel and unusual punishment analysis was applied by the Ninth Circuit to ban the use of the gas chamber: California executions must henceforth take place by lethal injection.[64]

Commerce Clause considerations, discussed above in connection with carjacking and child support, were applied to capital punishment by the Eastern District of Pennsylvania in late 1995.[65] The court upheld 18 U.S.C. §848(e)(1)(A), capital punishment for murder in the furtherance of a continuing criminal enterprise. Under this analysis, Congress can regulate the unlawful interstate traffic in narcotics, provided that the capital sentence is imposed only if the murder furthers the continuing criminal enterprise—not merely if it was committed by a person who happened to be involved in activities other than the underlying criminal enterprise.

[¶1910.3] Related Sentencing Issues

The recent trend has been more punitive—e.g., indefinite incarceration under appropriate circumstances; post-sentence sanctions such as civil commitment or community notification of the presence of a convicted sex offender.

The Western District of Washington has invalidated Washington's Code §71.09 [indefinite post-sentence civil commitment of convicted sexually violent predators],[66] finding a violation of due process because commitment (and indefinite incarceration) can occur without a showing that the committed person is mentally ill.

New Jersey's "Megan's Law" (community notification) has been upheld by the state's Supreme Court, which found that it satisfies due process, does not invade the privacy of committed sex offenders, is not an ex post facto law or cruel and unusual punishment.[67] However, it cannot be applied to individuals who were convicted and sentenced before the effective date of the law.[68]

California's "three strikes" law, which significantly increases sentences and reduces prosecutorial and judicial discretion in cases involving repeat offenders has been upheld by the state's Court of Appeals.[69] The court rejected various arguments (that the law violates separation of powers; that it imposes cruel and unusual punishment in violation of the state Constitution), and noted that 75% of voters favored the law, so it does not shock the conscience of a civilized society.

Another California law has been upheld by the U.S. Supreme Court[70]—this time, one permitting parole hearings every two or three years rather than annually in certain circumstances. The circumstances are a conviction of multiple homicides; denial of the initial application by the parole board; and that it would be unreasonable to expect that parole would be granted at a later, annual hearing.

Although the defendant committed his crime before the statute was passed, the Supreme Court did not find the law to operate ex post facto because it does not increase the punishment imposed for the crime; it only limits the possibility of mitigation of punishment via parole.

— ENDNOTES —

1. The text is reproduced at 63 LW 4379.

2. *Bailey v. U.S.*, #94-7448, 94-7492, 116 S.Ct. 501 (Sup.Ct. 12/6/95); below, 36 F.3d 106 (D.C.Cir.1994).

3. *Hubbard v. U.S.*, #94-172, 115 S.Ct. 1754, 131 L.Ed.2d 779 (Sup.Ct. 5/15/95).

4. *U.S. v. Bishop*, 66 F.3d 569 (3rd Cir. 9/7/95).

5. *U.S. v. Hampshire*, 21 Fam.L.Rep. 1432 (D.Kan. 6/14/95); *U.S. v. Sage*, 906 F.Supp. 84 (D.Conn. 10/3/95).

6. *U.S. v. Mussari*, 894 F.Supp.1360 (D.Ariz. 7/26/95); *U.S. v. Schroeder*, 21 Fam.L.Rep. 1463, *U.S. v. Parker*, 64 LW 2313 (E.D.Pa. 10/30/95).

7. *U.S. v. Robertson*, #94-251, 115 S.Ct. 1732, 131 L.Ed.2d 714 (Sup.Ct. 5/1/95).

8. *U.S. v. Shaboni*, #93-981, 63 LW 4001 (Sup.Ct. 11/1/94).

9. *Rutledge v. U.S.*, #94-8769, 64 LW 4238 (Sup.Ct. 3/27/96); below, 40 F.3d 879 (7th Cir. 1994).

10. *California v. Souza*, 885 P.2d 982 (Cal.Sup. 12/28/94).

11. *U.S. v. Botero-Ospino*, 71 F.3d 783 (10th Cir. 12/5/95).

12. 64 LW 3459.

13. *Colorado v. Redinger*, 906 P.2d 81 (Colo.Sup. 10/30/95).

14. *Pennsylvania v. Matos*, 64 LW 2585 (Pa.Sup. 2/26/96).

15. *Illinois v. James*, 645 N.E.2d 195 (Ill.Sup. 12/22/94).

16. *Wilson v. Arkansas*, #94-5707, 115 S.Ct. 1914, 131 L.Ed.2d 976 (Sup.Ct. 5/22/95).

17. *Hawaii v. Meyer*, 63 LW 2732 (Hawaii Sup. 4/11/95).

18. Compare *Illinois v. Mitchell* (Ill.Sup. 4/20/95) with *Connecticut v. Trine* (Ct.App. 4/18/95), both summarized at 63 LW 2695.

19. *U.S. v. Cusumano*, 67 F.3d 1497 (10th Cir. 10/4/95).

20. *Johnson v. Oklahoma*, 64 LW 2383 (Okla.Crim.App. 8/15/95).

21. *Colorado v. Sanders*, 904 P.2d 1311 (Colo.Sup. 11/6/95).

22. *U.S. v. Kow*, 58 F.3d 423 (9th Cir. 6/21/95).

23. 11 Cal.4th 354 (Cal.Sup. 10/12/95).

24. *Thompson v. Keohane*, #94-6615, 116 S.Ct. 457 (Sup.Ct. 11/29/95); 34 F.3d 1073 (9th Cir. 1994) *vacated and remanded.*

25. *California v. Stansbury*, 889 P.2d 588 (Cal.Sup. 3/9/95).

26. *California v. Smith*, 37 Cal.Rptr.2d 524 (Cal.App. 1/26/95). Also note that, although California allows a good-faith exception to the exclusionary rule, New Hampshire does not: see *New Hampshire v. Canelo*, 653 A.2d 1097 (N.H.Sup. 2/3/95).

27. *Midkiff v. Virginia*, 462 S.E.2d 112 (Va.Sup. 9/15/95).

28. *Trice v. U.S.*, 662 A.2d 891 (D.C.App. 7/24/95).

29. *Stewart v. U.S.*, 668 A.2d 857 (D.C.App. 12/21/95).

30. #94-8729, 116 S.Ct. 994 (Sup.Ct. 3/4/96).

31. See, e.g., *Louisiana v. Johnson*, 64 LW 2527 (La.Sup. 1/16/96). *U.S. v. Salinas*, 65 F.3d 551 (6th Cir. 9/27/95) treats a civil in rem forfeiture of drug proceeds (as distinct from property used to facilitate the narcotics transaction) as remedial rather than punitive, thus permitting a prosecution for the offense.

32. *In re P.S.*, 64 LW 2527 (Ill.Sup. 1/18/96); *U.S. v. Perez*, 70 F.3d 345 (5th Cir. 11/21/95); *U.S. v. Ursery*, 59 F.3d 568 (6th Cir. 7/13/95), cert. granted #95-345, 116 S.Ct. 1037, 1315.

33. *U.S. v. Smith*, 874 F.Supp. 347 (N.D.Ala. 1/20/95). *U.S. v. Parcel of Land (Altman)*, 63 LW 2403 (D.Mass. 12/2/94) holds that 21 U.S.C. §881(i) requires the court to enter judgment of forfeiture whenever the defendant concedes forfeiture—the court cannot stay the forfeiture, even if the result is that prosecution is rendered impossible by double jeopardy considerations. Also see *U.S. v. Martin*, 38 F.3d 534 (11th Cir. 1994) permitting cumulative punishment for the same conduct under different federal statutes.

34. See, e.g., *U.S. v. Smith*, 64 LW 2501 (8th Cir. 1/31/96); *U.S. v. One Residence*, 13 F.3d 1493 (11th Cir. 1994); *U.S. v. Millan*, 2 F.3d 17 (2d Cir. 1993). Also see *U.S. v. Stanwood*, 872 F.Supp. 791 (D.Ore. 12/16/94): jeopardy attaches in a civil forfeiture case when the final judgment of forfeiture is entered, so an individual who pleads guilty to related criminal charges after seizure but before final judgment of forfeiture cannot raise a double jeopardy argument.

35. *U.S. v. $405,089.23*, 33 F.3d 1210 (9th Cir. 1994), cert. granted #95-346, 116 S.Ct. 1039, 1315. Also see *U.S. v. 9844 S.Titan Court*, 64 LW 2543 (10th Cir. 2/5/95), finding that a drug offense can be a "lesser included offense" with respect to civil forfeiture, and also finding that in rem forfeiture of narcotics proceeds is punitive, so that criminal prosecution and a parallel forfeiture action are not a single proceeding for double jeopardy purposes.

36. *U.S. v. One Parcel of Property*, 64 LW 2533 (11th Cir. 2/14/96). But see *U.S. v. Chandler*, 36 F.3d 358 (4th Cir. 1994), stating that proportionality is not a factor in determining whether an in rem forfeiture is excessive or not.

37. 47 F.3d 669 (4th Cir. 3/2/95).

38. *U.S. v. Libretti*, #94-7427, 116 S.Ct. 356 (Sup.Ct. 11/7/95), affirming 38 F.3d 523 (10th Cir.1994).

39. *U.S. v. $19,047*, 63 LW 2389 (S.D.N.Y. 12/1/94).

40. *U.S. v. $814,254.76*, 51 F.3d 207 (9th Cir. 3/29/95).

41. *U.S. v. One Parcel of Real Estate*, 41 F.3d 1448 (11th Cir. 1/6/95). However, *U.S. v. One 1973 Rolls Royce*, 63 LW 2354 (3d Cir. 1994) takes the opposite view.

42. *U.S. v. Douglas (Lussier)*, 55 F.3d 584 (11th Cir. 6/21/95); *U.S. v. Bachner*, 877 F.Supp. 625 (S.D. Fla. 1/20/95).

43. *Cooper v. Oklahoma*, #95-5207, 64 LW 4255 (Sup.Ct. 4/16/96); below, 889 P.2d 293.

44. 64 LW 2421 (Tex.Crim.App. 12/13/95)

45. 57 F.3d 739 (9th Cir. 6/8/95).

46. *Virgin Islands v. Weatherwax*, 64 LW 2613 (3rd Cir. 3/13/96).

47. *Fields v. Murray*, 49 F.3d 1024 (4th Cir. 3/20/95).

48. *Kyles v. Whitley*, #93-7927, 115 S.Ct. 1555 (Sup.Ct. 4/14/95); 5 F.3d 806 (5th Cir. 1993) reversed and remanded.

49. *U.S. v. Posado*, 57 F.3d 428 (5th Cir. 6/20/95); *U.S. v. Galbreth*, 908 F.Supp. 877 (D.N.M. 10/4/95); *U.S. v. Crumby*, 895 F.Supp. 1354 (D.Ariz. 8/21/95); *U.S. v. Sherlin*, 67 F.3d 1208 (6th Cir. 10/18/95).

50. *U.S. v. Lech*, 64 LW 2179 (S.D.N.Y. 7/26/95).

51. #93-1660, 115 S.Ct. 1185, 131 L.Ed.2d 234 (Sup.Ct. 3/1/95). Nevertheless, *Florida v. White*, 660 So.2d 664 (Fla.Sup. 7/13/95) finds evidence inadmissible if it was seized under a warrant that was invalid because of the police department's negligent failure to update its computer system to remove outdated information.

52. #93-1340, 115 S.Ct. 797, 130 L.Ed.2d 697 (Sup.Ct. 1/16/95), on remand 54 F.3d 613.

53. *Tome v. U.S.*, #93-6892, 115 S.Ct. 696, 130 L.Ed.2d 574 (Sup.Ct. 1/10/95), on remand 61 F.3d 1446.

54. 63 LW 2630 (N.Y.App. 3/28/95).

55. *U.S. v. Yazzie*, 59 F.3d 807 (9th Cir. 6/9/95); *California v. Carey*, 41 Cal.Rptr.2d 715 (Cal.App. 5/22/95).

56. *Borawick v. Shay*, 68 F.3d 597 (2nd Cir. 10/17/95); *Lemmerman v. Fealk*, 534 N.W.2d 695 (Mich.Sup. 7/5/95). Also see *S.V. v. R.V.*, 64 LW 2626 (Tex.Sup. 3/14/96), denying the discovery rule in a recovered-memory incest case.

57. *Rise v. Oregon*, 59 F.3d 1556 (9th Cir. 7/18/95).

58. *Carlisle v. U.S.*, #94-9147, 64 LW 4293 (Sup.Ct. 4/29/96).

59. *U.S. v. Aguilar*, 63 LW 2763 (E.D.N.Y. 5/4/95).

60. *Schlup v. Delo*, #93-7901, 115 S.Ct. 851, 130 L.Ed.2d 808 (Sup.Ct. 1/23/95).

61. *Lonchar v. Thomas*, #95-5015, 64 LW 4243 (Sup.Ct. 4/2/96); 58 F.3d 590 (11th Cir. 1995) vacated and remanded.

62. *Felker v. Turpin*, #95-8836.

63. *Harris v. Alabama*, #93-7659, 115 S.Ct. 1031, 130 L.Ed.2d 1004 (Sup.Ct. 2/22/95).

64. *Fierro v. Gomez*, 64 LW 2548 (9th Cir. 2/21/96).

65. *U.S. v. Tidwell*, 64 LW 2436 (E.D.Pa. 12/22/95).

66. *Young v. Weston*, 898 F.Supp. 744 (W.D.Wash. 8/25/95).

67. *Doe v. Poritz*, 662 A.2d 367 (N.J.Sup. 7/25/95).

68. *Artway v. New Jersey Attorney General*, 876 F.Supp. 666 (D.N.J. 2/28/95).

69. *California v. Superior Court, San Diego County*, 37 Cal.Rptr.2d 364 (Cal.App. 1/13/95).

70. *California Department of Corrections v. Morales*, #93-1462, 115 S.Ct. 1597, 131 L.Ed.2d 588 (Sup.Ct. 4/25/95); on remand 56 F.3d 46.

— FOR FURTHER REFERENCE —

Ahlen, Michael J., "Opening Statements in Jury Trials: What Are the Legal Limits?" 71 *North Dakota L.Rev.* 701 (Summer '95).

Boland, Ryan A., "Sex Offender Registration and Community Notification," 30 *New England L.Rev.* 183 (Fall '95).

Grossman, Steven, "Proportionality in Non-Capital Sentencing," 84 *Kentucky L.J.* 107 (Winter '95).

King, Nancy J., "Portioning Punishment: Constitutional Limits on Successive and Excessive Penalties," 144 *U. of Pennsylvania L.Rev.* 101 (November '95).

Kirven, Gerald, "Capital Crime and Punishment: Shortening the Time Between Them," 42 *Federal Lawyer* 20 (November-December '95).

Nathanson, H.S., "Strengthening the Criminal Jury: Long Overdue," 38 *Criminal Law Q.* 217 (December '95).

Nunes, Jeffrey W., "Organizational Sentencing Guidelines: The Conundrum of Compliance Programs and Self-Reporting," 27 *Arizona State L.J.* 1039 (Fall '95).

Spears, David, "Turning the Tables: Introduction of Similar Act Evidence by a Defendant," *N.Y.L.J.* 2/21/96 p. 1.

Steiker, Carol S. and Jordan M., "Sober Second Thoughts: Reflections on Two Decades of Capital Punishment," 109 *Harv.L.Rev.* 355 (December '95).

Sullivan, J. Thomas, "The 'Burden' of Proof in Federal Habeas Litigation," 26 *U.Memphis L.Rev.* 205 (Fall '95).

Wiley, David L., "Beauty and the Beast: Physical Appearance Discrimination in American Criminal Trials," 27 *St. Mary's L.J. 193* (Fall '95).

DRUNK DRIVING CASES

[¶2001] The Ninth Circuit decided in mid-1995 that the Fourth Amendment does not require that an arrest be made before taking a blood sample without the consent of a person accused of driving while drunk. Certain limitations are imposed. There must be probable cause to suspect DUI; the police officer must have a reasonable belief that there is an emergency that threatens the destruction of evidence; and a reasonable procedure must be used to extract the blood.[1]

The Seventh and Eighth Circuits are in agreement:[2] it does not constitute a violation of the Americans with Disabilities Act to fire or demote an employee who has been arrested for drunk driving (i.e., has committed criminal misconduct). The employer would react the same way to the arrest of a non-alcoholic employee; and it is possible to have the disability of alcoholism without driving while intoxicated, so the employer is not guilty of discrimination.

BAC test results in a hospital record can be admitted in a civil suit under the medical records hearsay exception: neither the chain of custody nor the reliability of BAC testing has to be established.[3]

[¶2002] IMPLIED CONSENT LAWS

To no one's surprise, both Maryland and Hawaii courts ruled that suspending or revoking a license for failing or refusing to take a blood or breath test is not punitive in nature. Since it is not punitive, it cannot constitute double jeopardy.[4]

[¶2003] CHALLENGING THE POLICE CASE

Oregon has joined the states that accept Horizontal Gaze Nystagmus (HGN) testing for intoxication, finding it to be scientifically acceptable and not substantially more prejudicial than probative.[5]

[¶2004] PLEAS AND ALTERNATIVES

The Southern District of New York decided that the First Amendment ban on establishment of religion is violated by forcing a convicted drunk driver to attend Alcoholics Anonymous meetings as a condition of probation.[6] The court suggested but did not explicitly hold that it might be acceptable to give persons convicted of DUI the choice between AA and a sobriety program without spiritual content.[7]

New York's Court of Appeals said that the state's probation statute does not authorize a condition of probation requirement that a recidivist drunk driver put a "convicted DWI" sign on his or her license plate. Probation is supposed to be rehabilitative, rather than punitive, in nature, so public obloquy is not an appropriate condition of probation.[8]

— ENDNOTES —

1. *U.S. v. Chapel*, 55 F.3d 1416 (9th Cir. 5/26/95); on remand, 61 F.3d 913.

2. *Maddox v. University of Tennessee*, 62 F.3d 843 (6th Cir. 8/21/95); *Despears v. Milwaukee County*, 63 F.3d 635 (7th Cir. 8/21/95).

3. *Judd v. Louisiana*, 663 So.2d 690 (La.Sup. 11/27/95).

4. *Maryland v. Jones*, 340 Maryland 235 (Md.App. 10/16/95); *Hawaii v. Toyomura*, 904 P.2d 893 (Haw.Sup. 10/11/95).

5. *Oregon v. O'Key*, 899 P.2d 663 (Ore.Sup. 7/7/95).

6. *Warner v. Orange County Department of Probation*, 870 F.Supp. 69 (S.D.N.Y. 12/14/94).

7. This was the holding of *O'Connor v. California*, 855 F.Supp. 303 (C.D.Cal. 1994).

8. *New York v. Letterlough*, 86 N.Y.2d 259 (N.Y.App. 6/13/95).

— FOR FURTHER REFERENCE —

Feigl, Mark, "DWI and the Insanity Defense," 20 *Vermont L.Rev.* 161 (Fall '95).

Honts, Charles R. and Susan L. Amato, "Horizontal Gaze Nystagmus Test," 71 *North Dakota L.Rev.* 671 (Summer '95).

Hugel, David H., "Taking a Closer Look at the Double Jeopardy DWI Defense," 35 *Judges Journal* 16 (Winter '96).

Meyer, Stuart, "Abandoning Judicial Principles in DWI Cases," 68 *New York State Bar J.* 46 (February '96).

Sives, Nina J. and John Ekman, "Double Jeopardy: A New Tool in the Arsenal of Drunk Driving Defenses," 68 *Wisconsin Lawyer* 14 (December '95).

White, Katherine M., "Drunk Driving as Second-Degree Murder in Michigan," 41 *Wayne L.Rev.* 1433 (Spring '95).

EMPLOYER-EMPLOYEE RELATIONS

[¶2101] During the supplement period, the percentage of unionized workers in the economy continued to decline, so it is understandable that discrimination cases reviewed for this supplement outnumbered traditional labor law cases. Within the topic of employment discrimination, the most active issues included sexual harassment and age discrimination.

[¶2102] PRIVACY AND DUE PROCESS ISSUES

There is no statutory or general fiduciary duty to disclose the names and addresses of other retirement plan participants on request of a participant.[1]

[¶2103] FEDERAL LABOR LAW

In November, 1995, the Supreme Court found that a paid union organizer can nevertheless be a protected "employee" under the NLRA. Even under traditional agency principles, it is possible to be the "servant of two masters," and a rank-and-file employee who performs ordinary services for the employer in addition to receiving a union salary comes under the protection of the NLRA.[2]

In April, 1996, the Supreme Court upheld the NLRB's determination that members of "live-haul" crews who transport and process poultry were employees (and thus covered by federal labor laws) rather than exempt agricultural employees.[3]

It violates the NLRA for an employer to implement a managed care program unilaterally, substituting for the existing comprehensive health plan.[4] Bargaining is required for the change because it goes beyond the employer's reserved right to amend or modify the plan. The managed care program is an entirely new delivery system that is not reasonably comprehended within the system already agreed to by the union.

An employee's claim that he was unlawfully discharged in retaliation for filing a Worker's Compensation claim is not removable to federal court, because the claim does not require interpretation of the collective bargaining agreement. Thus, state remedies are not preempted by LMRA §301.[5]

Nor does LMRA §301 preempt state law claims (e.g., fraud, breach of contract, intentional infliction of emotional distress) in a case where employees charge that the employer promised them job security but instead fired them after a union decertification vote. In the Third Circuit's reading, an independent promise of job security, not the collective bargaining agreement, was involved, and CBA interpretation was not required to assess the nature and effect of the employer's promise.[6]

In two recent LMRA §301 cases, employees seemed likely to prevail on claims that the LMRA prevents the employer from terminating retiree health benefits in violation of the CBA.[7] LMRA §301 is itself preempted by the 1987 ERISA amendments that make the employer liable to the PBGC for benefits that are unfunded when a plan terminates. Therefore, according to the Sixth Circuit, the employees and the union cannot bring an LMRA §301 action to recover those non-guaranteed pension benefits.[8]

However, the NLRA does preempt a state statute that makes a successor employer liable under any predecessor's CBA that contains a successor clause, nor does federal labor law require the new employer to hire unwanted employees of the former employer. In this reading, the new employer should not be forced to abide by a CBA it did not bargain for.[9]

An employee can bring a Fair Labor Standards Act case in federal court without first arbitrating the wage claim under the CBA.[10] Apropos of arbitration, the Third Circuit upheld an arbitrator who read a CBA provision for discharge "for proper cause" to imply a system of progressive discipline. Therefore, the arbitrator was justified in suspending a driver who caused a rear-end collision rather than firing him immediately.[11] The Sixth Circuit read Federal Arbitration Act §1, excluding contracts of "seamen, railroad employees, or any other class of workers engaged in foreign or interstate commerce" very narrowly, to mean only workers who actively transport goods between states, not all workers whose jobs affect interstate commerce.[12]

Both the LMRA and the duty of fair representation are violated when a union hiring hall refers only applicants who are known to the union officials. Referrals must be based on consistent, objective standards.[13]

[¶2103.3] Controls on Strikes

On March 8, 1995, President Clinton issued an executive branch procurement policy forbidding procurement from companies that hire permanent replacements for lawfully striking workers. However, the D.C. Circuit has ruled that the executive order is preempted by the NLRA's permission to replace economic strikers under certain conditions. Furthermore, despite the lower-court ruling that judicial review was inappropriate, the D.C. Circuit viewed judicial review as appropriate in all cases alleging executive branch violation of a statute.[14]

The D.C.Circuit held that an employer acted reasonably by reinstating strikers but restricting them to well-supervised, non-sensitive positions that limited their movements within the plant. Special factors were present: the reinstated strikers were union activists who returned to work after the union had been decertified with the specific objective of advocating voting "union" in the rerun election. After the rerun election (which the union lost) the reinstated strikers quit their jobs and went back on strike. The employer was held to have substantial, legitimate business justification for the limitations on the returned workers (and thus did not discriminate against them). There had already been strike-related violence and vandalism, and sabotage and product tampering were deemed to be real threats.[15]

The Eighth Circuit has ruled that unfair labor practices occurring during an economic strike are not sufficient to convert the strike into an unfair labor practices strike except in the limited situation in which the unlawful conduct serves to prolong the strike.[16]

[¶2104.3] Electioneering

There is no NLRA violation in forbidding union representatives to enter the employer's property in order to distribute handbills telling potential condominium buyers that the employer used underpaid non-union labor. The employer's property rights clearly prevail over the union right of free speech—particularly since union organizing was not involved.[17] Nor is the NLRA violated if the employer refuses to let employees post union materials on the bulletin board used for personal notices—"The employer doesn't have to promote unions by giving them special access to bulletin boards."[18]

A union member-plaintiff who wins monetary damages in a case involving union democracy has conferred a "common benefit," justifying an award of attorneys' fees. It is not necessary for equitable relief to be ordered, as long as the damages can be expected to have a salutory effect on union governance by rendering union leaders less likely to suppress dissent among the rank-and-file.[19]

[¶2105] PROTECTION OF EMPLOYEES AGAINST DISCRIMINATION

During the supplement period, there were several important Supreme Court cases.[20] According to the Fifth Circuit, in order to infer discrimination from a plaintiff's prima facie case and rebuttal of the employer's defense, the trier of fact must decide that there is a conflict in substantial evidence that creates a jury question.[21]

The Third Circuit's reading of the post-*Hicks* burden on the plaintiff, where the defendant submits a defense of non-discrimination and moves for summary judgment, is to supply a preponderance of the evidence. There are four factors for the court to apply to see if a reasonable finder of fact could agree that the plaintiff submitted the preponderance of the evidence:

➤ Inference of discrimination from the prima facie case

➤ Can discrimination justifiably be inferred from the rejection of the defense's proffered reason?

➤ Strength of the inference that the defense tried to conceal discrimination

➤ Other available evidence.[22]

The high court ruled that "after-acquired evidence" (evidence discovered by the employer only after a discharged employee has charged the company with discrimination) does not absolutely bar remedies for the employee.[23] However, if the evidence is sufficiently damning, it means that the employer need not reinstate the employee or provide front pay in lieu of reinstatement. Duration of the back pay period might also be limited.

The Northern District of Iowa reads this to mean that post-discharge misconduct, as opposed to pre-discharge misconduct discovered after the discharge, is irrelevant and prejudicial, and therefore not admissible in the case.[24]

A number of cases involving several statutes assessed the potential liability of individual supervisors and employees. The Northern District of Illinois did permit individual liability of supervisors or managers under the Family and Medical Leave Act, finding that the FMLA resembles the Fair Labor Standards Act in contemplating that an individual will deal with multiple "employers," all of whom are potentially liable.[25] However, by and large the result has been that individuals are not considered to be "employers" with a potential Title VII or Americans with Disabilities Act liability.[26]

[¶2105.1] Title VII

It's a fact question—in other words, within the ambit of the jury—to determine whether a female manager's job remained open after her maternity leave, or whether the job was eliminated in a reorganization.[27]

On April 22, 1996, certiorari was granted in the case of *Robinson v. Shell Oil*, #95-1376, on the issue of whether a company can be sued by an ex-employee who claims that he was given a bad reference as retaliation for pressing claims of racial discrimination.

In late 1995, the Sixth Circuit decided a case involving a class of black employees. The employer entered into a five-year consent decree. One of the employer's several plants was sold. The employees were unsuccessful in having successor liability imposed on the purchaser. Although the decree refers to liability of parties, their agents, and successors, it also allows plant closings. The court accepted the employer's argument that selling the plant to another company is the equivalent of a plant closing.[28]

In mid-1995, the Third Circuit refused to allow four ex-employees who did not file timely EEOC charges to join a suit by five plaintiffs, alleging similar conduct, who did file the timely charges.[29] That Circuit also said that as long as one act within the 300-day period before filing of the charge can be alleged, earlier conduct can be proved to demonstrate a long-standing, persistent, ongoing pattern creating a hostile work environment.[30]

The EEOC was granted a preliminary injunction preventing an employer from requiring employees to sign and follow the company's "ADR Policy" instead of litigating claims of Title VII violations. The employer was also enjoined from requiring employees to pay the cost of ADR proceedings, and from interfering with the EEOC charges or Title VII actions.[31] However, if there is already a CBA in place that specifically makes sex and disability claims subject to arbitration, a union member cannot litigate Title VII or ADA claims against the employer.[32]

As noted above, sexual harassment is one of the most active litigation areas within Title VII. One of the most contentious areas is whether or not sexual harassment of one male by another male, or one female by another female, is cognizable.[33] On related issues, two recent cases find that sexually tinged horseplay or innuendo, directed by males against males, is not made "on account of sex" and therefore cannot be treated as sexual harassment.[34]

Inaction by the employer is considered ratification of the harasser's conduct, so the employer is still liable for failing to remedy harassment that it incorrectly thought had ended. The employer must take prompt, effective action to end harassment if it wishes to escape liability.[35]

As an example of effective employer action, see *Gary v. Long*,[36] where the employer established, enforced, and advertised effective anti-discrimination measures. In this case, a supervisor raped an employee; but this was clearly outside the scope of his employment, and the employee victim was reassigned following her complaint even though the employer did not find corroborating evidence of the charge.

The Ninth Circuit permits introduction of evidence of harassment of other employees in a quid pro quo sexual harassment case. The rationale is that it goes to motive and also refutes the employer's contention that the plaintiff was fired for a non-discriminatory reason.[37]

What if the fired party was not the alleged victim of harassment, but the accused harasser? The Seventh Circuit defines "gross misconduct" by an employee to include sexually harassing others. Therefore, it is not arbitrary or capricious to discharge such a person without severance benefits, even if the conduct was not serious enough to support a federal suit.[38]

The Colorado Supreme Court considers state common-law sexual harassment claims to be cumulative with the federal claims. Therefore, a plaintiff is not obligated to exhaust state-law administrative remedies with respect to common-law claims that could have been, but were not, brought under the state anti-discrimination statute.[39]

The Ninth Circuit said that state-court (California) claims for wrongful discharge and intentional interference with contract relations, contrary to the state policy forbidding religious discrimination, could not be removed to federal court.[40] (The employee filed in state court; the defendant employer got the case removed to federal court and was awarded summary judgment by the District Court.) The case neither asserted a federal cause of action nor depended on a federal question. The plaintiff's complaint did mention Title VII, but only to show that the state did have a public policy against religious discrimination. Title VII preemption of state law is not complete; only inconsistent state laws are preempted.

State court remedies are viable, e.g., for employees of companies too small to be covered by the federal statute. The employee can sue for wrongful discharge contrary to state public policy.[41] In Michigan, unemployment benefits serve to reduce damages in a contract action for wrongful discharge.[42]

[¶2105.2] Civil Rights Act of 1991

According to the First Circuit, the $200,000 cap on damages under 42 U.S.C. §1981a(b)(3) means a cap on the total damages (compensatory and punitive) against the employer, and this limit applies to the ADA as well as Title VII and the ADEA.[43]

The 90-day filing requirement applies to ADEA actions filed after the effective date of CRA '91, referring to discriminatory acts occurring earlier.[44] Furthermore, once the employee receives the right-to-sue notice, the suit must be filed strictly within the 90-day period, which is not tolled by an employee request that the EEOC reconsider its no-reasonable-cause determination.[45]

[¶2105.3] The Equal Pay Act

A job applicant who fails to mention a criminal conviction on a job application is barred from certain remedies, but not an EPA claim that she was paid less than comparable males. The after-acquired evidence of concealment of the conviction does not go to the defendant employer's state of mind (whether it acted in good faith and in the reasonable belief that the EPA was not violated). According to the Eleventh Circuit, the after-acquired evidence counts only if the back pay period terminated before the employee was fired.[46]

[¶2105.4] The Age Discrimination in Employment Act

In spring 1996, the Supreme Court resolved a vexing question by deciding that an ADEA plaintiff need not prove replacement by someone outside the over-40 protected group, as long as the replacement is much younger than the plaintiff.[47]

The Tenth Circuit said that there is no such thing as a disparate impact ADEA claim—ADEA plaintiffs must show that they themselves were the victims of disparate treatment.[48]

The Third Circuit said that the standard for jury instructions in an ADEA pretext case is not whether age was the sole cause of the employer decision, but whether age was a factor that played a determinative role in the employer's decision to discharge or otherwise disadvantage the employee.[49]

Several courts came to grips with international implications of the ADEA. According to the Southern District of Florida, foreign corporations are not pro tanto exempt from the ADEA; only their operations outside the United States are exempt.[50] The Eastern District of Pennsylvania said that the ADEA is irrelevant to a promotion outside the United States. The relevant worksite is the locus of the position sought by the plaintiff, not where she was working at the time she allegedly underwent age discrimination.[51] The D.C. Circuit reversed the District Court and found that a German employment contract, reflecting German practices, covering employees in Munich and enforceable in German courts, counts as a foreign "law." Therefore, the contract can lawfully reflect the German practice of mandatory retirement at age 65. The Munich Labor Court required mandatory retirement at 65 for the benefit of German workers who might be hired after the compulsory retirement of the American incumbents.[52]

The ADEA is not violated when enhanced severance benefits are offered to everyone who is affected by a Reduction in Force, regardless of age, in return for their release of all claims. Although people over 40 have an additional claim (under the ADEA), they do not necessarily have accrued claims that make their waiver more valuable than that of younger employees.[53]

Apropos of releases the Fourth Circuit has ruled that a release that fails to satisfy the Older Workers Benefit Protection Act is merely voidable, not void. The signing employee can ratify the voidable release by subsequent conduct, such as the acceptance of benefits under the release.[54]

See ¶2105.2, above, for discussion of the CRA '91 filing requirements.

[¶2105.5] Handicap/Disability Discrimination

In March, 1995, the EEOC published a guidance memorandum, "Compliance Manual Section 902: Definition of the Term 'Disability.'".[55] According to the memo, personality traits (such as a bad work attitude) are not an impairment, but an actual mental disorder such as a bipolar mood disorder is an impairment. Even if an employee is genuinely impaired, the employer can legitimately hold all employees to the same level of performance and conduct.

The memo also defines severe overweight (more than 100 pounds over the individual's normal weight) as an impairment, but being a few pounds overweight is not. In sum, the scope or perceived scope of an individual's condition, without consideration of mitigating measures, determines whether an impairment is present.

The Southern District of Indiana considered the ADA/labor law interface, and decided that the ADA duty to accommodate disabled employees does not require an employer to "bump" employees who have more seniority under the Collective Bargaining Agreement.[56]

The Southern District of Iowa did not deem procreation to be a "major life activity"—thus, it ruled that neither the ADA nor Title VII is violated when an employer's health plan excludes infertility treatment.[57]

The Eastern District of Pennsylvania said that claiming disability benefits for AIDS estops the claimant from also asserting that he or she is a "qualified employee" for ADA purposes.[58]

Coincidentally, on the same day both the Sixth and Seventh Circuits decided that the ADA is not violated when an employer demotes or fires an employee for drunk driving despite the employee's claimed alcoholism disability. The rationale is that the employees were guilty of criminal misconduct for which any employee, irrespective of disability, would have been discharged.[59]

[¶2105.6] Family and Medical Leave Act (FMLA)

The Family and Medical Leave Act of 1993, 29 U.S.C §2612(c), applies to all companies with 50 or more employees in each working day in 20 or more weeks of a year. Qualifying employees (those who have been employed there for at least 12 months, with at least 1,250 work hours in the preceding 12 months) must be permitted to take up to 12 weeks' unpaid leave per year without penalty, for personal or family health needs. Employees returning after a leave must be reinstated in the old job, or in a position of equivalent responsibilities, working conditions, and compensation. (There is an exception for top executives, who need not be reinstated if their absence has severely impaired corporate operations.)

FMLA leave is available when the employee needs hospitalization or continued medical treatment, or if the employee serves as caregiver for a spouse, child, or parent with a serious health condition. Leave must also be granted for the birth or adoption of a child. The leave can take the form of a reduced schedule or a period of several days at a time—it is not necessary that the employee be absent for an extended period to qualify for leave.

The statute contains a requirement that employees give advance notice of the need for non-emergency leave. Employers can require medical certification of the need for leave.

According to the Western District of Michigan, it is permissible to discharge an employee who was eligible for FMLA leave but failed to satisfy the regulations that require at least verbal notice to alert the employer to the presence of an FMLA claim.[60] However, the Fifth Circuit says that employees are entitled to the protections of the FMLA even if they fail to specifically invoke the statute when they apply for medical leave.[61] The District of Columbia District Court says that the 1995 FMLA regulations, including the employer's responsibility for notifying employees of eligibility requirements before leave begins, cannot be applied retroactively.[62] Furthermore, "hours of service" for computing eligibility for FMLA leave are hours actually worked, not vacation, holiday, sick leave, or maternity leave hours.

[¶2106]   OTHER LIMITATIONS ON EMPLOYMENT AT WILL

Attorneys with government jobs have a right of intimate association (under the First Amendment). Therefore, a state can withdraw a job offer to an attorney, based on her intention to undergo a religious commitment ceremony with her female lover, only if the state can show that refusal to employ the attorney is narrowly tailored to serve a compelling state interest. The Eleventh Circuit could not detect any such compelling state interest in punishing a religious ceremony related to sincere and long-held religious beliefs of both spouses.[63]

In a workplace too small to be covered by state anti-discrimination law, an employee who alleges sexual harassment can nevertheless bring a common-law tort suit for wrongful discharge in violation of public policy.[64]

— ENDNOTES —

1. *Hughes Action Committee v. Administrator of Hughes Non-Bargaining Retirement Plan*, 72 F.2d 686 (9th Cir. 12/15/95).

2. *NLRB v. Town & Country Electric Inc.*, #94-947, 64 LW 4022 (Sup.Ct. 11/28/95), *reversing and remanding* 34 F.3d 625 (8th Cir.1994).

3. *Holly Farms v. NLRB*, #95-210, 64 LW 4269 (Sup.Ct. 4/22/96).

4. *Loral Defense Systems-Akron*, 320 NLRB #54 (1/31/96).

5. *Humphrey v. Sequentia Inc.*, 58 F.3d 1238 (8th Cir. 6/28/95).

6. *Trans Penn Wax Corp. v. McCandless*, 50 F.3d 217 (3rd Cir. 2/28/95).

7. *Compare Golden v. Kelsey-Hayes Co.*, 64 LW 2458 (6th Cir. 1/18/96) [mandatory injunction granted obligating employer to restore benefits, but jury trial denied because money damages only incidental to equitable cause of action] *with Stewart v. KHD Deutz of America Corp.*, 64 LW 2574 (11th Cir. 2/28/96) [jury trial available even if LMRA claim is joined with ERISA claim for same monetary relief].

8. *United Steelworkers of America v. United Engineering Inc.*, 63 LW 2699 (6th Cir. 5/2/95).

9. *United Steelworkers of America v. St. Gabriel's Hospital*, 871 F.Supp. 335 (D.Minn. 12/20/94). Query whether the new employer should not be bound by the contract, which it was certainly aware of during the negotiations for the purchase.

10. *Tran v. Tran*, 54 F.3d 115 (2nd Cir. 5/5/95).

11. *Transportation Union Local 1589 v. Suburban Transit Corp.*, 51 F.3d 376 (3rd Cir. 3/16/95).

12. *Asplundh Tree Expert Co. v. Bates*, 57 F.3d 592 (6th Cir. 12/14/95).

13. *Plumbers Local 32 v. NLRB*, 50 F.3d 29 (D.C.Cir. 3/28/95).

14. Original order: see 63 LW 2575. Court decisions: *Chamber of Commerce of the U.S. v. Reich*, 897 F.Supp. 570 (D.D.C. 7/31/95) and 57 F.3d 1099 (D.C.Cir. 2/2/96).

15. *Diamond Walnut Growers Inc. v. NLRB*, 64 LW 2623 (D.C.Cir. 3/29/96).

16. *F.L. Thorpe & Co. v. NLRB*, 71 F.3d 282 (8th Cir. 12/1/95).

17. *Metropolitan District Council of Philadelphia v. NLRB*, 68 F.3d 71 (3rd Cir. 10/25/95); *United Food and Commercial Workers, Local 880 v. NLRB*, 64 LW 2471 (D.C.Cir. 1/26/96) is similar for distribution of union literature by non-employees to customers of the employer.

18. *Guardian Industries Corp. v. NLRB*, 49 F.3d 317 (7th Cir. 2/28/95).

19. *Radonich v. Senshyn*, 52 F.3d 28 (2nd Cir. 4/10/95).

20. Although it is before the supplement period, reference should also be made to *St. Mary's Honor Center v. Hicks*, 113 S.Ct. 2742 (1993), which increases the burden on the plaintiff. Instead of merely having to challenge the defendant's explanation that its conduct was not caused by discriminatory motives, the plaintiff must now prove affirmatively, by preponderance of the evidence, that discriminatory animus motivated the employer's conduct.

21. *Rhodes v. Guiberson Oil Tools*, 64 LW 2486 (5th Cir. 1/31/96).

22. *Sheridan v. DuPont*, 64 LW 2487 (3rd Cir. 1/31/96).

23. *McKennon v. Nashville Banner Pub. Co.*, #93-1543, 115 S.Ct. 879, 130 L.Ed.2d 852 (Sup.Ct. 1/23/95); on remand, 51 F.3d 272. This is an ADEA case, part of the predominance of age cases in employment discrimination litigation.

24. *Carr v. Woodbury County Juvenile Detention Center*, 905 F.Supp. 619 (N.D.Ia. 11/23/95).

25. *Freemon v. Foley*, 64 LW 2344 (N.D.Ill. 11/7/95).

26. *Williams v. Banning*, 72 F.3d 552 (7th Cir. 12/21/95) [supervisor, Title VII]; *Tomka v. Seiler Corp.*, 66 F.3d 1295 (2nd Cir. 9/27/95) [co-employee, hostile work environment sex discrimination]; *Stephens v. Kay Management Co.*, 66 F.3d 41 (E.D.Va. 12/7/95), *EEOC v. AIC Security Investigations*, 63 LW 2746 (7th Cir. 5/22/95) [supervisors, ADA].

27. *Quaratino v. Tiffany*, 71 F.3d 58 (2d Cir. 11/20/95).

28. *Huguley v. G.M. Corp.*, 67 F.3d 129 (6th Cir. 10/10/95).

29. *Whalen v. W.R. Grace & Co.*, 56 F.3d 504 (3d Cir. 6/2/95).

30. *West v. Philadelphia Electric Co.*, 45 F.3d 744 (3rd Cir. 1/19/95).

31. *EEOC v. River Oaks Imaging & Diagnostic*, 63 LW 2733 (S.D.Tex. 4/19/95).

32. *Austin v. Owens-Brockway Glass Container, Inc.*, 64 LW 2586 (4th Cir. 3/12/96).

33. Same-sex harassment is not cognizable: *Garcia v. Elf Atochem North America*, 28 F.3d 446 (5th Cir. 1994), *Hopkins v. Baltimore Gas & Electric*, 871 F.Supp. 822 (D.Md. 12/28/94), *Vandeventer v. Wabash National Corp.*, 867 F.Supp. 790 (N.D. Ind. 1994); *contra, Sardinia v. Dellwood Foods*, 64 LW 2329 (S.D.N.Y. 10/30/95); *King v. M.R. Brown Inc.*, 64 LW 2231 (E.D.Pa. 9/26/95); *EEOC v. Walden Book Co.*, 63 LW 2710 (M.D.Tenn. 5/4/95).

34. *McWilliams v. Fairfax County Board of Supervisors*, 72 F.3d 1191 (4th Cir. 1/1/96) [humiliating treatment of one heterosexual male by a group of other heterosexual males]; *Fox v. Sierra Development Co.*, 876 F.Supp. 1169 (D.Nev. 1/30/95) [pervasive homosexual innuendo in the workplace is not actionable by offended heterosexual male employee].

35. *Fuller v. Oakland, California*, 47 F.3d 1522 (9th Cir. 2/14/95).

36. 59 F.3d 1391 (D.C.Cir. 7/28/95).

37. *Heyne v. Caruso*, 69 F.3d 1475 (9th Cir. 11/8/95).

38. *Chalmers v. Quaker Oats Co.*, 61 F.3d 1340 (7th Cir. 8/15/95).

39. *Brooke v. Restaurant Services Inc.*, 906 P.2d 66 (Colo.Sup. 9/25/95).

40. *Rains v. Criterion Systems Inc.*, 64 LW 2616 (9th Cir. 3/26/96).

41. *Molesworth v. Brandon*, 64 LW 2587 (Md.App. 3/5/96).

42. *Corl v. Huron Casting Inc.*, 64 LW 2587 (Mich.Sup. 3/1/96).

43. *Hogan v. Bangor & Aroostook Railroad*, 61 F.3d 1034 (1st Cir. 8/18/95).

44. *St. Louis v. Texas Workers Compensation Commission*, 65 F.3d 43 (5th Cir. 9/26/95); *Vernon v. Cassadaga Valley Central School District*, 49 F.3d 886 (2nd Cir. 3/8/95).

45. *McCray v. Corry Mfg. Co.*, 64 LW 2122 (3rd Cir. 8/9/95).

46. *Wallace v. Dunn Construction Co.*, 62 F.3d 374 (11th Cir. 8/30/95).

47. *O'Connor v. Consolidated Coin Caterers Corp.*, #95-354, 64 LW 4243 (Sup.Ct. 4/1/96),*reversing and remanding* 56 F.3d 542.

48. *Ellis v. United Airlines*, 64 LW 2423 (10th Cir. 1/4/96).

49. *Miller v. Cigna Corp.*, 63 LW 2482 (3rd Cir. 1/23/95).

50. *EEOC v. Kloster Cruise Ltd.*, 888 F.Supp. 147 (S.D.Fla. 5/12/95).

51. *Denty v. SmithKline Beecham Corp.*, 907 F.Supp. 879 (E.D.Pa. 11/7/95).

52. *Mahoney v. RFE/RL Inc.*, 47 F.3d 447 (D.C.Cir. 2/28/95).

53. *Di Biase v. SmithKline Beecham Corp.*, 48 F.3d 719 (3d Cir. 2/16/95), reversing the District Court (62 LW 2655).

54. *Blistein v. St. John's College*, 64 LW 2502 (4th Cir. 1/26/96).

55. See 63 LW 2590.

56. *Eckles Consolidated Rail Corp.*, 890 F.Supp. 1391 (S.D.Ind. 7/5/95).

57. *Krauel v. Iowa Methodist Medical Center*, 64 LW 2304 (S.D. Ia. 10/2/95).

58. *McNemar v. Disney Stores*, 64 LW 2063 (E.D.Pa. 6/29/95).

59. *Maddox v. University of Tennessee*, 62 F.3d 843 (6th Cir. 8/21/95); *Despears v. Milwaukee County*, 63 F.3d 635 (7th Cir. 8/21/95).

60. *Reich v. Midwestern Plastic Engineering Inc.*, 64 LW 2087 (W.D.Mich. 7/22/95).

61. *Manuel v. Westlake Polymers Co.*, 66 F.3d 758 (5th Cir. 10/3/95).

62. *Robbins v. BNA Inc.*, 896 F.Supp. 18 (D.D.C. 8/15/95).

63. *Shahar v. Bowers*, 70 F.3d 1218 (11th Cir. 12/20/95).

64. *Collins v. Rizkana*, 652 N.E.2d 653 (Ohio Sup. 8/16/95).

— FOR FURTHER REFERENCE —

Biddle, Richard E., "Disparate Impact Reference Trilogy for Statistics," 46 *Labor L.J.* 651 (November '95).

Burns, Sarah E., "Evidence of a Sexually Hostile Workplace," 21 *N.Y.U. Review of Law and Social Change* 357 (June '94).

Daus, Matthew A., "Successful Mediation of Employment Discrimination Claims," *N.Y.L.J.* 4/8/96 p. 1.

Franke, Katherine M., "The Central Mistake of Sex Discrimination Law," 144 *U. of Pennsylvania L.Rev.* 1 (November '95).

Hamilton, Arthur, Judy Tansley and Peter A. Veglahn, "Wage Surveys and Anti-Trust Law," 46 *Labor Law J.* 763 (December '95).

Lind, Jessica, "The Prima Facie Case of Age Discrimination in Reduction-in-Force Cases," 94 *Michigan L.Rev.* 832 (December '95).

McCargo, Samuel E., "Responding to the Hostile Sexual Environment: Cure or Legal Defense?" 74 *Michigan Bar J.* 1168 (November '95).

Miller, Bruce A., "The Americans With Disabilities Act and the Unionized Workplace," 74 *Michigan Bar J.* 1180 (November '95).

Mishkind, Charles S., "The Use of After-Acquired Evidence in Employment Litigation After McKinnon," 23 *Employee Relations L.J.* 109 (Winter '95).

Olsen, Amy, "Family Leave Legislation: Ensuring Both Job Security and Family Values," 35 *Santa Clara L.Rev.* 983 (Summer '95).

Sand, Robert H., "Workplace Exposures and the Right to Sue for Medical Monitoring," 21 *Employee Relations L.J.* 143 (Winter '95).

Turner, Ronald, "The Color Complex: Intraracial Discrimination in the Workplace," 46 *Labor L.J.* 678 (November '95).

ENVIRONMENTAL LAW

[¶2201] On March 31, 1995, the EPA issued an announcement, "Voluntary Environmental Self-Policing and Self-Disclosure Interim Policy Statement".[1] The agency announced that it may refrain from pursuing criminal charges if a company voluntarily corrects and reports its violations. The EPA may also refrain from imposing punitive fines in addition to standard penalties. This announcement falls short of immunity for voluntary reporters; the agency still retains the option of pursuing ultimate penalties in appropriate cases—e.g., where the violations are particularly serious, harmful, or manifest a corporate philosophy of concealment of wrongdoing.

The policy refuses to treat corporate environmental audits as privileged business information (although a number of states have enacted such laws, or have pending bills).

It's clear that a fine or penalty paid to the government is not tax-deductible. Neither is an $8 million contribution to an environmental fund set up to alleviate the toxic effects of the pesticide kepone, in lieu of a criminal fine. (The original fine of $13.2 million was reduced to $5 million because the fund was created.) In the Third Circuit's analysis, the contribution to the fund was at the direction of the government, and hence nondeductible.[2]

The owners of land next to land where a major oil spill occurred must show physical encroachment on their property in order to assert a negligence or private nuisance claim for fear of future health damages or diminution in the value of their own property.[3]

Sale of contaminated property "as is" transfers environmental liability to the buyer only if the deed makes this clear. Requiring transfer of a fee simple subject to environmental regulations is not sufficient to shift liability to the buyer.[4]

As always, see ¶2515.1 for discussion of environment-related insurance issues.

[¶2202] FEDERAL ENVIRONMENTAL LAWS

In order to recover from the cleanup fund, claims must be presented under the Oil Pollution Act of 1990 (33 U.S.C. §2713); a claim must also be made before filing a private suit under the OPA.[5]

Also see P.L. 103-311, the Hazardous Materials Transportation Authorization Act, 49 U.S.C. §5101 (8/26/94), under which the DOT is directed to make the National Intelligent Vehicle-Highway Systems Program promote safe transport of hazardous materials, including rules for safely packaging hazmats in fiber drums.

[¶2203] SCOPE OF CERCLA

The Western District of New York requires active human agency in disposing of hazardous materials for CERCLA liability—mere passive release of substances does not subject the landowner to CERCLA §107 liability.[6]

The seller of a building that contains asbestos doesn't become a CERCLA liable party merely because a subsequent purchaser removes the asbestos. The Seventh Circuit said that the sale was not a disposal of hazardous materials that would make the seller an "arranger." Selling a building cannot be deemed an abnormally hazardous activity, nor can the seller reasonably foresee that the buyer's agents would cause a hazardous condition by mishandling asbestos removal.[7]

A significant CERCLA issue is identification of liable "operators" of contaminated facilities. According to the Sixth Circuit, the parent corporation can be deemed the owner of a facility owned by a subsidiary if, and only if, the corporate veil can be pierced.[8] In a case where the veil can be pierced, the Second Circuit says that a parent corporation that has "owner" liability can also have independent "operator" liability for the subsidiary's facility.[9]

An individual employee is not an owner, and therefore escapes CERCLA liability unless he or she falls into another category, such as "operator." The Eighth Circuit says that an employee (whether or not he or she is also an officer, director, or shareholder) must not only have authority to control hazardous waste disposal, but must actually exercise it in order to be liable as an "operator."[10]

The CERCLA cast of responsible characters also includes "arrangers" and "transporters." To be liable as an arranger, an officer or director of a company must have authority, and in fact exercise direct or indirect control over a subsidiary's disposal practices[11]—the same standard as the parent company's liability. To suffer liability as a "transporter," an officer or director must actually participate in the conduct that created the liability. It's not enough to manage the company; one must be aware of the company's substantial participation in choosing disposal facilities and accepting materials for transport.[12]

A company that is responsible for pollution cannot get CERCLA contribution from a company that owned the property at a time when there was neither disposal nor release of hazardous waste.[13] According to the Eighth Circuit, a federal consent decree that settles the liability of certain Potentially Responsible Parties (PRPs) and protects them against contribution claims from non-settling PRPs is serious enough to entitle non-settling PRPs to intervention as of right if they want to challenge the consent decree.[14]

[¶2204] THE CLEAN WATER ACT

The Ninth Circuit allows a CWA citizen suit to enforce a discharge permit's water quality standard, even if the standard is not expressed as end-of-pipe effluent limitations—in other words, regulations that are qualitative rather than quantitative can still be enforced by citizen suit.[15]

To convict a corporate officer under the CWA's criminal provision (§309(c)(2)), the prosecution must show that he knew the nature of his acts and performed them intentionally. Because, in 1987, Congress amended the statute to refer to "knowing" rather than "willful" actions, successful prosecution does not require proof that the actor knew that the conduct violated the statute. In this reading, the Congressional intent was to impose more, rather than fewer, criminal penalties.[16]

All CWA citizen suit plaintiffs who seek an attorneys' fee award must satisfy the statute's pre-suit notice requirement—one plaintiff can't satisfy the requirement on behalf of all.[17]

[¶2205] THE CLEAN AIR ACT

The Tenth Amendment is not violated, and state sovereignty is not abridged, when the Clean Air Act imposes sanctions such as loss of federal highway funds for failure to comply with the Act's requirements for a state permit program covering stationary sources of pollution.[18]

The Clean Air Act imposes a requirement of prompt notification to the EPA whenever an asbestos-containing structure is renovated. However, it is not clear whether failure to do so is a one-time violation or one that continues until abated, so the Ninth Circuit decided that, absent clear statutory guidance, only the penalty for a single-day violation can be imposed.[19]

[¶2206] RESOURCE CONSERVATION AND RECOVERY ACT

A current owner cannot bring a RCRA citizen suit against a former owner to recover money that was expended to clean up a site that once was but no longer is imminently hazardous. The Supreme Court decided this in the spring of 1996 because the RCRA citizen suit provision is drafted in terms of "restraining" contamination posing "imminent and substantial endangerment," which no longer exists (because of the cleanup). The Court felt that this distinction between CERCLA and RCRA shared liability concepts indicates an intention to limit the passage of RCRA liability back through the chain of title. This case[20] does not reach the question of whether a party who has properly commenced a citizen suit can get an injunction obligating someone else to pay future cleanup costs for a site that continues to be hazardous—but note that according to the Eighth Circuit, there is no implied private right of action under RCRA §7002 (the citizen suit provision) for recovery of the costs of cleaning up contaminated property.[21]

[¶2206.2] State Regulation of Solid Waste Disposal

The Ninth Circuit saw no Commerce Clause objection to a Washington State statute requiring everyone who collects and transports solid waste within the state to have a certificate of public convenience and necessity—even if they operate in interstate commerce.[22]

The Third Circuit similarly approved of a municipal flow control ordinance that sends solid waste to specific facilities—provided that the process of selecting the facilities is fair and does not discriminate against out-of-state businesses.[23]

However, the Eighth Circuit found a Commerce Clause violation in a state referendum about putting a large municipal solid waste facility in the state. In this reading, both the purpose and the effect are discriminatory, based on restrictions on bringing out-of-state waste into the state. Because non-discriminatory alternatives were available, the Court of Appeals did not find the state environmental interest compelling enough to justify the restriction on interstate commerce.[24]

[¶2207] OTHER FEDERAL ENVIRONMENTAL LAWS

To have standing in a citizen suit against the government for violation of the procedures of the Endangered Species Act, plaintiffs must assert an interest in preserving the species. Thus, ranchers and irrigation districts do not have standing.[25]

— ENDNOTES —

1. 60 FR 16875.

2. *Allied-Signal Inc. v. C.I.R.*, 1995 U.S.App. LEXIS 5130 (3rd Cir. 1995).

3. *Adams v. Star Enterprises*, 51 F.3d 417 (4th Cir. 4/6/95).

4. *New West Urban Renewal Co. v Westinghouse Electric Corp.*, 64 LW 2383 (D.N.J. 11/21/95).

5. *Boca Ciega Hotel Inc. v. Bouchard Transportation Co.*, 51 F.3d 235 (11th Cir. 4/17/95).

6. *Idylwoods Associates v. Mader Capital Inc.*, 64 LW 2580 (W.D.N.Y. 2/16/96).

7. *G.J. Leasing Co. v. Union Electric Co.*, 54 F.3d 379 (7th Cir. 5/4/95).

8. *U.S. v. Cordova Chemical Co.*, 59 F.3d 584 (6th Cir. 7/14/95).

9. *Schiavone v. Pierce*, 64 LW 2603 (2nd Cir. 3/14/96).

10. *U.S. v. Gurley*, 43 F.3d 1188 (8th Cir. 12/28/94).

11. *U.S. v. TIC Investment Corp.*, 68 F.3d 1082 (8th Cir. 10/16/95).

12. *U.S. v. USX Corp.*, 68 F.3d 811 (3rd Cir. 10/23/95).

13. *Joslyn Mfg. Co. v. Koppers Co.*, 40 F.3d 750 (5th Cir. 12/28/94).

14. *U.S. v. Union Electric Co.*, 64 F.3d 1152 (8th Cir. 8/30/95).

15. *Northwest Environmental Advocates v. Portland, Oregon*, 56 F.3d 979 (9th Cir. 6/7/95); *follows PUD No. 1 of Jefferson County v. Washington Department of Ecology*, 114 S.Ct. 1900 (Sup.Ct. 1994).

16. *U.S. v. Hopkins*, 53 F.3d 533 (2nd Cir. 4/28/95); *also see U.S. v. Weitzenhoff*, 35 F.3d 1275 (9th Cir. 1994).

17. *New Mexico Citizens for Clean Air and Water v. Espanola Mercantile Co.*, 72 F.3d 830 (10th Cir. 1/2/96).

18. *General Accident Insurance Co. of America v. New Jersey*, 64 LW 2618 (N.J. Sup. 3/26/96).

19. *U.S. v. Trident Seafoods Corp.*, 60 F.3d 556 (9th Cir. 7/12/95).

20. *Meghrig v. KFC Western Inc.*, #95-83, 64 LW 4135 (Sup.Ct. 3/19/96), *reversing* 49 F.3d 518 (9th Cir. 3/1/95).

21. *Furrer v. Brown*, 62 F.3d 1092 (8th Cir. 8/15/95).

22. *Kleenwell Biohazard Waste v. Nelson*, 48 F.3d 391 (9th Cir. 2/9/95).

23. *Harvey & Harvey Inc. v. Chester County, Pennsylvania*, 68 F.3d 788 (3rd Cir. 10/23/95).

24. *SDDS Inc. v. South Dakota*, 47 F.3d 263 (8th Cir. 2/6/95).

25. *Bennett v. Plenert*, 63 F.3d 915 (9th Cir. 8/24/95).

— FOR FURTHER REFERENCE —

Bannon, Alexander Laboutin and David L. Sfara, "Glowing Reports: Valuation of Contaminated Properties," 10 *Probate and Property* 22 (January-February '95).

Been, Vicki, "Analyzing Evidence of Environmental Justice," 11 *J. of Land Use and Environmental Law* 1 (Fall '95).

Cross, Frank B., "When Environmental Regulations Kill," 22 *Ecology Law Q.* 729 (November '95).

Mandiberg, Susan F., "The Dilemma of Mental State in Federal Regulatory Crimes: The Environmental Example," 25 *Environmental Law* 1165 (Fall '95).

Marino, Andrew A. and Lawrence E., "The Scientific Basis of Causality in Toxic Tort Cases," 21 *U. of Dayton L.Rev.* 1 (Fall '95).

Nooney, Kathleen L., "Living, Breathing and Working With the Indoor Air Quality Rules," 11 *Practical Real Estate Lawyer* 75 (November '95).

Sand, Robert H., "Workplace Exposures and the Right to Sue for Medical Monitoring," 21 *Employee Relations L.J.* 143 (Winter '95).

Simon, Ron, "Radiation Overexposure Claims: Fighting Defense Tactics Creatively," 32 *Trial* 26 (January '96).

Smith, G. Nelson III, "Nuisance and Trespass Claims in Environmental Litigation," 36 *Santa Clara L.Rev.* 39 (Winter '95).

Tupper, Stephen, "Barriers to Trade: The Environmental Claims of the Future," 8 *Environmental Claims J.* 133 (Winter '95).

ESTATE PLANNING AND ADMINISTRATION

[¶2301] During the supplement period, Congress offered some protection to charities via the Philanthropy Protection Act of 1995, P.L. 104-62 and the Charitable Gift Annuity Antitrust Relief Act of 1995, P.L. 104-63.

The former exempts charitable income pooled funds, such as those set up for charitable remainder trusts, from various securities laws by making it clear that they are not investment companies. Nevertheless, the funds are subject to federal anti-fraud securities laws, and donors are still entitled to disclosure of "material terms of the operation of the fund" within 90 days of making an irrevocable donation. (Funds that accept revocable donations are given three years to restructure.)

The latter makes it clear that it is not an antitrust violation for issuers of charitable gift annuities to use uniform rates, specifically those set by the American Council on Gift Annuities.

[¶2305] THE UNLIMITED MARITAL DEDUCTION

No marital deduction was allowed by the Fourth Circuit on trust assets passing to the surviving spouse under a settlement agreement relating to a dispute about the trust's terms. Under the settlement, the survivor received a life estate but no power of appointment. Crucially, the survivor's rights did not pass "from the decedent," and were obtained in her role as litigant rather than that of spouse.[1]

The surviving spouse's interest in QTIP property can be determined at the date of the QTIP election rather than the date of the deceased spouse's death. The surviving spouse as executor in this case could also be given discretion to determine the amount of the QTIP election, because once the election was made, the property was placed into a trust that could not be appointed away from the surviving spouse until after her death.[2]

[¶2307] VALUATION

The IRS issued Final Regulations for income, gift, and estate taxation of annuities, life or term interests, remainders, and reversions. The Final Regs. stipulate the situations in which the ordinary IRS §7520 valuation tables cannot be used.[3] The tables cannot be used if the transfer instrument does not give the beneficiary the degree of beneficial enjoyment traditionally applying to that type of property interest as defined by local law.

Nor can the tables be used to value transfers by the terminally ill, defined as persons with a 50% likelihood of dying within one year. However, if an individual survives the transfer by 18 months, it is presumed that he or she was not terminally ill at the transfer unless terminal illness is proved by clear and convincing evidence. Mere age does not make a person terminally ill—unless he or she has one or more illnesses which, separately or together, are life-threatening.

The Fifth Circuit requires the filing of a "recapture agreement," binding all heirs to maintain the special use (and repay tax benefits if it is not) as a condition of electing §2032A special use valuation. The recapture agreement must be enforceable under state law.[4]

The Court of Federal Claims valued "flower bonds" at their par value plus accrued interest on the owner's date of death—a valuation that was affirmed per curiam by the Federal Circuit.[5]

[¶2311] GENERATION-SKIPPING TRANSFER TAX

Final Regulations covering the GST were adopted by T.D. 8644, effective 12/27/95. See 1996-7 IRB 16.

[¶2313] ADMINISTERING THE ESTATE

Distributions made from a decedent's trust, after his death, to satisfy completed gifts that were enforceable pre-mortem debts are claims against the trust. Therefore, according to the District Court for the District of Massachusetts, they cannot be deducted from the estate as §2053 "claims against the estate." The distributions were mandatory, and therefore the decedent relinquished the power to revoke or amend those distributions within three years of death. The result is that the distributions made within three years of death were included in the trust's fair market value by §2038.[6]

[¶2316] TAX DUTIES OF FIDUCIARIES

According to the Eighth Circuit, the IRS could not appeal a District Court order removing a tax lien from a property, because the lien arose at the date of death, and thus had to be appealed within ten years of the date of death.[7] That is, the lien is durational, not limitational. The lien lasts exactly ten years after death; the government does not get ten years to file a claim after discovery of the existence of the claim.

[¶2326] CHECKLIST OF POST-MORTEM TAX PLANNING STEPS

Cash gifts made by a surviving spouse to disclaiming legatees prevented their disclaimers from being valid. Therefore, the estate could not claim the marital deduction for amounts passing to the surviving spouse because of the purported disclaimers—which, in any case, were not freely made because family members would be unlikely to alienate a rich relative.[8]

— ENDNOTES —

1. *Estate of Stanley Carpenter v. C.I.R.*, 52 F.3d 1266 (4th Cir. 5/9/95).

2. *Estate of Spencer v. C.I.R.*, 43 F.3rd 226 (6th Cir. 1/5/95). Although the IRS has litigated the validity of this "wait and see" approach several times, the Fifth and Eighth Circuits also permit "wait and see": *Estate of Clayton v. Comm'r*, 976 F.2d 1486 (5th Cir. 1992); *Estate of Robertson v. Comm'r*, 15 F.3d 779 (8th Cir. 1994).

3. T.D. 8630, 1996-3 IRB 19 (12/95), finalizing the Regs. proposed in 59 FR 30180 (6/10/94).

4. *Estate of Hudgins v. C.I.R.*, 57 F.3d 1393 (5th Cir. 6/28/95).

5. *Weld v. U.S.*, 55 F.3d 623 (Fed.Cir. 1995).

6. *White v. U.S.*, 75 AFTR2d 95-767 (D.Mass. 1995).

7. *U.S. v. Davis*, 52 F.3d 781 (8th Cir. 4/21/95).

8. *Estate of Louise Monroe*, 104 T.C. No. 16 (3/27/95).

— FOR FURTHER REFERENCE —

Barnhart, Timothy, "Updating Estate Plans: A Structured Review," 10 *Probate and Property* 15 (January-February '96).

Belkin, Eileen W., "Transferring the Personal Residence," 26 *Tax Adviser* 718 (December '95).

Blumenthal, Susan G., "Disclaimers Under Federal and Local Law," 11 *Tax Management Financial Planning J.* 275 (December 19, 1995).

Denby, Stephanie, "Creative Approaches to Get the Most Out of Your Trusts," 135 *Trusts and Estates* 41 (January '96).

Frankel, George, "Planning Strategies for Inherited IRA Withdrawals," 24 *Taxation for Lawyers* 231 (January-February '96).

Gillis, Michael R., "Charitable Contributions of Closely Held Stock," 26 *Tax Adviser* 723 (December '95).

Huffaker, John B., "Sale of Remainder Failed to Keep Full Value of Stock Out of Estate," 84 *J. of Taxation* 19 (January '96).

Kiziah, Trent S., "GST: Unscrambling the Code," 10 *Probate and Property* 28 (January-February '96).

Lusby, Roger W. III, "An Update on Crummey Powers," 26 *Tax Adviser* 722 (December '95).

Ng, Peter P.J., "The Ethics of Marketing Estate Planning Documents," 135 *Trusts and Estates* 20 (January '96).

Pohl, Amelia E., "Planning for Incapacity," 14 *Preventive Law Reporter* 6 (Winter '95).

Richter, Michael H., "Basis Adjustment for Gift Tax Paid," 26 *Tax Adviser* 722 (December '95).

Shumaker, Roger L., "The World Wide Web is a Prime Resource for Trust Professionals," 134 *Trusts & Estates* 16 (December '95).

Sollee, William L. and Paul J. Schneider, "Final Regs. on Eligible Rollover Distributions from Qualified Plans," 84 *J. of Taxation* 54 (January '96).

Teitell, Conrad, "'Five Percent Probability' Test for Annuity Trusts," 134 *Trusts and Estates* 58 (December '95).

Treacy, Gerald B., "Planning to Preserve the Advantages of Community Property," 23 *Estate Planning* 3 (January '96).

Wechsler, David A. and Lisa M. Weinstein, "Estate Planning Begins with Charity," 10 *Washington Lawyer* 44 (November-December '95).

Zabel, William D. and Kim E. Baptiste, "Asset Protection and Estate Planning," 134 *Trusts and Estates* 47 (December '95).

IMMIGRATION

[¶2401] P.L. 104-51 amends §101(b) of the Immigration and Nationality Act (8 U.S.C. §1101(b)) to change the vocabulary used in the Act's definition of "child." Children are now referred to as born "in wedlock" or "out of wedlock" rather than "legitimate" or "illegitimate."

Federal immigration law preempts California's Proposition 187, a 1994 initiative that denies illegal aliens state services or benefits. According to the District Court for the Central District of California, the state law is preempted to the extent that it conflicts with federal law or establishes a state scheme for the inherently federal area of regulation of immigration.[1]

[2401.1] Exclusion and Deportation

A Chinese immigrant was denied the asylum that he sought to protect himself from coerced abortion or sterilization in furtherance of China's limitation of families to one child. The Fourth Circuit did not find this an appropriate asylum petition because the immigrant could not prove that he was at individual risk because of his political opinions; the policy was applied to the population at large.[2]

Other Chinese asylum seekers, who jumped out of a smuggling vessel and swam ashore, did not achieve "entry" sufficient to entitle them to deportation proceedings in lieu of summary exclusion. The Third Circuit said[3] that "entry" requires a lack of official restraint and either admission by immigration officials or an intentional evasion of inspection.

A "Marielito"—a person expelled from Cuba's Mariel prison—had spent about a decade in various U.S. prisons as an excluded alien, because Cuba wouldn't take him back and no other country wished to admit him. The Ninth Circuit said[4] that there is no limitation on the duration of detention where there is no possibility of immediate deportation. Parole is the exception, not the rule; and cases are reviewed at least once a year to see if parole can be granted. In this reading, Congress knew about the potential for lengthy detention, but chose not to eliminate it.

An Eastern District of Virginia case involving another Marielito permits retention of an excludable alien in federal prison after completion of his sentence for an offense committed while on immigration parole.[5]

[¶2404] EXCLUSION AND DEPORTATION PROCEEDINGS

In April, 1995, the U.S. Supreme Court held that a motion to reconsider a final deportation order of the Board of Immigration Appeals does not toll the running of the statutory 90-day period for seeking judicial review of the decision.[6]

According to the Tenth Circuit, an immigrant can be deported on the basis of an aggravated felony conviction; a separate showing of dangerousness to the community is not required to support deportation.[7] On the other hand, aliens who have been convicted of federal offenses, which are also deportable offenses, cannot use mandamus to get themselves deported before they finish their prison sentences.[8]

The Eighth Circuit rejected a Due Process challenge to the 10-day time limit for filing an administrative appeal of a deportation order. The court agreed that potential deportees who live in remote areas can be inconvenienced in satisfying that brief time period, but they don't have to use regular mail; the form can be sent to the INS office by UPS or Federal Express.[9]

The Seventh Circuit found the INS unreasonable in denying suspension of deportation without considering the aliens' community service within the United States, or the hardship to their child.[10]

[¶2405] EMPLOYER SANCTIONS

Executive Order 12989, 61 FR 6091 of February 13, 1996 debars federal contractors who knowingly hire illegal aliens from getting further federal contracts.

— ENDNOTES —

1. *League of United Latin American Citizens v. Wilson*, 908 F.Supp. 755 (C.D.Cal. 11/20/95).

2. *Chen v. Carroll*, 48 F.3d 1331 (4th Cir. 3/6/95); *Zhang v. Slattery*, 55 F.3d 732 (2nd Cir. 5/19/95) is similar.

3. *Yang v. Maugans*, 68 F.3d 1540 (3rd Cir. 10/24/95).

4. *Barreia-Echavarria v. Rison*, 44 F.3d 1441 (9th Cir. 1/12/95).

5. *Cruz-Elias v. U.S. Attorney General*, 870 F.Supp. 692 (E.D.Va. 12/8/94). The court saw no statutory or Due Process objections, in light of the facts that his status was reviewed at least annually, and that no other country wished to admit him.

6. *Stone v. INS*, #93-1199, 115 S.Ct. 1537, 131 L.Ed.2d 465 (Sup.Ct. 4/19/95).

7. *Al-Salehi v. INS*, 47 F.3d 390 (10th Cir. 2/8/95).

8. *Hernandez-Avalos v. INS*, 50 F.3d 842 (10th Cir. 3/9/95). The Ninth Circuit agrees: *Campos v. INS*, 62 F.3d 311 (9th Cir. 8/4/95).

9. *Talamantes-Penalver v. INS*, 51 F.3d 133 (8th Cir. 3/30/95).

10. *Salameda v. INS*, 70 F.3d 447 (7th Cir. 11/9/95).

— FOR FURTHER REFERENCE —

Gotcher, James R., "Computers and Information Technology in an Immigration Practice," 96 *Immigration Briefings* 1 (January '96).

Hirson, David, "Immigrant Investors Five Years After," 95 *Immigration Briefings* 1 (November '95).

Macko, Lia, "Acquiring a Better Global Vision," 9 *Georgetown Immigration Law J.* 545 (Summer '95).

Mailman, Stanley, "The Employer as Immigration Inspector," *N.Y.L.J.* 4/22/96 p. 3.

Raufer, Susan, "In-Country Processing of Refugees," 9 *Georgetown Immigration Law J.* 233 (Spring '95).

Tessier, Kevin, "Immigration and the Crisis in Federalism," 3 *Indiana J. of Global Legal Studies* 211 (Fall '95).

Theodoredes, Pamela, "Detention of Alien Juveniles," 12 *New York Law School J. of Human Rights* 393 (Spring '95).

INSURANCE

[¶2501] The National Banking Act (12 U.S.C. §92) permits national banks in small towns (population under 5000) to act as agents for life and property insurance. This somewhat staid statute has given rise to not one but two Supreme Court cases during the supplement period.

The first, *NationsBank of North Carolina N.A. v. VALIC*[1] upholds the Commissioner of Currency's determination that banks can also sell annuities because this is "within the incidental powers necessary to the business of banking," and furthermore that annuities are investment instruments rather than insurance for this purpose.

The later case holds that a Florida statute forbidding insurance sales by banks is preempted by §92; the federal law does specifically relate to the business of insurance, so it falls within the McCarran-Ferguson Act exemption.[2] The Sixth Circuit found that §92 also preempts a Kentucky statute that prevents bank holding companies from serving as insurance agents. The statute is not entitled to the McCarran-Ferguson exemption because it keeps willing sellers out of the insurance business rather than merely regulating the insurance business.[3]

The Seventh Circuit says that a bank located in a small town has the further right to sell insurance in other, larger towns and cities.[4]

Viatical settlement—the procedure under which a terminally ill person assigns his or her life insurance to a settlement company, in return for a lump sum or continuing payments representing the discounted value of the insurance benefit—has been held to be an investment contract that is subject to regulation under the Securities Act of 1933 §2(1).[5] In general, insurance is exempt from securities law regulation, but the District Court held that there is no transfer of risk to an insurer and therefore the viatical settlements fall outside the insurance category.

[¶2508] LEGAL ASPECTS OF BENEFICIARY DESIGNATION

A divorcing couple's separation agreement was incorporated into their decree. A clause in the agreement stating that the spouses had no rights in the other's estate "as heirs or otherwise" was not sufficient to terminate the husband's rights as named beneficiary of the wife's insurance. (She never changed the beneficiary designation.) According to the Nevada Supreme Court, specific divestiture in policy rights is required.[6]

[¶2509] LIFE INSURANCE TAXATION

According to the Fifth Circuit, a Qualified Terminable Interest in Property (QTIP) existed, and the Tax Court should not have placed 100% of the $650,000 proceeds of term life insurance purchased with community funds into the insured husband's gross estate. (The uninsured wife predeceased him, and the proceeds were payable to his estate.) Under Texas community property law, when the husband died, 50% of the policy proceeds belonged to the wife's residuary trust. The policy remained community property even though the husband continued to renew the policy after the wife's death—he did not create new, separate policies.[7]

[¶2515] LIABILITY INSURANCE

According to the New Jersey Superior Court, it is contrary to state public policy to allow a company to insure against punitive damages, even if the company's liability is only vicarious.[8] In this analysis, punitive damages are supposed to act as a deterrent, but cannot do so if insurance coverage is available to shift liability.

In a recent Wisconsin case, a child was injured by a meatgrinder. The injured child's family sued the manufacturer, who countersued the child's mother (and the family's homeowner's insurance policy) for negligent supervision. The state's Supreme Court permitted the enforcement of the family exclusion clause in a third-party contribution claim, because of the serious risk of collusion in intrafamily tort cases.[9]

[¶2515.1] Liability Insurance and Environmental Claims

Several familiar issues were once again the subject of court decisions. At the end of 1995, the D.C. Circuit ruled that the CGL pollution exclusion clause's reference to "sudden and accidental" events unambiguously excludes coverage for gradual pollution, with the result that the federal government and not the insurer became responsible for a $100 million dioxin cleanup.[10]

However, where a personal injury policy does cover wrongful entry and does not exclude pollution, then the insurer can be made to cover government-mandated cleanup costs.[11] According to the Sixth Circuit, an insured's cleanup costs, incurred after getting a CERCLA "PRP letter" (identifying the insured as a party potentially responsible for cleanup costs), are considered damages sought in a suit. Therefore, they are covered by the CGL. Furthermore, these costs are not subject to the "own property" exclusion, because the state owns the groundwater—the insured property owner does not.[12]

In a case of first impression in the state, the Oklahoma Supreme Court also applied the CGL exclusion to disposal of hazardous waste, on the usual grounds that "sudden" refers to abruptness and immediacy; "accidental" refers to the release itself, not the result that the release has the effect of causing pollution.[13]

The Eleventh Circuit deemed the term "discharge" in the CGL to be susceptible to more than one meaning. As a result, the policyholder was entitled to defense and indemnity when inhalation of a vapor "emission" from an adhesive product caused death, because of the ambiguity as to whether this "emission" was a "discharge."[14] The Second Circuit also found ambiguity in the CGL pollution exclusion—this time, whether the exclusion is limited to environmental pollution or covers the situation in which wrongful death and other injuries resulted from the release of carbon monoxide due to a landlord's negligent maintenance of a heating system.[15]

In the Second Circuit, if the insured can prove by a preponderance of the evidence that asbestos-caused disease was triggered continuously throughout the disease process, then coverage will correspondingly be triggered continuously. If several insurance policies are involved, coverage is prorated based on which insurer was liable at each particular time. The policyholder remains liable for the periods in which it was without insurance coverage. With respect to property damage, each time that asbestos-containing material is installed is an occurrence for which another deductible may properly be imposed.[16]

[¶2518] PROPERTY INSURANCE

See Rev.Rul. 95-22, 1995-1 C.B. 145, for circumstances under which gain does not have to be recognized when insurance proceeds are received in connection with a Presidentially proclaimed natural disaster.

[¶2530] SUPPLEMENTARY BENEFITS UNDER LIABILITY INSURANCE

In a Michigan case, a child sexually coerced another child on two occasions. In the first, the child was six years old; in the second, he was nine years old. The state Supreme Court required the parents' homeowner's insurance to treat these actions as "occurrences" covered by the policy. Although the child intended to obtain sexual gratification by his actions, he did not intend to harm the other child.

Absent proof of subjective intent to harm, he could neither be said to expect nor intend the injuries. Nor could summary judgment be granted based on the characterization of the child's activities as "intentional acts." Although adults are presumed to intend injury when they sexually assault children, no presumption obtains when both the actor and victim are children. Therefore, the jury must decide the question of whether a reasonable child of the actor's age would foresee injury resulting from his activities.[17]

The no-fault automobile policy covering injury to a family member or pedestrian, caused by an object "propelled by or from an automobile" is broad enough to provide PIP benefits in the case of a drive-by shooting.[18]

[¶2531] HEALTH INSURANCE

Because the cost of health care is so high, it is unusual for anyone to pay out-of-pocket for such care. Usually payment is made by a third party—either

Medicare or Medicaid (see ¶3903, 3904 in the main volume) or private health insurance. Although some people purchase insurance as individuals, or through affinity groups (such as bar associations), the commonest form of health insurance is through a plan sponsored by the employer. Many ex-employees are entitled to assume individual payment for continuation of their group insurance plans for a period of months or years, as provided by the federal statute COBRA (the Comprehensive Omnibus Budget Reconciliation Act of 1985-6).

Traditionally, the employer furnished the entire premium for the plan, which either reimbursed employees for their medical expenses or paid on an indemnity basis ($X for a particular service or health condition or per day of hospitalization), subject to a copayment responsibility. The distinction between reimbursement and indemnity is that reimbursement pays back the employee or other insured person for expenses incurred. Indemnity provides the insured with money that can, but need not be, used to pay medical expenses.

Today, however, there is an ever-increasing likelihood that an employer's group health plan (EGHP) will either offer managed care as an option, or require employees to get their care from a managed care entity (see below). Furthermore, employees are required to assume an increasing share of the cost of insurance, both through premiums they pay and through the copayments (deductibles and coinsurance) they are required to assume.

Sometimes employers (especially large companies) will self-insure. That is, instead of purchasing health insurance policies, they will set aside reserves to be used when employees encounter health expenditures of a type covered by the health plan. An insurance company may take a limited role in administering such a plan; it is then called a TPA (third party administrator) or ASO (administrative services only) organization vis-a-vis the employer.

EGHPs are considered welfare benefit plans for ERISA purposes. Therefore, in many instances employees will not have state-law remedies against the insurer or the employer because ERISA preempts the state law—even though ERISA has very little to say on the subject of welfare benefits.

In the spring of 1995, the Supreme Court upheld a New York statute requiring hospitals to collect a surcharge (to be used to pay for the care of the uninsured and destitute) on hospital bills if the patient was covered by a commercial insurer or certain HMOs, but exempting patients covered by Blue Cross/Blue Shield from the surcharge. The Supreme Court rejected the argument that ERISA preempts the state statute, because the surcharges do not "relate to" employee benefit plans, but rather to hospital financing; states can properly regulate hospital costs even if the regulation has an indirect economic effect on benefit plans. The exemption is intended to help out Blue Cross plans in their role as insurer of last resort.[19]

Health insurance policies are generally drafted to exclude "experimental" drugs and procedures, so a frequent litigation issue is when a treatment has become accepted enough to be removed from the experimental class. High-dose chemotherapy for breast cancer has been characterized as non-experimental by the Fourth Circuit, ruling that therapy need only be accepted by the scientific community; the person seeking coverage need not demonstrate a statistically significant chance of a cure.[20]

However, another case also involving CHAMPUS (the federal agency that finances the medical care of civilian dependents of military personnel) found that CHAMPUS was not arbitrary or capricious when it characterized the high-dose chemotherapy as experimental, and thus denying coverage was no violation of the Administrative Procedures Act.[21]

Another breast cancer patient succeeded in obtaining a preliminary injunction, given the likelihood of success on her claim that high-dose chemotherapy is an accepted treatment. Thus, her health plan violated the ADA by covering high-dose chemotherapy for certain cancers but denying it for breast cancer.[22]

Also note that a union welfare fund settled a major EEOC case involving discrimination against persons with AIDS by agreeing to pay at least $1 million and extend coverage for PWAs. The settlement applies to the 13 named plaintiffs and any plan member who responds within 45 days to a mailed notice disclosing the settlement. However, emotional distress damages are limited to $50,000 per person.[23]

[¶2531.1] Policy Design

Health insurance policies are usually written as either basic medical insurance or major medical insurance. A basic medical insurance plan covers, e.g., hospital expenses (room and board, drugs, laboratory tests, etc.), surgical fees, and other physician fees. In general, hospital expenses are covered based on a certain amount per day, up to a certain number of days (e.g., 30 days per year; 90 days per year; even 365 days per year). There are two basic payment approaches: reimbursing the insured for the actual cost of hospital care, up to $X per day; or a service benefit, paying whatever the hospital's charge may be for a semi-private room.

Surgical expenses are paid according to a surgical schedule; reasonable and customary fees; or a relative value scale. A surgical schedule sets a "price" for a long list of procedures. The insured receives either what the surgeon actually charges or the amount on the schedule—whichever is less. The reasonable and customary approach pays the full amount of the actual fee, provided that it is comparable to what other surgeons in the same area charge. A relative value scale compares the seriousness of various operations, and compensates more highly for the more serious procedures than the trivial ones.

Nonsurgical doctor bills (e.g., office visits; care by physicians in the hospital when the patient is not undergoing surgery) are usually compensated at a certain amount per visit.

A major medical plan requires the insured person to assume a significant deductible, but offers a very high level of coverage (e.g., up to $1 million in lifetime benefits). A major medical policy can supplement a basic policy; or a person who is very risk-tolerant or very short of cash might purchase a major medical policy as his or her only form of health insurance coverage.

As a general rule, health insurance policies pay only for costs incurred "as a result of injury or sickness," and only for medically necessary services. Thus, elective procedures such as cosmetic surgery are not covered. Nor are experimental procedures that are not scientifically accepted. This is a major litigation area: in many instances, coverage of an expensive procedure will be denied, leading to a charge of bad faith (or wrongful death) by the person seeking coverage or his or her family or survivors.

Health policies usually contain a preexisting condition waiver—i.e., for a period such as six months or a year after the policy becomes effective, coverage will be denied for conditions for which the insured was already under treatment, or for which a reasonable person would have sought treatment, and which was not disclosed on the application. (Policies are also conventionally written to exclude disclosed preexisting conditions.)

It is unusual for a sick person to collect the full cost of medical care. Usually, payments do not begin until a deductible has been satisfied (for the calendar year or for each sickness or injury), and the insured is usually required to pay a coinsurance amount. Also, to avoid anyone earning a profit on illness, if there are two or more policies that might pay for the care, benefits are coordinated—i.e., there are rules determining the responsibility of each policy, making sure that the insured never collects over 100% of the cost of care.

[¶2531.2]   Policy Renewals

Health insurance policies may fall into any one of five categories of renewability. A cancelable policy offers the least stability and protection for the insured: it permits the insurer to increase premiums at any time permitted by state regulators, and to terminate the policy at any time by notifying the insured and returning any premiums that were paid in advance.

An optionally renewable policy's premium can be raised for an entire class of insureds, but not for a particular insured who has made large claims. The policy can be terminated on a date set by the contract—typically, the policy anniversary. A conditionally renewable policy can be terminated by the insurer because of conditions named in the contract, such as ceasing to become employed or reaching a triggering age—but not deterioration in health. Here, too, premium increases must be applied to a whole class or not at all.

A guaranteed renewable policy must be renewed until a specific age (typically 65, the age of Medicare eligibility, or age 60) as long as the insured continues to maintain premium payments. Only class-wide premium increases are permitted. Noncancelable health insurance policies are rare. They continue until the insured reaches age 65, and the insurer retains neither the right to terminate the coverage nor to increase the premium.

[¶2531.3]   Managed Care Entities

Managed care developed as a response to continuing double-digit annual increases in the cost of insured medical care. A managed care entity is an organization (typically an insurance company or division of an insurance company) that administers the provision of medical care under terms other than conventional fee-for-service care rendered by any provider of the patient's choice. There are many managed care entities currently operating, many hybrid entities, and the lines of demarcation are not always clear-cut.

Theoretically, managed care entities will lower the cost of health care by "gatekeeper" mechanisms that prevent health care consumers from over-using care, and by removing providers' incentives to over-treat or over-prescribe. The risk of the pure fee-for-service plan is that providers, given an economic incentive to expand the care furnished, will drive up the bill by ordering unnecessary services for purely financial reasons. The risk of the pure managed care plan is that providers, given an economic incentive to restrict treatment, will impair patients' health by withholding necessary services.

At first, managed care entities were absolved of liability on various theories (they did not furnish care, and thus could not commit malpractice, etc.). However, there is an increasing trend to make the managed care entity liable if, for instance, it is negligent in selection or supervision of participating physicians, or if utilization review activities deny access to necessary care, with resulting harm to the would-be patient.

The Health Maintenance Organization, or HMO, might be called the "traditional" mode of managed care. Patients ("lives") who are covered by an HMO are expected to get most or all of their care through the HMO. In exchange for this limitation, they will be insulated from major out-of-pocket expenses: they may receive treatment without explicit cost, or at a small out-of-pocket copayment, within the system.

Depending on the arrangement, patients may be denied reimbursement, or reimbursed at a lower rate, if they seek care outside the HMO's pool of physicians, hospitals, diagnostic facilities, and other resources. However, full reimbursement will typically be available for emergency care outside the network, or if it is agreed that the patient needs a type of specialized care that is not available within the HMO network.

Usually, patients will be required to see a "gatekeeper" family physician before being referred to an HMO specialist. Advance authorization is generally required for surgery; second opinions are generally required before authorization will be granted; and utilization review is generally used to determine if a continued stay in a hospital, nursing facility, or rehabilitation facility continues to be appropriate.

Typically, HMOs are capitated plans. That is, health care providers receive a fee for each subscriber ("per head") for each month, whether or not a particular subscriber receives health care services in that month, or the level or intensity of the services.

In a "staff model" HMO, the physicians, nurses, physical therapists, etc., are salaried employees of the HMO itself. In a "group model" HMO, care is provided by medical groups with diverse specialties, who contract with the HMO.

The "IPA" (Individual Practice Association) model provides services under a contract between the HMO and physicians or medical groups who practice independently. The IPA itself, as an entity, is usually a business corporation with physicians as stockholders and officers.

The general rule is that the IPA HMOs do not own hospitals, imaging centers, etc.; usually, they enter into contractual arrangements for the use of existing facilities. However, IPAs often provide utilization management, quality assurance, and retrospective review of services performed by the association members. Vertical integration (direct ownership of facilities) is common among staff and group model HMOs.

A "closed panel" HMO is limited to a certain number of physicians. A rule of thumb is that the key figure is the number of primary care (family) physicians affiliated with the HMO—and that approximately one primary physician is required for every 1600 HMO members. The panel will have many primary physicians for every specialty physician.

One of the most controversial aspects of the arrangement between HMOs and providers is the frequent use of mechanisms that shift the financial risk of providing treatment to the provider. Depending on the contract, providers may be given incentives (such as payments from a risk pool) if utilization falls below a defined amount—or they may be forced to pay penalties if utilization is higher.

The HMO itself can be organized in many ways. The first HMOs, some of which are still operating (e.g., Kaiser Permanente; Harvard Community Health Plan) are non-profit organizations, staffed by health care workers (including physicians) who are salaried employees.

The Preferred Provider Organization (PPO) is a business company, generally a conventional for-profit corporation but perhaps a non-profit or non-corporate proprietary entity, created either by insurers, by providers, or by a coalition. The preferred providers are "members" of the entity, under contract with but not employees of the PPO. The provider contract specifies the rate schedule for provision of services to covered patients.

The general rule is that PPOs do not require licensure as health care facilities, but there may be circumstances under which licensure is mandated. Depending on circumstances, the PPO may be the actual payor for the care, or may merely be an administrative entity that does business with the payors. Patients covered by a PPO usually get to choose their own providers, but receive discounts if they use one of the preferred providers within the network.

An "open-panel" PPO will permit any qualified physician who is willing to accept the plan's fee schedule to join the panel. Some states have passed "any willing provider" laws that obligate PPOs to accept physicians unless there is some valid reason (e.g., professional sanctions; incomplete training) for rejecting them. "Any willing provider" laws protect physicians against the risk of being forced out of practice if most of the patients in an area are covered by managed care plans, and if those plans deny admission to physicians for improper reasons (e.g., racial or sex discrimination).

The Point of Service (POS) plan is a hybrid that has some features of the HMO and some of the PPO. POS plans give patients more choice of provider, with different reimbursement schedules depending on whether the provider selected is within or outside the network. For instance, the patient might be responsible only for a 10% copayment if a network provider is chosen, but for 40% outside the network.

A Physician-Hospital Organization (PHO) offers a combination of hospital and medical services, on a risk basis, to HMOs or other managed care entities. PHOs can be set up as for-profit or non-profit organizations. Usually, the PHO is jointly owned by a hospital and by a group of doctors affiliated with that hospital and providing care there. In turn, the doctors may organize themselves into an IPA or other business entity. PHOs generally do not enter into capitation arrangements, because state law often treats such arrangements as insurance contracts that require licensure (and regulation) as an insurance company.

The Exclusive Provider Organization is an insurance arrangement, under which the employer's plan covers only care that is provided by one of the designated providers, not care from "outsiders" selected by the patient. Although, from the patient's point of view, the EPO and the HMO operate similarly, the two have different legal structures. An HMO is regulated by special state laws covering only HMOs; EPOs are treated as insurance products regulated under the insurance law.

A management services organization is a legal entity, usually a corporation, that owns and operates medical offices, office equipment, diagnostic equipment, and other items needed for a group medical practice. The MSO may also provide support staff and administer managed care contracts. MSOs may be owned by the physicians (free-standing) or by a health care organization (hospital-affiliated or HMO-affiliated). Because the MSO does not furnish medical services, it can be owned and operated by individuals who are not licensed physicians or other health care providers.

[¶2532] LONG-TERM CARE INSURANCE

Long term care (LTC) is the provision of services, either at home or in institutions, to aged or disabled individuals who have a continuing need for assistance. The problem requiring assistance may be physical (e.g., paraplegia), cognitive (e.g., Alzheimer's Disease), or both. Some frail elderly people require LTC even though they have no specific acute illness.

Although some health insurance policies have some coverage of home care or physical therapy, usually the coverage can be triggered only if there has been some accident or acute illness. The Medicare system covers acute health care, but not LTC. Since the 1980s, there has been a growing variety of specialized policies covering LTC.

Long-Term Care Insurance (LTCI) policies can be purchased to cover nursing home care; nursing home care plus home care; home care only; or a broad spectrum of LTC services, adding adult day care and innovative housing services to institutional and home care.

Although some companies offer LTCI to their employees (and often their employees' parents as well) as an employee benefit, and there are some other ways of purchasing group LTCI, usually LTCI policies are purchased by individuals.

The general legal requirement is that LTCI policies must be guaranteed renewable (i.e., if the insured person keeps up premium payments, the employer can neither terminate the policy nor refuse to renew it on the basis of deterioration in the insured's health). Furthermore, although the premium can be raised for an entire class of policyholders, insurers are not permitted to raise individual premiums because of health status or claims history. Generally speaking, once the insured selects a policy, the premium for that policy will be based on entry age and will not rise unless a class-wide premium increase has been granted.

At first, LTCI benefits were expressed in dollars per day (e.g., $50 or $100 a day). Often, the home health care benefit was set at 50% of the benefit for treatment in a nursing home (e.g., $120/$60 per day). However, it is possible to purchase policies with different ratios, or with equal daily benefits for nursing home and home care. It is also possible to purchase policies with an option to buy increased coverage without proof of insurability, or with an automatic increase to keep pace with the ever-increasing cost of medical care. A more recent trend is for the insurer to adopt disability principles and treat the coverage as a "pot of money"—so benefits that are not used on a particular day after coverage has been triggered can be applied to later needs.

Lifetime LTCI coverage can be purchased. So can coverage for a term of years (two to five years is typical). State law usually imposes a minimum duration (typically one or two years) for policies sold as LTCI policies. Some policies provide benefits as soon as coverage is triggered, but most impose a waiting period. Of course, the shorter the waiting period and/or the longer the duration of the coverage, the higher the premium, because the insurer undertakes more risk.

Eligibility for LTCI benefits depends on "triggering" the coverage. Most policies now on the market use an ADL trigger, a cognitive trigger, or a combination of the two. ADL means "Activities of Daily Living," such as dressing, bathing, eating, or using the toilet. Coverage becomes available under an ADL trigger based on the insured person's need for assistance in these areas. A cognitive trigger makes benefits available based on the presence of Alzheimer's Disease or other condition that impairs mental acuity.

— ENDNOTES —

1. #93-1612-, -1613, 115 S.Ct. 810, 130 L.Ed.2d 740 (Sup.Ct. 1/18/95); on remand, *VALIC v. Clarke*, 49 F.3d 128.

2. *Barnett Bank of Marion County v. Nelson*, #94-1837, 116 S.Ct. 1103 (Sup.Ct. 3/26/96); 43 F.3d 631 (11th Cir. 1/30/95) *reversed*.

3. *Owensboro National Bank v. Stephens*, 44 F.3d 388 (6th Cir. 12/29/94).

4. *NBD Bank NA v. Bennett*, 67 F.3d 629 (7th Cir. 10/4/95).

5. *SEC v. Life Partners Inc.*, 898 F.Supp. 14 (D.D.C. 8/30/95).

6. *Ohran v. Sierra Health & Life Ins. Co.*, 63 LW 2788 (Nev.Sup. 5/25/95).

7. *Estate of Cavenaugh*, 75 AFTR2nd 2049 (5th Cir. 5/10/95).

8. *Johnson & Johnson v. Aetna Casualty & Surety Co.*, 667 A.2d 1087 (N.J.Super. 12/11/95).

9. *Whirlpool Corp. v. Ziebert*, 539 N.W.2d 883 (Wis.Sup. 11/16/95).

10. *Charter Oil Co. v. American Employers' Insurance Co.*, 69 F.3d 1160 (D.C.Cir. 11/14/95).

11. *Martin Marietta Corp. v. Insurance Co. of North America*, 47 Cal.Rptr.2nd 670 (Cal.App. 12/5/95).

12. *Anderson Development Co. v. Travelers Indemnity Co.*, 49 F.3d 1128 (6th Cir. 3/20/95).

13. *Kerr-McGee Corp. v. Admiral Insurance Co.*, 905 P.2d 760 (Okla.Sup. 10/3/95).

14. *Bituminous Casualty Corp. v. Advanced Adhesive Technology*, 64 LW 2544 (11th Cir. 1/23/96).

15. *Stoney Run Co. v. Prudential-LMI Commercial Insurance Co.*, 47 F.3d 34 (2nd Cir. 1/31/95).

16. *Stonewall Insurance Co. v. Asbestos Claims Management Corp.*, 64 LW 2447 (2nd Cir. 12/13/95).

17. *Fire Insurance Exchange v. Diehl*, 64 LW 2622 (Mich.Sup. 3/19/96).

18. *Lindstrom v. Hanover Insurance Co.*, 649 A.2d 1272 (N.J.Sup. 12/19/94).

19. *New York State Conference of Blue Cross/Blue Shield Plans v. Travelers Insurance Co.*, #93-1408, -1414, -1415, 115 S.Ct. 1671, 131 L.Ed.2nd 695 (Sup.Ct. 4/26/95).

20. *Wilson v. Office of CHAMPUS*, 65 F.3d 361 (4th Cir. 9/15/95).

21. *Smith v. Office of CHAMPUS*, 66 F.3d 905 (7th Cir. 9/26/95).

22. *Henderson v. Bodine Aluminum Inc.*, 64 LW 2199 (8th Cir. 9/27/~).

23. *EEOC v. Mason Tenders District Council Welfare Fund*, 64 LW 2400 (S.D.N.Y. 12/14/95).

— FOR FURTHER REFERENCE —

Abney, David L., "Insurance Company Assumptions, Consumer Realities and Judicial Rules of Interpretation," 32 *Arizona Attorney* 19 (February '96).

Christensen, Burke A., "Consumers Take 'Atomic' View of Life Insurance Policies," 135 *Trusts and Estates* 69 (January '96).

Fleming, Peter D., "Helping Clients Protect Against Risk," 18 *J. of Accountancy* 61 (January '96).

Fredman, James, "COBRA Continuation Coverage," 28 *J. of Health and Hospital Law* 264 (November-December '95).

Golub, Ira M., "Multiemployer Group Health Plans and COBRA," *21 J. Pension Planning and Compliance* 1 (Winter '96).

Quinn, Michael Sean and L. Kimberly Steele, "Insurance Coverage Options," 44 *Defense L.J.* 591 (Winter '95).

Rappaport, Michael B., "The Ambiguity Rule and Insurance Law," 30 *Georgia L.Rev.* 171 (Fall '95).

Richmond, Douglas R., "Lost in the Eternal Triangle of Insurance Defense Ethics," 9 *Georgetown J. of Legal Ethics* 475 (Winter '96).

Royle, Lia B., "Insurance Company Bad Faith in Settlement," 4 *Nevada Lawyer* 22 (March '96).

Silver, Charles and Kent Syverud, "The Professional Responsibilities of Insurance Defense Lawyers," 45 *Duke L.J.* 255 (November '95).

Witte, Philip D., "A Map for the Insurance Coverage Maze," 16 *California Lawyer* 65 (January '96).

INTELLECTUAL PROPERTY

[¶2601] As has been the case for many years, much of the activity in intellectual property in the supplement period involved new technology—particularly computers. However, old-fashioned questions such as trade dress continued to occupy the courts and legislatures.

Congress passed several relevant measures during the supplement period. P.L. 103-349, the Plant Variety Protection Act Amendments of 1994 (10/6/94) conforms United States law to the International Convention for the Protection of New Varieties of Plants.

P.L. 104-41, the Biotechnical Process Patents Act, amends 35 U.S.C. §103 with respect to the conditions under which a biotechnical process will not have to undergo a separate review of non-obviousness. In other words, if it uses or produces a patentable composition of matter, the separate review can be by-passed. The legislation was necessary because, absent the change, patent host cells could be used in offshore manufacturing and then imported into the United States if the process patent were not issued.

[¶2602] PATENTS

In April, 1996, the Supreme Court affirmed a 1995 ruling of the Federal Circuit, holding that construction of a patent claim (determining the meaning and scope of the claims that allegedly were infringed) is a matter of law—in other words, exclusively within the duties of the court. The jury's function is to compare the construed claim to the allegedly infringing device. The Supreme Court said "judges, not juries, are the better suited to find the acquired meaning of patent terms."[1]

Under the "doctrine of equivalents," making a trivial change or slight improvement does not prevent a finding of patent infringement. The Federal Circuit says that it is a jury question whether "equivalents" infringement occurred (even though "equivalents" is an equitable doctrine). The minute differences between the two inventions must be proved, but the plaintiff is not required to prove bad faith by the infringer.[2]

Infringement of a plant patent means asexual reproduction of the actual patented plant, not merely creating a plant with the same essential characteristics.[3]

[¶2611] ASSIGNMENT VS. LICENSING OF PATENTS

On April 6, 1995, the Department of Justice and the Federal Trade Commission adopted joint guidelines for intellectual property licensing.[4] The transactions will be considered acceptable, and not inhibiting competition, if the licensing entities collectively control 20% or less of each relevant market, and the license does not contain restraints that are facially anticompetitive. These guidelines do not apply in circumstances under which the DOJ/FTC merger analysis guidelines apply. A license that does not satisfy the guidelines is not necessarily an antitrust violation, as long as the license does not have anticompetitive effect.

[¶2613] REMEDIES FOR PATENT INFRINGEMENT

An antitrust allegation (that a patent was obtained fraudulently and used to destroy competition) does not operate as a compulsory counterclaim in an infringement suit involving that patent.[5]

[¶2614] DURATION OF PATENT

For drug patents in force on June 8, 1995, term extensions are added to the expiration date prescribed by the Uruguay Round Agreements Act—not the date 17 years from the granting of the initial patent.[6]

[¶2615] TRADEMARKS AND TRADE NAMES

The Federal Trademark Dilution Act, P.L. 104-98 (1/16/96) amends Lanham Act §43 (15 U.S.C. §1125) by adding a new sub-section. Once a mark becomes "famous," owners of the mark who demonstrate that it is equitable and reasonable can get an injunction against subsequent commercial use of a mark or trade name that dilutes the famous mark.

Factors in determining which marks qualify include the inherent or acquired distinctiveness of the mark; the duration and extent to which the owner has used and publicized it; the channels of trade in which it is used; the degree of recognition; and the nature and extent of use of similar marks by third parties. If another entity engages in willful dilution of the famous mark (lessening the public ability to distinguish which goods are sold under that mark) Lanham Act §35 and §36 remedies are available.

In early 1995, the Supreme Court settled a vexing question by deciding that color alone can be a registrable trademark (here, a green-gold shade used for dry cleaners' pressing pads) provided that it is nonfunctional and has secondary meaning.[7]

An earlier Supreme Court case[8] allows protection of inherently distinctive trade dress even without proof of secondary meaning. The Eighth Circuit says trade dress is protectible even if it is not "striking in appearance" or "memorable," provided that it is fanciful or arbitrary (not mandated by the nature of the product). Where the trade dress is dictated by the nature of the product, secondary meaning does have to be proved to protect the trade dress.[9]

The Seventh Circuit ruled that if comparison of competing products does not make it clear that consumers are likely to be confused by duplication of a color trademark, the manufacturer who claims that its color trademark is infringed must produce "some" evidence of actual confusion.[10]

Trade dress that is limited to useful product features as defined by Lanham Act §43(a) cannot be protected—useful features are not non-functional (the key characteristic of a trademark) and are properly covered by a utility patent, not a trademark.[11]

[¶2632] PROTECTION OF TRADE SECRETS

In the view of the Ninth Circuit, alleged misappropriation of trade secrets does not "arise out of" breach of a licensing agreement, but is a separate tort. Therefore, a tort suit is not barred by the licensing agreement's arbitration clause.[12]

[¶2636] SCOPE OF COPYRIGHT LAW

A sculpture incorporated into the structure of a building was created as a work for hire. Thus, the Visual Artists' Rights Act of 1990 did not prevent the building owner from dismantling the artwork.[13]

Copyrighting a collection (e.g., a group of songs) protects individual copyrightable works within the collection, even if they are not listed individually on the copyright registration form.[14]

A party who copies something that is, in turn, an unauthorized copy of primary material is still liable to the copyright owner of the infringed material, even though the copy and not the primary material was directly copied.[15]

[¶2641] FAIR USE

The Sixth Circuit permitted a copy shop that compiled "coursepacks" of academic articles to assert a fair use/educational use defense unless the copyright holder could show meaningful likelihood of harm to the potential market for the works. The coursepack consists of excerpts adding up to 5-30% of the content of the original work; the court did not feel that the "heart" of the work was necessarily contained there. The rationale was that professors would not assign the original work if the coursepack were not available, so the market for the original was not impaired.[16]

[¶2643] MUSIC RECORDING RIGHTS

P.L. 104-39, the Digital Performance Right in Sound Recordings Act of 1995 amends 17 U.S.C. §§106 and 114. Because of these amendments, creators and performers do not have a comprehensive right to control public performance. Instead, they are given a "carefully crafted and narrow performance right, applicable only to certain digital transmissions of sound recordings." Thus, copyright owners can control performance of their works as part of an interactive service (e.g., over the Internet). The amendments apply only to digital audio, not conventional analog audio and not digital transmission of an audiovisual work. Congress anticipated that digital transmission ("audio on demand" or "pay per listen") would become a common commercial medium, so a limited performance right is justified. However, conventional, free, advertising-supported radio or similar transmissions are not covered by the amendments.

A plaintiff owned the copyright to sound recordings, but not the underlying composition. The defendant synchronized the recording into the soundtrack for a television show. The Second Circuit decided[17] that synchronization of previously recorded sounds with an audiovisual work is part of the rights granted under Copyright Act §114(b) to the owner of the rights of the sound recording.

This is true even though it would have been permissible to use the recording in a live broadcast: the synchronization constituted a commercial use, not mere time-shifting. If the work were sufficiently altered, the synchronization might also constitute an unauthorized derivative work. However, the plaintiff did not have an exclusive performance right, so the TV stations who played the broadcast containing the soundtrack were not liable to him.

The licensing organizations ASCAP and BMI have a procedure for using undercover investigators to detect unauthorized public performances of copyrighted music. New York passed a statute requiring landlords to be notified of the investigations within 72 hours of the initial deployment of the investigator. However, the Southern District of New York found that the state statute was preempted by the federal Copyright Act, and granted a preliminary injunction forbidding enforcement of the statute.

The rationale was that Congress established a three-year statute of limitations for copyright infringement suits, so that is the proper time frame for notifying an alleged infringer. The District Court was also troubled by the state statute's potential for "dueling damages," because it permits a damage award if an accused infringer does not receive the 72-hour notice. The court also deemed that the 72-hour notice requirement would prevent ASCAP and BMI from carrying out their enforcement mission.[18]

[¶2646] NEW TECHNOLOGY AND COPYRIGHT

In order to make the Quattro spreadsheet compatible with Lotus 1-2-3, Borland International copied the Lotus menu tree but not the underlying code. The First Circuit (reversing the District Court) ruled that a computer program's menu tree (the arrangement of almost 500 commands into more than 50 menus and submenus) is a "method of operation," and consequently not copyrightable subject matter.[19] This is a question of immense importance to software companies (and to software users who seek compatibility with other products), so it is understandable that certiorari has been granted to settle once and for all the copyrightability of menu elements.

In early 1996, a company that spent a lot of money compiling a CD-ROM phone directory was out of luck when a competitor decided to put the contents of the directory on the Internet. The competitor downloaded the CDs and added its own search engine, then uploaded to the Internet. The Western District of Wisconsin[20] ruled that no copyrightable subject matter existed. Furthermore, the only copying was from the CDs to the hard drive of the competitor's computer, which the court treated as personal use. Although the CDs were sold with the conventional shrink-wrap license, which imposes various draconian rigors on the purchaser, the court found the license unenforceable as a contract of adhesion, imposed contrary to the UCC without adequate notice to the purchaser.

The Church of Scientology has instituted several cases protesting the unauthorized posting of copyrighted Scientology materials on computer bulletin boards (BBS) and the Internet. The District Court for the District of Colorado denied the church a preliminary injunction. It treated posting of the materials on an Internet bulletin board as fair use because it was non-commercial; did not harm the church financially; and occurred in the context of discussion and criticism of Scientology.[21] In contrast, the Northern District of California found that a BBS or Internet service provider can be contributorily liable for copyright infringement once placed on notice that certain posts were infringing but nevertheless failing to remove them.[22]

Where the operator of a BBS allowed users to download copyrighted software, the federal wire fraud statute cannot be used to press criminal copyright infringement charges (17 U.S.C. §506(a). Unlike wire fraud, criminal copyright infringement requires proof of personal financial advantage to the infringer. In this case, the infringer did not benefit financially by giving access to the software.[23]

— ENDNOTES —

1. *Markman v. Westview Instruments Inc.*, 52 F.3d 967 (Fed.Cir. 4/5/95), *aff'd* #95-26, 64 LW 4263 (Sup.Ct. 4/23/96).

2. *Hilton Davis Chemical Co. v. Warner-Jenkinson Co. Inc.*, 62 F.3d 1512 (Fed.Cir. 8/8/95).

3. *Imazio Nursery Inc. v. Dania Greenhouses*, 69 F.3d 1560 (Fed.Cir. 11/3/95).

4. See 63 LW 2654.

5. *Hydranautics v. Film Tec Corp.*, 70 F.3d 533 (9th Cir. 11/15/95).

6. *Merck & Co. v. Kessler*, 903 F.Supp. 964 (E.D.Va. 10/16/95).

7. *Qualitex Co. v. Jacobsen Products Co.*, #93-1577, 115 S.Ct. 1300, 131 L.Ed.2d 248 (Sup.Ct. 3/28/95).

8. *Two Pesos Inc. v. Taco Cabana Inc.*, 503 U.S. 957 (Sup.Ct. 1992).

9. *Stuart Hall Co. v. Ampad Corp.*, 51 F.3d 780 (8th Cir. 4/7/95).

10. *Libman Co. v. Vining Industries, Inc.*, 69 F.3d 1360 (7th Cir. 11/16/95).

11. *Elmer v. ICC Fabrication Inc.*, 67 F.3d 1571 (Fed.Cir. 10/10/95). *Vornado Air Circulation Systems Inc. v. Duracraft Corp.*, 58 F.3d 1498 (10th Cir. 7/5/95)

denies protection to the spiral shape of the grill of a household fan because it is a non-functional product configuration that was a significant inventive component of an invention for which a utility patent was issued.

12. *Tracer Research Corp. v. National Env. Services Co.*, 42 F.3d 1292 (9th Cir. 12/19/94).

13. *Carter v. Helmsley-Spear Inc.*, 71 F.3d 77 (2nd Cir. 12/1/95).

14. *Szabo v. Errisson*, 68 F.3d 940 (5th Cir. 11/20/95).

15. *Lipton v. Nature Co.*, 71 F.3d 464 (2nd Cir. 11/28/95).

16. *Princeton University Press v. Michigan Document Services*, 64 LW 2516 (6th Cir. 2/12/96).

17. *Agee v. Paramount Communications Inc.*, 59 F.3d 317 (2nd Cir. 6/26/95).

18. *ASCAP v. Pataki*, 64 LW 2613 (S.D.N.Y. 3/20/96).

19. *Lotus Development Corp. v. Borland International*, 49 F.3d 807 (1st Cir. 3/9/95), aff'd without opinion, #94-2003, 116 S.Ct. 1062 (Sup.Ct. 1/16/96).

20. *Pro CD Inc. v. Zeidenberg*, 908 F.Supp. 640 (W.D.Wis. 1/4/96).

21. *Religious Technology Center v. FACTNET Inc.*, 901 F.Supp. 1519 (D.Colo. 9/15/95).

22. *Religious Technology Center v. Netcom*, 907 F.Supp. 1361 (N.D.Cal. 11/21/95).

23. *U.S. v. LaMacchia*, 871 F.Supp. 535 (D.Mass. 12/28/94).

— FOR FURTHER REFERENCE —

Carroll, Amy E., "Not Always the Best Medicine: Biotechnology and the Global Impact of U.S. Patent Law," 44 *American U.L.Rev.* 2433 (August '95).

Cavazos, Edward A. and G. Chin Chao, "System Operator Liability for a User's Copyright Infringement," 4 *Texas Intellectual Property L.J.* 13 (Fall '95)

Garcia, Julie Arthur, "Trademark Dilution: Eliminating Confusion," 85 *Trademark Reporter* 489 (September-October '95).

Hamilton, Gary W., "Trademarks on the Internet: Confusion, Collusion, or Dilution?" 4 *Texas Intellectual Property Law J.* 1 (Fall '95).

Jevens, Thomas J., "Some Tips on Software Licenses," 41 *Practical Lawyer* 43 (December '95).

Prowda, Judith Beth, "Parody and Fair Use in Copyright Law," 17 *Communications and the Law* 53 (September '95).

Rooklidge, William C. and Matthew F. Weil, "The Application of Experimental Use to Design Patents," 77 *J. of the Patent and Trademark Office Society* 921 (December '95).

Skon, Linda, "Copyright Protection of Computer User Interfaces," 27 *Arizona State L.J.* 1063 (Fall '95).

MATRIMONIAL MATTERS

[¶2901] During the supplement period, issues involving both traditional and non-traditional families were assayed—although not necessarily resolved; simple questions such as the constitutionality of federal law about interstate child support received conflicting answers.

This supplement adds discussion of adoption, an increasingly active area of litigation. Many of these cases involve the same-sex partners of biological parents. On the related issue of whether same-sex couples can marry, the District of Columbia Court of Appeals found no Constitutional barrier to limiting the issuance of marriage licenses to male-female couples.[1] Advocates both of gay marriage and of traditional families paid profound attention to Hawaii, which was widely believed to be about to enact a statute permitting same-sex marriages, which would then be entitled to full faith and credit in other jurisdictions.

[¶2902] ANTENUPTIAL AGREEMENTS

At least in Louisiana, a premarital waiver of the right to permanent alimony will not be enforceable, on the theory that the state has an interest in preventing divorced persons from becoming public charges.[2]

A Montana case[3] makes waiver of the right of election in the future spouse's estate enforceable as long as general information about the future spouse's net worth is disclosed, and as long as the antenuptial agreement includes a general statement that fair disclosure was made. It is not necessary for the proponent of the antenuptial agreement to show that specific asset-by-asset disclosure was made.

[¶2907] INCOME TAX CONSEQUENCES

U.S. v. Williams[4] is doubly unusual: as a Supreme Court income tax case, and as a Supreme Court domestic relations case. When the Williamses divorced, Mrs. Williams was awarded the family home. Nevertheless, the IRS imposed a lien on all of Mr. Williams' property. Mrs. Williams, under protest, paid the tax to get the IRS lien removed from the house. The Supreme Court gave her standing, under 28 U.S.C. §1346, to bring suit in federal District Court for recovery of tax alleged to have been assessed or collected erroneously or illegally. The court rejected the IRS' contention that only the person against whom the tax was assessed has standing in this situation.

Another tax-deficient ex-husband had a Code §6321 lien imposed on all his property. However, the one-time family home did not fall into this category, because it had been awarded entirely to the ex-wife under the divorce decree.

Even though the decree was not recorded until after the lien was attached, the house was nevertheless not the property of the ex-husband and thus was not subject to the lien.[5]

Where the parties did not intend payments to terminate at the recipient wife's death, payments described as "alimony as division of equity" that must be "paid in full" constitute property settlements, not alimony. Consequently, such amounts are neither deductible by the payor nor gross income to the payee.[6]

According to the Tax Court, a distribution, made prior to a divorce decree, to the wife's IRA did not constitute a tax-free rollover.[7]

[¶2907.1] Liability for Tax on a Joint Return

Two other Tax Court cases deal with interesting joint-return questions. *Shackelford*[8] finds that an annulment does not relate back to the beginning of the marriage for tax purposes. Therefore, a person who held himself or herself out as married in a particular year cannot file a return as a single person for that year, even if the marriage was later annulled.

A divorced wife who received a property distribution in excess of normal support was held to have benefited by her ex-husband's tax shelter investments, even though tax shelter limited partnership interests per se were not distributed to her. Because of the benefit she received, she was not permitted to claim innocent spouse status when the shelters were disallowed.[9]

In contrast, the Second Circuit did permit innocent spouse characterization of a spouse who was aware of tax shelter transactions, because the spouse's limited education and financial experience precluded imputation of knowledge that tax liability had been substantially understated. In this reading, the innocent spouse reasonably relied on the common perception that legitimate tax shelters were available, as well as the assurances of her husband and recommendations from an accountant and tax shelter expert.[10]

[¶2913.1] Interspousal Torts

Even prior to finalization of the divorce, breaking into the home of an estranged spouse constitutes burglary and criminal trespass.[11]

[¶2926] FACTORS INFLUENCING ALIMONY AWARD

Given societal changes and changing attitudes toward permanent alimony, it is understandable that several cases in the supplement period deal with rehabilitative alimony. Mississippi permits a divorce court to specify a time-limited period for periodic rehabilitative alimony, even though ordinarily periodic alimony is indefinite and vests as it becomes due; rehabilitative periodic alimony is for a limited period of time and vests as it accrues.[12]

A Florida case holds that, absent agreement to the contrary, remarriage is merely a factor in determining whether there has been a change of circumstances justifying termination of rehabilitative alimony—termination upon remarriage is not automatic.[13] The Arizona Court of Appeals held that spousal support cannot be terminated simply by characterizing cohabitation as a de facto marriage; the trial court must examine the economic effect of the live-in relationship.[14]

Illinois considers smoking and weight to be inappropriate issues for consideration as to the extension of rehabilitative maintenance.[15]

Even if a divorcing wife does not require maintenance at the time of divorce, the Wisconsin Court of Appeals says that the court can keep the issue open in case her chronic kidney condition creates a need for maintenance in the future.[16]

[¶2927] COMMUNITY PROPERTY

In California, post-separation disability benefits are not community property, even if the insurance policy paying the benefits was purchased with community funds, and even if the intention was to safeguard the community's financial position.[17]

Community-property-like principles have been applied to a cohabiting couple in a long-term, stable, quasi-marital relationship. Thus, there is a rebuttable presumption that property acquired during the relationship is jointly owned, irrespective of title. (The presumption can be overcome by showing acquisition with funds that would have been separate if the couple had been married.[18])

[¶2928] EQUITABLE DISTRIBUTION OF PROPERTY

A bankruptcy court (which is a federal court, of course) has discretion to lift the automatic stay so that the non-debtor spouse's equitable distribution action against the debtor spouse can proceed in state court.[19]

Nor does the automatic stay prevent distribution of 50% of the debtor's pension, under a decree granted before the Chapter 13 bankruptcy petition, because the pension funds have become the non-employee spouse's sole and separate property and not a claim on the debtor's estate. However, spousal support payments come from the debtor's income, which is property of the bankruptcy estate. Thus, the bankruptcy trustee cannot make support payments without getting relief from the automatic stay.[20]

For many couples, the family home and the potential pension rights of one or both spouses are the most significant assets—if not the only significant assets—to be divided. Thus, the continuing presence of these issues in court is to be expected.

During the supplement period, the Fourth Circuit permitted a separation agreement, which was incorporated into the divorce decree, to waive the non-employee spouse's interest in ERISA pension plan proceeds.[21] In contrast, a provision in an incorporated decree waiving all rights to the ex-spouse's estate, as heir or otherwise, has been held insufficiently explicit to waive an interest in the pension plan.[22]

A non-vested pension was valued, and the non-employee spouse given a sum equal to her interest right away, rather than waiting for the interest to vest in 1996. The rationale is that the non-employee spouse has the option of accepting the risk of non-vesting. The Alaska Supreme Court's methodology for valuing anticipated pension benefits is reduction to present value, with upward adjustment for inflation and discount using the market interest rate.[23]

However, the Eighth Circuit found the obligation to pay a set amount to the spouse, in settlement of the pension interest, is dischargeable in bankruptcy if embodied in a pre-petition divorce decree—even if installment payments are supposed to continue after the bankruptcy filing.[24] In this analysis, the obligation was not a QDRO (because it was not directed to the plan administrator) and was not linked to the retirement income actually to be earned by the employee spouse. Instead, the non-employee spouse's interest was reduced to an amount certain to be paid from the bankruptcy debtor's assets. Therefore, it was a simple and dischargeable pre-petition debt rather than non-dischargeable support or maintenance.

Where the employee spouse acquired a retirement fund prior to the marriage, the enhancement in the fund's value during the marriage is divisible marital property only to the extent that it derives from employer contributions, labor of the spouses, or funds of the spouses. The portion deriving from investment appreciation, inflation, or management by others is separate property of the employee spouse.[25]

As for a more basic form of retirement benefit, the Iowa Court of Appeals decided that a property settlement should not be adjusted to reflect the difference in the size of Social Security benefits that the spouses can expect after retirement.[26]

For a spouse serving in the military, post-divorce promotions do not increase the marital portion of the nonvested pension—although passive appreciation, such as Cost of Living increases, does serve to increase the marital share.[27] Future Social Security benefits can be considered in setting alimony, but not in distributing marital property; Iowa says that the Social Security Act preempts state law in this context.[28]

Indiana and Washington State disagree about unvested options in the stock of a spouse's employer. Indiana says that unvested options that can be exercised only contingent on working for the employer when they vest are not marital property, because of their contingent nature.[29] Washington says that unvested options acquired during marriage but vesting post-separation are part community property, part separate property. Vested stock options are acquired when granted (either before or after the marriage), and the time of acquisition determines their community status.[30]

A QDRO can issue ordering the plan administrator to pay part of the monthly benefit to satisfy alimony obligations (as distinct from equitably distributing the pension interest)—this has been deemed to constitute enforcement of the court's alimony award rather than an unlawful modification of the property award.[31]

QDROs can be issued in connection with a welfare plan, not just a pension plan (e.g., an agreement to maintain the children of the marriage as beneficiaries of group insurance invalidates the later designation of the second wife as beneficiary).[32] A divorce decree in which the wife waives her interest in the husband's life insurance prevails over plan documents that continue to name her as beneficiary.[33] According to the Eighth Circuit, federal common law, rather than the ERISA anti-alienation provision (here read to apply only to pension benefits, not welfare benefit plans) applies to an ex-wife's claim to the life insurance policy of which she was named as irrevocable beneficiary in the divorce decree.[34]

Yet another perpetual question is the correct treatment of divorcing spouses' business interests and professional practices. Late in 1995 New York's highest court altered its policy and permitted a professional license to be assigned independent value as a marital asset—it is no longer deemed to merge into the professional practice.[35] In Oklahoma, the goodwill of a professional practice is divisible, if it is marketable as distinct from the professional reputation of the practitioner.[36]

Illinois drew a distinction between "personal" and "enterprise" goodwill in the division of a car dealership conducted as a partnership. Enterprise goodwill is divisible, but personal goodwill is not, because it duplicates other elements used in allocating property.[37]

An attorney undergoing a divorce has separate property in the part of a contingent fee that relates to work done on the case after the spouses separated. It is not necessary to apply a legal fiction that the lawyer resigned from his law firm on the date of the separation.[38]

[¶2928.1] Attorneys' Fees

According to the District Court for the Central District of California, ERISA preempts a state domestic relations law that requires pension plans to pay attorneys' fees in connection with QDROs.[39]

Some recent cases treat the obligation to pay fees to one's ex-spouse's attorney as being in the nature of maintenance—and therefore not dischargeable in bankruptcy.[40]

The conduct of divorce attorneys also received some attention. According to the West Virginia Supreme Court, sexual relations with a divorce client is not by itself a breach of professional responsibility—but the attorney can be disqualified from further representation of the client if ethical rules, such as those respecting conflict of interest, are violated.[41]

A divorce lawyer can be sued for malpractice for failure to advise clients on well-established principles of law, such as the substantive law about termination of the alimony obligation upon remarriage of the alimony recipient.[42]

[¶2929] PAYMENTS FOR SUPPORT OF MINOR CHILDREN

During the supplement period, there were two items of federal legislation involving child support. P.L. 103-383, the Full Faith and Credit for Child Support

Orders Act, 28 U.S.C. §1 denies a state court the power to modify the order of another state court requiring the payment of child support unless either of two conditions is met. First, the recipient of the payments can reside in the state where the modification is sought; second, the recipient can consent to the modification being heard in the courts of the first state.

P.L. 104-35, the Child Support Retrieval Systems Act, 42 U.S.C. §654(24) gives states an extra two years (to 1997) to implement electronic data processing and information retrieval systems within state plans for assuring that spousal and child support are paid (thus preventing the designated payees from becoming public charges).

An earlier piece of federal legislation, 1992's Child Support Recovery Act, 18 U.S.C. §228, was litigated in several District Courts. Some courts found that the measure, which makes it a criminal offense to willfully fail to pay past-due obligations to support a child who lives in another state, was Constitutional,[43] while others found that Congress had exceeded its Commerce Clause powers and blundered into an area where states either have established their own criminal laws, or have refrained from legislating.[44]

Arrears of child support assigned by the intended recipient to a non-governmental collection agency cannot be discharged in the intended payor's bankruptcy—because the transfer was merely an assignment for collection, not a true assignment that would be non-dischargeable.[45]

The Constitutionality of a South Dakota law forbidding issuance or renewal of a driver's license to persons who have over $1,000 in child support arrears was upheld.[46] The court was persuaded by the state's argument that depriving a non-payor of a driver's license makes it harder to change jobs or move to avoid detection.

Pennsylvania has a statute permitting a court order obligating divorcing parents to contribute to the cost of their children's college education. In February of 1995, the Superior Court upheld this statute (even though married parents are not obligated to support "children" over 18); in October, the state Supreme Court found it unconstitutional.[47] In the interim, the Superior Court held that actual education expenses, not counting personal expenses of the college student, should be used to calculate the obligation—not the Child Support Guidelines.[48]

[¶2931] UNIFORM RECIPROCAL ENFORCEMENT OF SUPPORT ACT

A custodial parent cannot use URESA to increase a foreign support order as long as the out-of-state parent is current in payments under a valid foreign order.[49]

[¶2932] CHILD CUSTODY

A man who was led to believe that he was the father of a child born to his wife in wedlock is an "equitable parent" who is entitled to seek custody of the child, even if, in fact, he was not the father of the child.[50] This stress on relationship rather than genetics was also applied in a Pennsylvania case in which the "best interests of the child" standard was applied in a custody battle between parents and the grandparents who actually took care of the children. Parenthood was viewed as a significant factor, but the court refused to presume that parents are the best individuals to receive custody.[51]

A divorcing wife was given "custody" of *in vitro* pre-embryos; it was held that her soon-to-be ex-husband does not have a right to prevent the use of his sperm for procreation.[52]

New York's highest court established a new principle in March, 1996, ruling that the focus in an application for relocation of custodial parent and child to another state must be in the child's best interests—not whether or not the non-custodial parent will be deprived of meaningful access to the child.[53]

A father who has joint custody can be guilty of custodial interference if he secretly removes and hides his daughter; violating the other joint custodial parent's right to physical custody is a criminal act.[54]

In light of the extremely low risk of infection posed by casual contact, the Kentucky Court of Appeals decided[55] that the custodial parent's cohabitation with an HIV+ stepparent is not, taken by itself, grounds for modifying custody in favor of the non-custodial parent.

Once again, there were numerous cases dealing with lesbian mothers, e.g., the South Dakota Supreme Court's determination that it was not an abuse of discretion to grant custody to a mother living with a female life partner, in that cohabitation was not per se contrary to the best interests of the children.[56] To the Virginia Supreme Court, a lesbian mother is not per se unfit, but custody was nevertheless granted to the child's grandmother because the mother, for reasons including "active lesbianism" that could subject the child to social condemnation, offered a home less suitable than the grandmother's.[57]

In contrast, the New York Family Court awarded custody to the lesbian partner of a deceased mother, in preference to the child's grandmother and the deceased mother's ex-husband; the mother died shortly after the child's birth, and her life partner had provided a home for the child for four years.[58]

[¶2932.1] Surrogate Motherhood

In a case where a sister served as the gestational surrogate for the implanted egg of her sister (who had suffered a hysterectomy), fertilized with the sperm of the sister's husband, the married couple were ruled the natural and legal parents of a legitimate child. They were deemed to be the parents of the child (notwithstanding the sister's gestation of the embryo) because they are the genetic parents who have not waived their rights and who intend to raise the child as their own.[59]

An Arizona statute has been voided on Equal Protection grounds. The law permitted the biological father, but not the biological mother, of a child born pursuant to a surrogate parenting contract to rebut the presumption that the husband of the surrogate mother is the legal father of the child. Instead, the would-be adoptive mother must be given access to a "maternity" proceeding just as a sperm donor can assert his paternity in court. (The case arose because the potential adopters under the surrogacy contract got a divorce.[60])

[¶2932.2] Visitation

Two cases upheld laws (from Wyoming and New Mexico) that give grandparents visitation rights. Although the parents have the primary role in determining whom their children will associate with, the best interests of the child may give the children a right of association with their grandparents.[61]

Similarly, a mother's former lesbian partner, who took a step-parental role, can petition for visitation, according to the Wisconsin Supreme Court.[62] The court has equitable authority to hear the case and decide if visitation is so strongly in the child's best interest as to override the mother's right to control association with the child.

[¶2933] UNIFORM CHILD CUSTODY JURISDICTION ACT

According to the Utah Court of Appeals, the UCCJA does not apply to proceedings for termination of parental rights.[63]

[¶2935] ADOPTION

Adoption is the creation of a parent-child relationship. Once adopted, a child has the same status as a child born into the family: he or she becomes a distributee of relatives who die intestate, for example. Adoptions occur in several legal postures. In some cases, the biological parents of an infant surrender custody of the infant—to an adoption agency, or directly to potential adoptive parents. The adoption is then finalized by a court order approving the validity of the surrender and the suitability of the adoptive parents.

Children may become available for adoption if the parental rights of their biological parents are terminated, e.g., in cases of severe abuse. There is a strong presumption of parental fitness; parental rights can be terminated only on clear and convincing evidence (although unfitness—unlike criminal assault charges—need not be proved beyond a reasonable doubt.[64])

More than half of the adoptions in the U.S. are stepparent adoptions: the new spouse of a natural parent assumes legal parenthood of the children. If the other natural parent is still alive, he or she must surrender parental rights for the adoption to proceed. In general, a stepparent adoption terminates the biological parent's child support obligation, but does not extinguish the obligation to satisfy arrears of support.[65]

Most adoptions are of infants or young children, but it is generally legally possible for one adult to adopt another. A number of cases authorize adult adoption for estate planning purposes.[66] Adoption of an adult requires consent by the adoptee, adopter, and adopter's spouse. State law may require consent of the biological parent whose rights are terminated, or proof that the adoption creates a genuine parent-child relationship rather than giving legal sanction to a non-marital liaison.

However, an Idaho case from early 1995 denies a stepparent adoption of an 18-year-old. The stepchild was willing to be adopted, but his biological father objected. Idaho has no specific procedure for adult adoptions, and the court was unwilling to overcome the objections of the biological father.[67]

In a sense, adoption traditionally was analyzed more like a property transaction than as a matter of family law. For instance, parental rights cannot be surrendered in the abstract: either rights must be surrendered to an adoption agency, or directly to a stepparent or other potential adoptive parent.[68]

A child cannot have more than two legal parents, so it is not possible for, e.g., a stepfather to adopt his wife's child without the biological father surrendering his rights. This argument has also been used to deny adoption to some lesbian couples, on the grounds that the biological mother would have to surrender her parental rights for her life partner to be able to adopt the baby.[69]

However, there is a trend to reject this "exclusivity theory" and to permit the biological mother's life partner to adopt as a stepparent.[70] Another possibility is joint adoption by the couple (or by unmarried couples, whether male or heterosexual), where one partner has already given birth to or adopted a child. Here again, the rights of the biological mother are not forfeited by the adoption.[71]

If the adoptee is handicapped or has other special needs, agreements for assistance must be entered into before entry of the final decree of adoption.

[¶2935.1] The Placement Process

Traditionally, the adoption process was controlled by adoption agencies. When nonmarital births were shrouded in shame and secrecy, the agency played an important role as an intermediary between women surrendering babies for adoption and prospective adoptive parents. Both parties usually preferred not to be aware of the identity of the other.

Today, there is much greater acceptance of single parenthood (biological or adoptive), and in many cases the potential adoptive parents prefer to deal directly with pregnant women seeking to place infants for adoptions. All of the states except Colorado, Connecticut, Delaware, and Massachusetts allow "direct placement" adoptions that do not involve agency intervention.

State laws set strict limits on what payments can be made to whom in connection with an adoption. It is permissible for prospective adopters to pay maternity expenses, legal expenses, and living expenses incident to the mother's pregnancy, delivery, and the adoption itself. However, it is illegal for payment of expenses to be made contingent on the mother consenting to the adoption and surrendering her parental rights.

There are also statutory and ethical constraints imposed on the activities of "intermediaries" or "facilitators" (including attorneys) who are involved in the adoption process but who are not licensed adoption agencies. It is unethical for an attorney to receive a fee for procuring a child for adoption (as distinct from getting a fee for performing legal services in connection with the adoption).[72]

Some states criminalize deliberate fraud (accepting money with no intention of surrendering the infant for adoption), but potential adoptive parents are at risk and cannot recover payments they made to a pregnant woman who experiences a genuine change of heart about the advisability of adoption.

If it is proved that improprieties occurred (such as excessive or inappropriate payments), but the adoption is nevertheless in the best interests of the child, the adoption will probably be allowed to proceed, with other sanctions imposed on the guilty parties as necessary.[73] However, the Ninth Circuit has held that there is no due process right enforceable under 42 U.S.C. §1983 in the society of one's grandchildren. Thus, grandparents had no protectable liberty interest in preventing their daughter from surrendering her children for adoption by a third party.[74]

A number of states consider "wrongful adoption" (e.g., negligent material misrepresentation of fact about the infant's heritage or medical history) to be a tort for which compensatory damages may be recovered.[75]

In many instances, the birth mother is a minor. The adoption court may, on its own motion, develop evidence about the validity of her consent, or appoint a Guardian ad Litem to safeguard her interests.[76] A number of cases[77] require appointment of counsel for indigent biological parents in adoption cases, on the same terms as counsel would be appointed in an abuse-based proceeding to terminate parental rights.

An adoption is a legal proceeding, and the court's approval for the adoption will not be given unless a home study has been performed by a court-appointed investigator to determine the suitability of potential adopters. This requirement is waived for stepparent adoptions. Adoptions are not finalized for a period such as three months, six months, or a year. The court retains ongoing jurisdiction to protect the adoptee. In cases where an adoption agency is involved, the proceeding for termination of the biological parents' parental rights may be distinct from the adoption proceeding. The two proceedings are usually joined in direct placement cases.

There is an increasing trend to permit "open adoptions," where the birth mother and adopters are aware of each other's identity. In some cases, the birth mother is given the option of visiting the child, and the child is aware of the birth mother's identity.[78]

In most states, an adopted child will be able to get some health and genetic information about his or her birth parents, with identifying data removed. A number of states maintain registries that adoptees and people who surrendered children for adoption can contact and find out if the other is interested in meeting or providing information.

Generally speaking, a birth mother will not be permitted to consent to adoption until after the baby's birth, although some states do permit consent before the birth (which does not become effective unless confirmed after the birth). A valid consent must be written and witnessed, or made orally before a judge or court-appointed referee.

The National Conference on Commissioners of Uniform State Law's Uniform Adoption Act §2-406 requires that consent for direct placement or relinquishment of a child to an agency must evidence, in plain language, consent to transfer of legal and physical custody and extinguishment of parental rights. It must be made in the parent's native language.

The document must specify that consent is generally final and irrevocable except under the circumstances specified in the document itself—and cannot, for example, be set aside if a visitation agreement is violated. The Uniform Act provides a 192-hour period after birth, during which consents given before the infant's birth can be revoked.

If the biological father of the baby is known, he will generally be entitled to notice of the adoption proceeding, and to participate in it, although he will probably not be given outright veto power over the adoption.[79] Some states (e.g., Arizona, Indiana, Iowa, New York, Oregon) maintain Putative Father Registries; in order to contest an adoption, the father must sign the registry and admit paternity (thus making himself potentially responsible for support of the child.)

The biological father's right to re-open an adoption that has already occurred will probably depend on his actions vis-a-vis the child. A father who never provided support or took an interest in a child is unlikely to be permitted to overturn an adoption.[80]

[¶2935.2] Interstate and Choice of Law Issues

The federal Adoption Assistance and Child Welfare Act of 1980, 42 U.S.C. §§620-628, 670-676 requires, as a condition of receiving federal AFDC funding, that states must make assistance payments to persons who adopt special-needs children who would not be adoptable absent such a subsidy.

The Multiethnic Placement Act, 42 U.S.C. §5115a, inspired by the controversy over placing children for adoption in homes where the parents are of a different race than the children, imposes limits on racial matching policies in adoption or foster care agencies that are publicly funded.[81]

By the late 1980s, all of the states had adopted the Interstate Compact on Placement of Children (ICPC), to protect children placed across state lines. The "sending agency" has to transmit the Form ICPC-100A, Interstate Compact Placement Request, to the welfare department official designated as Compact Administrator in the receiving state. (The transmission may have to be routed through the Compact Administrator in the sending state, as well.) A social and case history of the child and a home study of the potential adopters is attached to the form. Placements of children with relatives in other states is exempt from the ICPC process. However, several appellate cases hold that the Uniform Child Custody Jurisdiction Act and/or Parental Kidnapping Prevention Act prevail over the ICPC.[82]

In early 1995, a Colorado court used the Uniform Dissolution of Marriage Act to determine that a child should remain with adoptive parents rather than being returned to the birth mother, who wanted the child returned about six months after a private placement. The court said the UDMA was applicable because the adoptive parents had physical custody for more than six months, and furthermore that UDMA custody did not terminate parental rights, so there was no requirement of determining unfitness of the birth mother.[83]

— ENDNOTES —

1. *Dean v. District of Columbia*, 635 A.2d 307 (D.C.App. 1/19/95).

2. *McAlpine v. McAlpine*, 650 So.2d 1142 (La.Sup. 2/9/95).

3. *Thies v. Lowe*, 903 P.2d 186 (Mont.Sup. 9/21/95).

4. #94-395, 115 S.Ct. 1611, 131 L.Ed.2d 608 (Sup.Ct. 4/25/95).

5. *Thomson v. U.S.*, 66 F.3d 160 (8th Cir. 9/19/95).

6. *Linda Hoover*, T.C. Memo 1995-183, 4/20/95.

7. *Rodoni v. C.I.R.*, 64 LW 2116 (Tax Ct. 7/24/95).

8. T.C. Memo 1995-484 (1995).

9. *Stiteler*, T.C. Memo 1995-279 (6/21/95).

10. *Friedman v. C.I.R.*, 53 F.3d 523 (2nd Cir. 4/26/95).

11. *Colorado v. Johnson*, 906 P.2d 122 (Colo.Sup. 11/14/95).

12. *Hubbard v. Hubbard*, 63 LW 2803 (Miss.Sup. 6/1/95).

13. *Vaccato (Pustizzi) v. Pustizzi*, 648 So.2d 1206 (Fla.App. 1/11/95).

14. *Van Dyke (Steinle) v. Steinle*, 21 Fam.L.Rep. 1262 (Ariz.App. 3/28/95).

15. *In re Offer*, 657 N.E.2d 694 (Ill.App. 10/31/95).

16. *Grace v. Grace,* 63 LW 2803 (Wis.App. 6/1/95).

17. *In re Elfmont*, 891 P.2d 136 (Cal.Sup. 4/10/95).

18. *Connell v. Francisco*, 127 Wash.2d 339, 898 P.2d 831 (Wash.Sup. 7/20/95).

19. *Roberge v. Roberge*, 188 Bank. 366 (E.D.Va. 11/7/95).

20. *Debolt v. Comerica Bank*, 177 Bank. 31 (Bank. W.D. Pa. 12/23/94).

21. *Estate of Altobelli v. IBM*, 64 LW 2573 (4th Cir. 2/28/96).

22. *Ohran v. Sierra Health & Life Insurance Co.*, 895 P.2d 1321 (Nev.Sup. 5/25/95).

23. *Wainwright v. Wainwright*, 888 P.2d 762 (Alaska Sup. 1/13/95).

24. *In re Ellis*, 72 F.3d 628 (8th Cir. 2/18/95).

25. *Thielenhaus v. Thielenhaus*, 21 Fam.L.Rep. 1176 (Okla.Sup. 1/31/95).

26. *In re Boyer*, 21 Fam.L.Rep. 1272 (Ia.App. 3/30/95).

27. *In re Hunt*, 63 LW 2788 (Colo.Sup. 5/15/95).

28. *In re Boyer*, 63 LW 2671 (Ia.App. 3/30/95).

29. *Hann v. Hann*, 655 N.E.2d 566 (Ind.App. 9/20/95).

30. *In re Short*, 125 Wash.2d 865, 890 P.2d 12 (Wash.Sup. 2/23/95).

31. *Bruns v. Iowa District Court for Linn County*, 21 Fam.L.Rep. 1396 (Ia.App. 5/30/95).

32. *Metropolitan Life Ins. Co. v. Wheaton*, 42 F.3d 1080 (7th Cir. 12/14/94).

33. *Metropolitan Life Ins. Co. v. Barlow*, 884 F.Supp. 1118 (E.D.Mich. 4/18/95).

34. *Equitable Life Insurance Society v. Crystal* 21 Fam.L.Rep. 1561 (8th Cir. 9/29/95).

35. *McSparron v. McSparron*, 64 LW 2389 (N.Y.App. 12/7/95). It's interesting to note that here, each spouse had a professional license (one doctor, one lawyer), so the net effect was limited.

36. *Traczyk v. Traczyk*, 896 P.2d 1277 (Okla.Sup. 3/21/95).

37. *In re Talty*, 652 N:E.2d 330 (Ill.Sup. 6/22/95); *In re Head*, 652 N.E.2d 1246 (Ill.App. 6/30/95) uses the "enterprise goodwill" concept in the valuation of a professional practice. *Also see Endres v. Endres*, 532 N.W.2d 65 (S.D.Sup. 5/17/95), treating the goodwill of a business as marital property.

38. *White v. Williamson*, 453 S.E.2d 666 (W.Va.Sup. 12/21/94). The divorcing wife in this case, also an attorney, was awarded rehabilitative alimony for the time she spent raising the couple's children rather than practicing law.

39. *AT&T Management Pension Plan v. Tucker*, 64 LW 2224 (C.D.Cal. 8/17/95).

40. *Holliday v. Kline*, 65 F.3d 749 (8th Cir. 9/12/95); *In re Miller*, 55 F.3d 1487 (10th Cir. 5/19/95); *Brown v. Brown*, 21 Fam.Law Rep. 1148 (Bank. M.D.Fla. 11/22/94). However, the Sixth Circuit disagrees: *In re Perlin*, 30 F.3d 39 (6th Cir. 1994).

41. *Musick v. Musick*, 453 S.E.2d 361 (W.Va.Sup. 1/25/95).

42. *McMahon v. Shea*, 657 A.2d 938 (Pa.Super. 2/23/95).

43. *U.S. v. Sage*, 906 F.Supp. 84 (D.Conn. 10/3/95); *U.S. v. Hampshire*, 21 Fam.L.Rep. 1432 (D.Kan. 6/14/95).

44. *U.S. v. Mussari*, 894 F.Supp. 1360 (D.Ariz. 7/26/95); *U.S. v. Parker*, 64 LW 2313 (E.D.Pa. 10/30/95). The Uniform Interstate Family Support Act has been adopted in Arizona, Arkansas, Colorado, Delaware, Idaho, Illinois, Kansas, Maine, Massachusetts, Minnesota, Montana, Nebraska, New Mexico, North Dakota, Oklahoma, Oregon, South Carolina, South Dakota, Texas, Virginia, Washington, Wisconsin, and Wyoming.

45. *Smith v. Child Support Enforcement*, 21 Fam.L.Rep. 1287 (D.Utah 4/13/95).

46. *Thompson v. Ellenbecker*, 21 Fam.L.Rep. 1571 (D.S.D. 9/18/95).

47. *Byrnes v.Caldwell*, 654 A.2d 1125 (Pa.Super. 2/9/95); *Curtis v. Kline*, 21 Fam.L.Rep. 1583 (Pa.Sup. 10/10/95).

48. *Bolton v. Bolton*, 657 A.2d 1270 (Pa.Super. 4/25/95).

49. *Alabama ex.rel. Robertson v. Robertson*, 21 Fam.L.Rep. 1183 (Ala.Civ.App. 2/10/95).

50. *In re Gallagher*, 539 N.W.2d 479 (Ia.Sup. 10/25/95).

51. *Rowles v. Rowles*, 668 A.2d 126 (Pa.Sup. 12/19/95).

52. *Kass v. Kass*, 21 Fam.L.Rep. 1172 (N.Y.Sup. 1/23/95). *Contra, Davis v. Davis*, 842 S.W.2d 588 (Tenn.Sup. 1992).

53. *Tropea v. Tropea*, 64 LW 2619 (N.Y.App. 3/26/96).

54. *Strother v. Alaska*, 891 P.2d 214 (Ala.App. 3/3/95). *Oregon v. Fitouri*, 133 Ore.App. 672, 893 P.2d 556 (Ore.App. 4/12/95) reaches a similar conclusion even where the custody order was not granted until after the father removed the child outside the United States.

55. *Newton v. Riley*, 899 S.W.2d 509 (Ky.App. 6/9/95).

56. *Van Driel v. Van Driel*, 525 N.W.2d 37 (S.D.Sup. 12/7/94).

57. *Bottoms v. Bottoms*, 63 LW 2704 (Va.Sup. 4/21/95).

58. *In re Astonn H.*, 64 LW 2351 (N.Y.Fam.Ct. 11/1/95).

59. *Belsito v. Clark*, 67 Oh.Misc.2d 54 (Ohio Comm.Pleas 11/14/94).

60. *Soos v. Maricopa County Superior Court*, 63 LW 2390 (Ariz.App. 12/8/94).

61. *Michael v. Hertzler*, 900 P.2d 1144 (N.M.App. 6/2/95); *Ridenour v. Ridenour*, 64 LW 2163 (Wyo.Sup. 8/4/95).

62. *Holtzman v. Knott*, 533 N.E.2d 419 (Wis.Sup. 6/13/95).

63. *T.B. v. M.M.J.*, 908 P.2d 345 (Utah App. 11/22/95).

64. *Santosky v. Kramer*, 455 U.S. 745 (1982).

65. *In re Marriage of Ramirez*, 840 P.2d 311 (Az.App. 1992); *Michels v. Weingartner*, 848 P.2d 1010 (Kan.App. 1993). The recipient parent's agreement to forgive the arrears in exchange for the delinquent payor's consent to the stepparent adoption is probably illegal as against public policy: *Stambaugh v. Child Support Enforcement Administration*, 17 Fam. Law Rep. 1447 (Maryland App. 1991). On a related issue, see *Shasta County ex.rel. Caruthers v. Caruthers*, 38 Cal.Rptr. 18 (Cal.App. 2/3/95), finding that a child—who is not a party to the paternity action—is not barred by the mother's settlement with the biological father. The mother has no right to terminate the child's right to a relationship with—or support from—the father unilaterally.

66. *In re Fortney's Estate*, 611 P.2d 599 (Kan.App. 1980); *In re Adoption of Swanson*, 623 A.2d 1095 (Del. 1993).

67. *In re Adoption of Chaney*, 887 P.2d 1061 (Ida.Sup. 1/5/95).

68. See, e.g., *Green v. Sollenberger*, 338 Md. 118, 656 A.2d 773 (1995). *Peregood v. Cosmides*, 663 So.2d 665 (Fla.App. 10/27/95) gives a child, even a young minor, standing to challenge a sham adoption in which the mother surrendered and then adopted her child in order to terminate the father's parental rights. The rationale is that a purported adoption that forfeits support from the father, and places the child in economic jeopardy, is not in the child's best interests.

69. *In re Angel Lace M.*, 516 N.W.2d 678 (Wis.Sup. 1994); *In re Adoption Petition of Bruce M.*, 20 Fam.Law Rep. 1307 (D.C.Super. 1994), *In re Dana (G.M.)*, 624 N.Y.S.2d 635 (A.D.2d Dept. 4/3/95).

70. *In re Jacob*, 64 LW 2294 (N.Y.App. 11/2/95) [whether unmarried couple is heterosexual or homosexual]; *In re Adoption Petition of K.H. and R.Z.*, 21 Fam.L.Rep. 1535 (Colo.Dist.Ct. 7/26/95).

71. *In re M.M.D.*, 662 A.2d 837 (D.C.App.6/30/95); *In re Adoption of Minor Child*, 21 Fam.Law Rep. 1332 (D.C.Super. 5/4/95); *In re Petition of K.M. and D.M.*, 653 N.E.2d 888 (Ill.App. 7/18/95); *In re Adoption by H.N.R.*, 666 A.2d 535 (N.J.Super. 10/27/95).

72. Also see *Rushing v. Bosse*, 652 So.2d 869 (Fla.App. 3/8/95) granting standing to a child to sue the lawyers for the adoptive parents for malpractice and malicious prosecution. (One of the lawyers also served as intermediary.) The adoptive parents falsified Florida residence, with the result that the child was removed from her grandmother and unlawfully adopted out of state. The court found the child to be the intended beneficiary of the client's actions, thus able to sue the attorney for malpractice despite the lack of privity (particularly in light of an attorney-intermediary's obligation to act in the best interests of the child). The malicious prosecution cause of action could proceed because legal machinery was misused for an unlawful purpose. However, the intentional infliction of emotional distress claim was dismissed; the mother's transportation of the child for adoption purposes was not deemed to be reckless or an outrageous violation of the standards of a civilized community.

73. *In re Anonymous*, 16 Fam.Law Rep. 1165 (NY Surr. 1990); *Yopp v. Bate*, 237 Neb. 779, 467 NW2d 868 (1991).

74. *Mullins v. Oregon*, 57 F.3d 789 (9th Cir. 6/12/95). In this instance, the grandparents had not established a custodial or quasi-parental relationship with the grandchildren; in fact, they seldom saw them.

75. See, e.g., *Mohr v. Massachusetts*, 421 Mass. 147 (Mass Sup.Jud.Ct. 8/14/95); *Mallette v. Children's Friend & Services*, 21 Fam.Law Rep. 1433 (R.I.Sup. 1995); *Juman v. Louise Wise Services*, 620 NYS2d 371 (N.Y.A.D. 1995) [intentional tort only]; *Gibbs v.Ernst*, 647 A.2d 881 (Pa. Sup. 1994).

76. *Adoption of Thomas*, 408 Mass. 446, 559 NE2d 1230 (1990).

77. *In re Adoption of Taylor*, 570 NE2d 1333 (Ind.App. 1991); *In re Adoption of Fanning*, 310 Ore. 514, 800 P.2d 773 (1990); *Appellate Defenders, Inc. v. Cheri*

S., 35 Cal.App.4th 1819, 42 Cal.Rptr.2d 195 (1995). Certiorari has been granted on April 1, 1996, (as #95-853, 116 S.Ct. 1349) in the case of *M.L.B. v. S.L.J.*, on the issue of waiver of fees for indigent persons appealing termination of parental rights.

78. See, e.g., *South Dakota ex.rel. S.A.H.*, 21 Fam.Law Rep. 1517 (S.D.Sup. 8/16/95), permitting the trial court to order an open adoption, with visitation by the birth mother, where this is found to be in the best interests of the child. Factors in the determination include the child's need to know his or her background, whether open adoptions would render adoption more or less attractive overall, and how openness would affect the adoptee's integration into the new, adoptive family.

79. The adoption agency is a quasi-state actor in the adoption process, so its activities vis-a-vis the biological father are subject to Constitutional scrutiny: *Swayne v. LDS Social Services*, 795 P.2d 637 (Utah 1990); *In re Adoption of Doe*, 572 So.2d 986 (Fla. 1990); *In re Adoption of BBC*, 831 P.2d 197 (Wyoming 1992).

80. *In re Dearing*, 98 Oh.App.3d 197, 648 NE2d 57 (1994).

81. Also see HHS' "Policy Guidance: Race, Color, or National Origin as Considerations in Adoption and Foster Care Placements," 60 FR 20272 (4/25/95).

82. See, e.g., *In re Zachariah K.*, 6 Cal.App.4th 1025, 8 Cal.Rptr.2d 423 (1992); *JDS v. Franks*, 893 P.2d 732 (Ariz. 1994); *In re Adoption by TWC*, 270 N.J.Super. 225, 636 A.2d 1083 (1994).

83. *C.R.S. v. T.A.M.*, 21 Fam.Law Rep. 1173 (Colo.Sup. 1/30/95).

— FOR FURTHER REFERENCE —

Appell, Annette Ruth, "Blending Families Through Adoption," 75 *Boston U.L.Rev.* 997 (September '95).

Basi, Bart A. and Ed Rodnam, "Retirement Plan Rules Supersede Premarital Contract," 24 *Taxation for Lawyers* 226 (January-February 1996).

Behling, Paul L., "Not All Domestic Relations Orders Satisfy QDRO Rules," 24 *Taxation for Lawyers* 212 (January-February '96).

Bergmann, Barbara R. and Sherry Wetchler, "Child Support Awards: State Guidelines vs. Public Opinion," 29 *Family Law Q.* 483 (Fall '95).

Garrison, Marsha, "How Do Judges Decide Divorce Cases? An Empirical Analysis of Discretionary Decision Making," 74 *North Carolina L.Rev.* 401 (January '96).

Hagan, Martin J., "Planning Through an Older Client's Changing Marital Status," 134 *Trusts and Estates* 38 (December '95).

Morgan, Laura W., "Adoption by Gay Couples," 8 *Divorce Litigation* 15 (January '96).

Swisher, Peter Nash and Melanie Diana Jones, "The Last-in-Time Marriage Presumption," 29 *Family Law Q.* 409 (Fall '95).

Turner, Brett R., "The Effect of Interspousal Transfers Upon Classification of Separate Property in Divorce Cases," 8 *Divorce Litigation* 1 (January '96).

Vincent, Maggie, "Mandatory Mediation of Custody Disputes," 20 *Vermont L.Rev.* 255 (Fall '95).

[¶3201] During the supplement period, some of the most heavily litigated issues were related to AIDS—issues relating to liability for infected blood products and for incorrect reporting of HIV test results. Medical issues relating to products liability for medical devices were also prominent.

In late 1995, Arizona abolished parental tort immunity. The new test is whether the parent acted reasonably and prudently, but the child was nevertheless injured.[1]

[¶3202] INTENTIONAL TORTS

A California plaintiff who alleges intentional interference with prospective economic relations must prove that the defendant's conduct was wrongful in some way other than its inconvenience to the plaintiff; disruption of an existing, bargained-for contract is treated more seriously than prevention of a potential contract.[2]

[¶3202.3] Intentional Inflictions of Mental Distress (or Anguish)

In Montana, negligent infliction of emotional distress can be a separate tort provided that the defendant's negligent act or omission reasonably could be foreseen to result in serious emotional distress to the plaintiff. The distress must be so severe that a reasonable person could not be expected to endure it. The same standard is used for intentional infliction of mental distress, but intentional conduct can subject the tortfeasor to punitive damages.[3]

In Alaska, negligent infliction of emotional distress (where there is no physical injury) is cognizable only if there is a pre-existing contract or fiduciary duty that obligates the actor not to disrupt the plaintiff's life. If there is no such duty, only intentional infliction of emotional distress is actionable.[4]

This case involved an incorrect HIV+ diagnosis. In Florida, the impact rule applies, so an HIV misdiagnosis does not entitle the plaintiff to emotional distress damages unless some physical injury results. However, unnecessary medical treatment with serious side effects would qualify as physical injury.[5]

The California Court of Appeals denied emotional distress damages to homeowners who live near power lines. The homeowner plaintiffs failed to submit adequate scientific evidence that electric and magnetic fields generated by the power lines are "more likely than not" to cause cancer. Fear, without scientific justification, is not actionable. In this reading, property damage claims that rely on public perception of danger should be raised before the state public utility commission, not in court.[6]

A three-year statute of limitations, and not the discovery rule, was applied in a Wisconsin case in which the plaintiff knew that a coercive sexual relationship with a priest was coercive when it occurred (27 years earlier) but did not perceive the emotional damage caused by the relationship until 1992.[7]

[¶3203] NEGLIGENCE

Mandamus issued in the Seventh Circuit to decertify a nationwide class of HIV+ hemophiliacs who alleged negligence by a manufacturer of blood products. The writ was granted because the court deemed the manufacturer to be at risk of irreparable harm because of intense pressure to settle the case.[8]

In another AIDS-related blood product case, the Third Circuit permitted a suit against the American Red Cross alleging negligence in connection with a blood transfusion. The Red Cross is not entitled to sovereign immunity.[9]

The Florida rule is that the "economic loss" rule (which says that no damages are available when a defective product causes economic loss, but no other damages, when it malfunctions) bars negligence claims. This is true even if economic loss is the plaintiff's only claim, so the suit must be dismissed. The court considers economic loss a contract concept, not one properly raised in a tort suit.[10]

[¶3203.3] Medical Malpractice

Once plaintiffs receive the cap limit against the hospital under EMTALA (the statute banning "patient dumping"—discharge of patients who are too sick to leave the hospital), they are not permitted to receive the cap limit again in a malpractice suit involving the same injuries against a hospital physician.[11]

[¶3203.4] Other Tort Reform Statutes

The Tenth Circuit has upheld Kansas' $250,000 cap on non-economic loss in personal injury cases. The Tenth Circuit found that the limitation does not violate Equal Protection or the Americans with Disabilities Act.[12]

[¶3205] PRODUCTS LIABILITY

The Third Circuit has held,[13] in a case involving implanted heart valves, that the federal Medical Device Amendments of 1976 preempt state-law claims for negligent design, negligent manufacture, strict products liability, breach of implied warranty of merchantability, and fraud on the FDA. However, certain state law claims were not preempted: those involving breach of express warranty and advertising fraud.

Federal jurisdiction issues were also involved in a breast implant case. The Northern District of Texas decided that a co-defendant could not get the case removed from Texas state court to federal court merely because of the bankruptcy of co-defendant Dow Corning.[14]

Nor can a bankruptcy court enjoin a personal injury suit against the purchaser of all of a manufacturer/Chapter 11 debtor's assets, where retailers and wholesalers of the firearms manufactured by the debtor did not have notice of the transfer and had no opportunity to comment on the reorganization plan.[15]

In a Ninth Circuit case, a woman who developed the autoimmune disorder lupus sued the manufacturer of the collagen implants for negligence, battery, breach of warranty, strict liability, and other claims. The manufacturer's position was that the implants are Class III medical devices pre-approved by the FDA, and thus the claims are preempted by the Medical Device Amendments. The Ninth Circuit was not persuaded, finding that state common-law claims of general applicability are not preempted; the approval process is not a "specific requirement applicable to a particular device" that would preempt state-law regulation. Furthermore, Congress would not want to replace state common law's role in compensating the injured.[16]

The Medical Device Amendments preempt state tort claims based on a manufacturer's failure to comply with the amendments themselves.[17]

A hospital doctor who implants a medical device (in this case a jaw prosthesis) is not "selling" the device and thus cannot be held strictly liable for defects in the device.[18]

Wisconsin does not allow evidence of comparisons between the defendant's product (in this case, a three-wheeled All Terrain Vehicle) and dissimilar products such as minibikes, trailbikes, and snowmobiles. Nor may the risks of using an ATV be compared to hazards of other recreational activities (e.g., swimming, scuba diving, horseback riding) because the comparisons are not relevant enough and are too likely to confuse the jury.[19]

Under Michigan law, a manufacturer does have a duty to warn if it finds out about a manufacturing defect that was not discoverable at the time of manufacture. The duty is satisfied by the mere warning, though—there is no duty to recall or repair the products.[20]

The family of a child injured by a meatgrinder sued the manufacturer. The manufacturer countersued the child's mother (i.e., the family's homeowner's insurance carrier) for negligent supervision. The Wisconsin Supreme Court permitted enforcement of the family exclusion clause in a third party contribution claim, because of the serious risk of collusion in family claims.[21]

[¶3205.1] Warranty Aspects of Products Liability

The test for breach of implied warranty is whether the product satisfies minimal safety standards for the product's intended purpose—whether or not the manufacturer behaved reasonably. This test can be satisfied even if the plaintiff cannot prove strict product liability (which requires proof that a reasonable manufacturer would have decided that the danger outweighed the utility of the product).[22]

[¶3205.2] Statute of Limitations Problems

The District of Columbia Court of Appeals did not permit the use of market share liability principles to charge 14 petroleum companies with the leukemia death of two mechanics who were exposed to petroleum products of uncertain brand. The exposure took place over a 20–30 year period; it was not proven that all the petroleum brands used the same formula; and leukemia is not necessarily caused by exposure to benzene.[23]

[¶3206] THE WRONGFUL DEATH ACTION

The Northern District of Illinois did not permit expert testimony on the hedonic value of life in a wrongful death case. The purported expert testimony did not use scientific methods or procedures, and in any event the jury's burden is to value a specific decedent's life, not the average value of life. The testimony is not "helpful" to the jury, and thus cannot be admitted under F.R.Evidence 702.[24]

There is no independent cause of action in New Mexico for the wrongful death of a non-viable fetus occurring when a pregnant woman is involved in an accident.[25]

[¶3207] PREMISES LIABILITY

A range of liability issues affecting owners and tenants of property has been identified as the legal topic of "premises liability." Liability may arise in many contexts:

➤ Presence of hazardous substances on the premises

➤ Discharge, escape, or transportation of hazardous substances away from the premises to areas owned by potential plaintiffs or where potential plaintiffs are affected (e.g., being poisoned by toxic fumes)

➤ Personal injury to a person employed on the premises (involving occupational safety and Workers' Compensation issues)

➤ Personal injury to a user of the premises (e.g., "slip and fall")

➤ Lack of adequate security on the premises, rendering users of the premises vulnerable to crime

➤ Failure to comply with the Americans with Disabilities Act (ADA)—which can lead to private suits or administrative enforcement

➤ Violation of a zoning regulation

➤ Improper use of the premises (e.g., sale of alcoholic beverages to minors; perpetrating or even tolerating the sale of illegal drugs)

Depending on the severity of the incident and who is involved, consequences may range from a small fine to a multimillion-dollar judgment. Property used in connection with illegal activities is subject to forfeiture—even if the owner is not the perpetrator of the crime.

Premises liability risk is frequently shifted through the purchase of insurance. However, as discussed in ¶2515.1, it is likely that environmental premises liability will not be covered by the conventional business insurance policy, although it may be covered by special (and expensive) environmental risks insurance.

[¶3207.1] Environmental Premises Liability

The use or generation of solid waste on the premises may give rise to liability under several federal statutes. Under CERCLA (the "Superfund" law; see ¶2203), business owners have an obligation to report the use of hazardous substances on the premises. As that paragraph discusses, quite a few current or past parties in the chain of ownership or use of the premises may have liability under CERCLA, either directly or by contribution.

In a limited number of cases, an innocent landowner may be exempt from CERCLA liability, if a buyer or seller of contaminated property had no actual knowledge of the contamination, and furthermore if the contamination was not discoverable by a reasonable party exercising due diligence.

Since 1986, CERCLA has contained a Title III, Emergency Planning and Community Right to Know Act (EPCRA). Premises on which potentially hazardous substances are used must notify local agencies (and must respond to queries from the interested public) about the substances used on the premises and the amount of toxic substances routinely emitted each year in a controlled fashion (e.g., vapors exiting a smokestack). The facilities must also develop an emergency plan for coping with unplanned releases. There is a notification procedure in case of such an emergency release.

As discussed in ¶2206, RCRA regulates the on-premises storage of solid waste as well as the transportation of such substances off the premises and their storage or disposal elsewhere. Many non-hazardous substances are covered by RCRA; its reach is not limited to substances conventionally considered polluting or toxic.

Depending on the use of the premises, it may be necessary to obtain a permit for the discharge of pollutants into the air or water. This is, of course, more likely if the premises are used for manufacturing than if they are offices or retail stores.

However, almost any type of older building may contain asbestos, because this material was very commonly used for insulation and fire protection. As a general rule, the mere fact that asbestos is in place on premises does not give rise to liability (although concealing the presence of asbestos may give the buyer a cause of action against the non-disclosing seller). It is probably safe to leave intact asbestos in place, although continued monitoring by a qualified asbestos removal firm is a good idea.

Removing asbestos is an extremely hazardous practice, because asbestos fibers are released into the air and persons on the premises are endangered by breathing these fibers. Asbestos removal must always be done by EPA-certified firms that are bonded and have adequate insurance. Most of the states license asbestos firms and certify workers who handle removal.

It is usually necessary to get a special local building permit to remove asbestos or to undertake any demolition or alteration which has the effect of exposing asbestos. On the federal level, the National Emission Standards for Hazardous Air Pollutants program (NESHAP) requires a notification to be filed with the nearest EPA Regional Office at least 10 days before start of any building work that exposes asbestos.

In general, workers who suffer illness because of asbestos exposure are barred from suing the employer because of Worker's Compensation exclusivity. In some cases, however (especially if the allegation is one of emotional rather than physical injury; if the employer was guilty of outrageous conduct, or perhaps even of negligence), the injured worker will be permitted to sue. In some cases, Worker's Compensation will prevent a damage award to the employee, but will require the employer to pay for continuing medical monitoring of the employee's condition. Of course, Worker's Compensation exclusivity does not bar a suit against the non-employer owner of the property where the allegedly harmful asbestos exposure occurred.

A number of suits have been brought—although few have succeeded—alleging the existence of an actionable "sick building syndrome." The theory is that some buildings contain building materials that off-load toxic vapors, and that the building's ventilation system is inadequate to clear these vapors. The tenant of a "sick building" may be able to sue the landlord for breach of the lease's covenant of quiet enjoyment; fraud damages may be available if there was misrepresentation as to the condition of the premises. The landlord might be liable for latent defects in the premises, provided that the landlord knew or should have known about the latent defect; failed to inform the tenant; and the tenant had no reasonable means of discovering or protecting against the risk.

[¶3207.2] Occupational Safety and Premises Liability

The federal Occupational Safety and Health Act (OSHA), administered by the Occupational Safety and Health Agency—also called OSHA—obligates employers to make routine annual reports of their safety record. If a workplace illness or injury does occur, a report to OSHA must be made within a short time of the incident. However, employers with fewer than 10 employees, and retail, service, and financial industries (deemed non-hazardous) are exempt from OSHA's record-keeping requirements.

Under OSHA's general duty clause, there is an obligation to maintain a safe workplace, where the risk of injury or occupational disease is reduced as much as possible. The CFR contains both general industry standards and special standards for the construction industry. OSHA also includes provisions about the use of

Material Safety Data Sheets (MSDS) to inform workers about the presence of toxic materials on the premises, and how to handle these materials safely. Employees must be given training in working with toxic materials without endangering themselves or accidentally releasing the substances into the outside environment.

[¶3207.3]   Premises Liability for Accidents, Crimes

Although strict liability is imposed in unavoidably dangerous situations (e.g., the use of explosives; much construction work; some uses of electricity), in general the liability standard is the negligence of the owner or operator of the premises. A premises owner or tenant may also be liable for incidents occurring near but not on the premises (e.g., the sidewalk or parking lot). The owner or tenant may also be liable for public or private nuisance—for instance, if vapors are transmitted to nearby areas; if patrons of a bar or restaurant are noisy or disruptive to the public.

In the conventional "slip and fall" accident scenario, there will be liability only if the premises were defective, and the defendant furthermore had both actual or constructive notice of the defect and a reasonable chance to remedy it. For instance, a patron who slips in a pool of water on a store floor can prevail by proving that the water was there for an hour—but not if the spill occurred three seconds before the accident.

If an employee, customer, or other person on or near the premises becomes a crime victim, the business owner or landlord may have liability. If the perpetrator is an employee, then the employer may be liable either if the crime is in the scope of the employee's employment (a very unlikely scenario!) or if the employer was negligent in hiring or supervision of the criminal. If the crime was committed by a third party, premises liability depends on whether the crime was foreseeable or not, and on whether there were reasonable precautions that could have been taken to prevent the crime, but were omitted. Foreseeability, in turn, depends on local conditions—a carjacking is far more predictable in Los Angeles than in Peoria.

— ENDNOTES —

1. *Broadbent v. Broadbent*, 907 P.2d 43 (Ariz.Sup. 11/14/95).

2. *Della Penna v. Toyota Motor Sales U.S.A.*, 11 Cal.4th 376 (Cal.Sup. 10/12/95).

3. *Sacco v. High Country Independent Press Inc.*, 63 LW 2768 (Mont.Sup. 5/19/95).

4. *Chizmar v. Mackie*, 63 LW 2767 (Alaska Sup. 5/19/95).

5. *R.J. v. Humana of Florida, Inc.*, 652 So.2d 360 (Fla.Sup. 3/2/95). Also see *Heiner v. Moretuzzo*, 652 N.E.2d 664 (Ohio Sup. 8/16/96) denying a cause of action for negligent infliction of emotional distress in a false-positive HIV case

where there is no physical "peril." Physical injury is not required, but the plaintiff must either be imperiled or observe someone else's peril.

6. *San Diego Gas & Electric Co. v. Superior Court of Orange County*, 38 Cal.Rptr.2d 811 (Cal.App. 2/28/95).

7. *Pritzlaff v. Archdiocese of Milwaukee*, 533 N.W.2d 780 (Wis.Sup. 6/27/95).

8. *In re Rhone-Poulenc Rorer Inc.*, 63 LW 2579 (7th Cir. 3/16/95).

9. *Marcella v. Brandywine Hospital*, 47 F.3d 618 (3rd Cir. 2/15/95).

10. *Airport Rent-a-Car Inc. v. Prevost Car Inc.*, 650 So.2d 628 (Fla.Sup. 6/15/95).

11. *Power v. Alexandria Physician's Group Ltd.*, 63 LW 2749 (E.D.Va. 5/18/95).

12. *Patton v. TIC United Corp.*, 64 LW 2562 (10th Cir. 2/16/96).

13. *Michael v. Shiley Inc.*, 46 F.3d 1316 (3rd Cir. 2/7/95).

14. *McCratic v. Bristol-Myers Squibb & Co.*, 183 Bank. 113 (N.D.Tex. 6/14/95).

15. *Western Auto Supply Co. v. Savage Arms Inc.*, 43 F.3d 714 (1st Cir. 12/14/94).

16. *Kennedy v. Collagen Corp.*, 67 F.3d 1153 (9th Cir. 10/17/95).

17. *Talbott v. C.R. Bard Inc.*, 63 F.3d 25 (1st Cir. 8/14/95).

18. *Cafazzo v. Central Medical Health Services Inc.*, 668 A.2d 521 (Pa.Sup. 11/28/95).

19. *Bittner v. American Honda Motor Co.*, 533 N.W.2d 476 (Wis.Sup. 6/21/95).

20. *Gregory v. Cincinnati Inc.*, 450 Mich.1 (Mich.Sup. 8/15/95).

21. *Whirlpool Corp. v. Ziebert*, 539 N.W.2d 883 (Wis.Sup. 11/16/95).

22. *Denny v. Ford Motor Co.*, 64 LW 2377 (N.Y.App. 12/5/95).

23. *Bly v. Tri-Continental Industries Inc.*, 663 A.2d 1232 (D.C.App. 8/21/95).

24. *Ayers v. Robinson*, 63 LW 2763 (N.D.Ill. 5/23/95).

25. *Miller v. Kirk*, 905 P.2d 194 (N.M.Sup. 10/17/95).

— FOR FURTHER REFERENCE —

Bernstein, Anita, "How Can a Product Be Liable?" 19 *Trial Diplomacy J.* 27 (January-February '96).

Conley, Cole H., "A State Law Theory for Products Liability Claims," 30 *Georgia L.Rev.* 267 (Fall '95).

Fischer, David A., "Causation in Fact in Product Liability Failure to Warn Cases," 17 *J. of Products and Toxics Liability* 271 (Fall '95).

Geistfeld, Mark, "Placing a Price on Pain and Suffering: A Method for Helping Juries Determine Tort Damages for Nonmonetary Injuries," 83 *California L.Rev.* 773 (May '95).

Haig, Robert L. and Steven P. Caley, "Successfully Defending Product Liability Cases," 19 *Trial Diplomacy J.* 27 (January-February '96).

Luntz, Harold, "Fear of Disease as Damage in Negligence," 3 *Torts L.J.* 212 (December '95).

Lutz, Sharon, "Breast Cancer Litigation: When is the Physician Liable?" 31 *Trial* 46 (December '95).

SECURITIES REGULATION

[¶3801] The supplement period has not been a happy one for would-be securities plaintiffs. The trend (both in Congress and in the courts) has been to deny the existence of private rights of action and in general to restrict access to litigation.

P.L. 104-62 and -63 were enacted in 1995 to offer a safe harbor for certain charitable annuities used in estate planning. Charitable income pooled funds, such as those used in connection with charitable remainder trusts, are held not to be investment companies, and are exempt from other securities provisions. Donors are still entitled to disclosure of material terms of the operation of the fund within 90 days of making a donation. Such funds are exempt from all provisions (except anti-fraud) of '33 and '34 Acts.

[¶3801.1] Securities Litigation and Settlement

An early 1996 Supreme Court decision requires a federal court to give full faith and credit to a Delaware court release of class-action '34 Act claims, with respect to parties who failed to either object or opt out.[1]

According to the Second Circuit, you cannot get benefit-of-the-bargain damages under Securities Act §11, but you can get such damages under Exchange Act §10 if the damages can be established with reasonable certainty.[2]

[¶3802] THE SECURITIES ACT OF 1933

Viatical settlement contracts, under which a terminally ill person in effect sells his or her life insurance policy for a percentage of its death benefit, have been held to be "securities" requiring registration because they fit under the definition of "investment contracts" contained in §2(1) of the Securities Act. The contracts do not qualify for the insurance exemption because there is no transfer of risk to an insurer.[3]

The first cautious steps are being taken for the use of the Internet (especially its World Wide Web component) in the issuance and sale of securities. Rules are evolving for making initial public offerings in electronic form; for delivering prospectuses electronically instead of on paper; and for creating a small-scale "securities exchange" for very small stocks that are not available on other exchanges. Of course, it's impossible to have an "intrastate" offering on an electronic system that is accessible throughout the world.[4]

[¶3805] THE SECURITIES EXCHANGE ACT

In 1994, the Supreme Court made it clear that there is no private remedy for "aiding and abetting" a §10(b) violation.[5] Because Connecticut's Uniform Securities

Act is based on §10(b) and Uniform Securities Act §101, there is no state-law cause of action for aiding and abetting, either.[6]

Early in 1995, the Supreme Court limited the application of §12(2) of the Exchange Act (material misrepresentation or omission of fact in a prospectus or oral communication) to public offerings made by an issuer or controlling shareholder. A private secondary sale of substantially all of a close corporation's stock was not covered. Statements in the contract of sale—whether true or false—do not constitute a "prospectus."[7]

In mid-1995, the Supreme Court struck down[8] §27A of the '34 Act (which, in turn, was enacted to revive suits barred under the 1991 *Lampf Pleva* decision).[9] The Supreme Court, which could hardly have been expected to like Congress' attempt to overturn its ruling, held that the statute violates the separation of powers doctrine because it makes the federal courts re-open final judgments that were entered before the enactment of §27A.

There is no private right of action for injunctive relief under §13(a) of the '34 Act, so a shareholder cannot use this provision to sue to compel a corporation and its officers to file quarterly and annual reports.[10]

Early in 1996, the Second Circuit ruled that 10b-5's disclosure requirement was satisfied by a statement that market share was an important consideration in business strategy. The issuing corporation did not omit material fact by not disclosing that it intended to cut prices (a departure from its usual price-hike strategy).[11]

The Fourth Circuit did not permit use of the misappropriation theory (improper use of material non-public information secured by breach of fiduciary duty) in a 10(b) action. The rationale is that a 10(b) action is premised on deception of a market participant. Although misappropriation involves deception, it seldom involves misrepresentation or nondisclosure.[12]

A lender who finances an LBO but does not control everyday operations or management policies is not an Exchange Act §20(a) "controlling person," and thus is not liable under 10b-5 if the LBO borrower is guilty of fraud.[13]

[¶3805.1] Regulation of Broker-Dealers

Defining the scope of securities arbitration remained a vital question during the supplement period.

Punitive damages can be awarded under an arbitration agreement that incorporates an SRO's rules by reference, and if the rules permit punitive damages. The Supreme Court held this even if the arbitration agreement also contains a choice of law provision calling for submission to the law of a state which does not permit arbitral punitive damages.[14]

Speaking of choice of law, Federal Arbitration Act (FAA) §4 allows a petition to compel arbitration in any district, with arbitration to be held in that district. However, according to the Seventh Circuit, §4 does not overrule the arbitration agreement's forum selection clause. Nor may the District Court where the petition was filed enjoin arbitration in the district which is proper under the arbitration agreement.[15]

The arbitrator, and not a federal court, determines if an investor's claims against a securities brokerage are timely.[16] The Fifth Circuit's view is that this is a question of procedural arbitrability and not a substantive eligibility requirement that a court must determine before the brokerage must submit to arbitration.

Securities firm employees who sign the U-4, the standard employment agreement, cannot be compelled to arbitrate their Title VII claims instead of litigating them. The U-4's arbitration clause requires arbitration of disputes that are arbitrable under Self-Regulatory Organization rules, but the SRO (in this case, the NASD) did not specifically mandate arbitration of employment discrimination claims; so employees did not make a knowing waiver of the right to bring discrimination suits.[17]

Class arbitration cannot be ordered unless the underlying agreement specifically permits it; FAA §4 calls for enforcement of the arbitration agreement in accordance with its terms.[18] Nor can expedited arbitration be compelled under either state law or the FAA unless expedited arbitration is specifically mentioned in the arbitration agreement.[19]

[¶3805.2] Regulation of the Proxy Process

The Second Circuit permits an attorneys' fee award to shareholders who win a Rule 14a-8 action and mandate inclusion of their proposal in the proxy statement—even if, when the vote is held, the proposal is defeated overwhelmingly. The court found that a common benefit was created because the shareholders at least got the chance to exercise their franchise by considering (and rejecting) the proposal.[20]

If a proxy statement includes discussion of the history of a merger at all, it is incomplete if it fails to disclose that a bid even higher than the accepted bid was made earlier but rejected by the Board of Directors.[21]

[¶3805.3] Williams Act Disclosure (Tender Offers)

Section 14(d)(7) of the '34 Act requires a bidder who raises a bid to pay the increased amount to all shareholders who tender. The Ninth Circuit says that tendering shareholders who do not get the increased amount have an implied private right of action.[22]

[¶3808] PRIVATE SECURITIES LITIGATION REFORM ACT OF 1995

This statute, P.L. 104-67, was vetoed by President Clinton on December 19, 1995, but re-passed over his veto on December 22, 1995. The PSLR adds a new §27, "Private Securities Litigation," to 15 U.S.C. §77a et.seq. (the Securities Act of 1933) and also amends §21 of the Exchange Act of 1934. The legislation's objective is to discourage frivolous securities litigation and provide a safe harbor for "forward-looking statements" such as earnings projections that do not pan out.

The bulk of the statute deals with securities class actions. (These provisions are effective for actions commenced on or after December 22, 1995.) The party with the greatest financial interest in the proposed relief is rebuttably presumed to be the "most adequate plaintiff" who must lead the class action. The court hearing the class action must approve the most adequate plaintiff's selection of counsel for the class.

Within 20 days of the filing of the complaint, the plaintiff who files the complaint must notify class members using a wire service or "widely circulated business publication." The legislative history shows that electronic means, such as e-mail, are acceptable forms of notice. The court then designates the most adequate plaintiff within 90 days of the publication of this notice.

Liability of multiple defendants is proportionate, not joint and several; Congress was concerned about the pressure on defendants with no or minimal culpability to settle strike suits to avoid the specter of being liable for the full amount of a massive judgment.

The PSLR Act states that there is no express private right of action against those who aid or abet securities law violations; this complements the 1994 Supreme Court decision in *Central Bank of Denver v. First Interstate Bank*, discussed above, that there is no implied private right of action under 10b-5 for aiding and abetting. Nor can securities fraud serve as a predicate offense for civil RICO claims; and no one—even the SEC—can bring a conspiracy case against a trader who allegedly participated in a market manipulation scheme.[23]

The 1995 legislation resolves the question of "loss causation" by requiring plaintiffs to demonstrate that the misstatements or omissions alleged in the complaint—and not market conditions—caused their damages. New pleading requirements are imposed. Fraud plaintiffs must specify each statement alleged to be misleading, why it is misleading, plus facts giving rise to a strong inference that the defendant acted with the requisite state of mind to constitute fraud.

Unless exceptional circumstances (e.g., terminal illness of a vital witness), discovery will be stayed pending the ruling on a motion to dismiss. Of course, a motion to dismiss will be filed in nearly every case, so plaintiffs' ability to achieve discovery during the interim period is eliminated.

The PSLR Act retains the one-year/three year statute of limitations provided by *Lampf Pleva*.

If the court deems a securities suit to be abusive, the plaintiff class can be ordered to pay reasonable attorneys' fees of the defendant(s). In a securities class action, the plaintiff class—or their attorneys—can be required to provide undertakings for payment of these attorneys' fees. On the other hand, fees to be recovered by attorneys for prevailing plaintiffs are limited to a reasonable percentage of the damages and prejudgment interest actually paid to the plaintiffs. Funds disgorged in an SEC suit or administrative action are not considered part of the fund generated by the private suit, and therefore do not affect the plaintiffs' attorneys' fees.

[¶3808.1] Safe Harbor

There is a safe harbor for oral or written forward-looking statements. Such statements are not actionable unless they are material (bearing in mind that plaintiffs must show loss causation to prevail). Nor are statements actionable if they are accompanied by "meaningful cautionary statements" about the factors that could prevent the predictions from coming true. Finally, there is no liability unless the plaintiff can prove that the maker of the statement had actual knowledge that it was false or misleading. If the statement was made by a corporation or other entity, the standard is whether the statement was made by or with the approval of an executive officer of the entity who knew the statement to be false or misleading.

— ENDNOTES —

1. *Matsushita Electric Industrial Co. v. Epstein*, #94-1809, 116 S.Ct. 873, *reversing and remanding* 50 F.3d 644.

2. *McMahan & Co. v. Wherehouse Entertainment*, 64 F.3d 1044 (2nd Cir. 9/13/95).

3. *SEC v. Life Partners Inc.*, 898 F.Supp. 14 (D.D.C. 8/30/95).

4. See Bradford P. Weirick, "Securities Law," *Nat.L.J.* 5/6/96 p. B5; Michael Selz, "Small Stock Issuers Find a New Market on the Internet," *Wall St. J.* 5/14/96 p. B2.

5. *Central Bank of Denver v. First Interstate Bank of Denver*, #92-854, 114 S.Ct. 1439, 128 L.Ed.2d 119 (Sup. Ct. 1994); *on remand, First Interstate Bank of Denver v. DBLKM Inc.*, 28 F.3d 112.

6. *Connecticut National Bank v. Giacomi*, 233 Conn. 304, 659 A.2d 1166 (Sup. 5/30/95).

7. *Gustafson v. Alloyd Co.*, #94-404, 115 S.Ct. 1061, 131 L.Ed.2d 21 (Sup.Ct. 2/28/95), *on remand* 53 F.3d 333.

8. *Plaut v. Spendthrift Farm*, #93-1121, 115 S.Ct. 1447, 131 L.Ed.2d 328 (Sup.Ct. 4/18/95).

9. *Lampf Pleva Lipkind Prupis & Petigrow v. Gilbertson*, 501 U.S. 350 (1991).

10. *Gray v. Furia Organization Inc.*, 896 F.Supp. 144 (S.D.N.Y. 8/22/95).

11. *San Leandro Emergency Medical Group Profit Sharing Plan v. Philip Morris Co.*, 64 LW 2473 (2nd Cir. 1/25/96). Maybe it serves them right for investing in a cigarette company anyway.

12. *U.S. v. Bryan*, 58 F.3d 933 (4th Cir. 6/27/95).

13. *Paracor Finance Inc. v. G.E. Capital Corp.*, 64 LW 2593 (9th Cir. 3/13/96).

14. *Mastrobuono v. Shearson Lehman Hutton Inc.*, #94-18, 115 S.Ct. 1212, 131 L.Ed.2d 76 (Sup.Ct. 3/6/95), *on remand* 54 F.3d 779.

15. *Merrill Lynch v. Lauer*, 49 F.3d 323 (7th Cir. 3/1/95).

16. *Smith Barney v. Boone*, 47 F.3d 750 (5th Cir. 3/20/95).

17. *Prudential Insurance Co. v. Lai*, 42 F.3d 1299 (9th Cir. 12/20/94).

18. *Champ v. Siegel Trading Co.*, 55 F.3d 269 (7th Cir. 5/18/95).

19. *Salvano v. Merrill Lynch*, 647 N.E.2d 1298 (N.Y.App. 2/21/95).

20. *Amalgamated Clothing and Textile Workers Union v. Wal-Mart Stores*, 54 F.3d 69 (2nd Cir. 4/20/95).

21. *Arnold v. Society for Savings Bancorp Inc.*, 650 A.2d 1270 (Del.Sup. 12/28/94).

22. *Epstein v. MCA Inc.*, 50 F.3d 644 (9th Cir. 2/27/95).

23. *SEC v. U.S. Environmental Inc.*, 897 F.Supp. 117 (S.D.N.Y. 8/24/95).

— FOR FURTHER REFERENCE —

Bloomenthal, Harold S., "The Private Securities Litigation Reform Act: How Safe is the Safe Harbor?" 18 *Securities and Federal Corporate Law Report* 89 (January '96).

Jaconette, James I., "The Fraud-on-the-Market Theory in State Law Securities Fraud Suits," 46 *Hastings L.J.* 1967 (August '95).

Karmel, Roberta S., "Is the Shingle Theory Dead?" 52 *Washington & Lee L.Rev.*1271 (Fall '95).

O'Mullen, Michael P., "Seeking Consistency in Judicial Review of Securities Arbitration," 64 *Fordham L.Rev.* 1122 (December '95).

Robertson, Robert A., "Personal Investing in Cyberspace and the Federal Securities Laws," 23 *Securities Regulation L.J.* 347 (Winter '96).

Schulz, David B., "Indemnification of Directors and Officers Against Liabilities Under Federal Securities Laws," 78 *Marquette L.Rev. 1043* (Summer '95).

Simkin, Morris N., "MD&A: When to Include Forward-Looking Statements," *N.Y.L.J.* 5/16/96 p. 5.

Steinberg, Marc I., "Securities Litigation Developments: The 'Bespeaks Caution' Doctrine and Related Defenses," 23 *Securities Regulation L.J.* 447 (Winter '96).

Weirick, Bradford P., "Securities Law" [Internet offerings] *Nat.L.J.* 5/6/96 p. B5.

Welle, Elaine E., "Limited Liability Company Interests as Securities," 31 *Land and Water L.Rev.* 153 (Winter '96).

TAX ENFORCEMENT

[¶4101] In late 1995, Congress was engaged in creating a budget package that would reconcile two seemingly contradictory objectives: eliminating the deficit and reducing taxes. Perhaps because of this difficult balancing act, 1995 came and went without a budget, with various stopgap measures being passed to keep the federal government from shutting down.

Thus, although it was anticipated that taxpayers (especially middle and upper-income taxpayers) would receive relief, such as a preferential tax rate for capital gains and an increased unified gift/estate tax credit, there was no major legislative development in 1995. (A budget bill was passed in the spring of 1996, but major measures dealing with government entitlements and tax relief were deferred until the fall.)

The IRS did announce[1] that non-binding mediation could be used to assist the settlement of issues in some cases within the Appeals administrative process, as long as the case had not been docketed in any court. The procedure is optional; the mediator's role is to facilitate settlement between the taxpayer and the IRS Appeals personnel.

However, taxpayer rights suffered a blow in the Fifth Circuit.[2] This case holds that a Federal Tort Claims Act suit cannot be brought against the IRS for releasing confidential taxpayer information about the plaintiff in violation of Code §6103. The rationale is that the IRS' press releases about the taxpayer's conviction for filing a fraudulent tax return were not actionable under Texas tort law as either invasion of privacy or negligence per se.

The Fifth Circuit said that although the FTCA does waive sovereign immunity, it does so only if a private person would be liable for the same conduct under state law. Texas does have a tort of disclosure of embarrassing private information, but the facts disclosed in this case, to the extent they were non-public, were not deemed embarrassing by the court.

In the supplement period, both the Ninth and Eleventh Circuits examined the position of the "responsible person" who is accused (under Code §6672) of failure to collect and remit employment tax. The "responsible person" penalty has been held to be penal in nature, rather than a revenue measure. Thus, the payor cannot deduct it, whether as a non-business bad debt or under any other theory.[3] The standard as to whether nonpayment was "willful" is reckless disregard for the obligation to pay the tax.[4] In this context, use of a jury instruction drawn from an instruction on gross negligence is acceptable, because gross negligence is more serious than simple negligence and therefore does not permit the jury to convict on too low a showing.

The distinction between punitive and revenue measures arose in another context: civil fraud penalties assessed on unreported narcotics income. According to the Fourth Circuit, this addition to tax is imposed to secure revenue, not as punishment, and therefore imposing the civil fraud penalty is neither an excessive fine forbidden by the Eighth Amendment, nor does criminal prosecution for the narcotics abuse constitute double jeopardy.[5]

Interest imposed on an income tax deficiency is a non-deductible personal expense; a business expense deduction is unavailable.[6]

Even though the tax shelter limited partnerships in question were not distributed to a divorced woman, she was held not to qualify for innocent spouse relief because she benefited from her ex-husband's tax shelters by receiving property in excess of normal support she would otherwise have received[7]—but innocent spouse relief was allowed in another tax shelter case based on reliance on the spouse who purchased the tax shelters, the accountant, and the financial adviser.[8]

The IRS is not obligated to follow its "John Doe" summons procedure (requiring court authorization) if the lawyer, rather than the client, is the target of investigation. Thus, the IRS can serve the lawyer with a summons to learn the names of clients that were omitted from Form 8300 [reporting of large cash transactions]. The identity of clients, and the nature of their fee agreements, is not generally privileged.[9]

[¶4101.1] Bankruptcy and Tax Enforcement

Another aspect of the §6672 penalty on the "responsible person" was explored by *Bronson v. U.S.*,[10] which treats imposing the penalty contrary to the automatic stay as merely voidable, not void. Thus, the taxpayer must pay unless action is taken within the bankruptcy proceeding to void the assessment.

The Tenth Circuit says that res judicata will not be applied to keep the IRS from presenting additional claims for taxes in a year in which the bankruptcy court has already determined an amount of taxes. Although this might seem to impair the debtor's chance at a fresh start, that's the way the court reads the rules.

The taxpayer was not entitled to equitable estoppel, because the IRS did not affirmatively mislead him (the court considers the possibility of estoppel against the federal government to be an open question in any event). In this reading, the IRS was not guilty of misconduct in failing to inform the debtor that further claims might be made; a reasonable debtor would assume that collection of all non-dischargeable taxes would be sought.[11]

Under Bankruptcy Code §523(a)(1)(C), willful attempts to evade or defeat claims (e.g., taxes) are not dischargeable. However, evasion is worse than simple non-payment. (Non-payment would include a situation in which limited funds are used to pay other debts.) The mere fact that the taxpayer knew that the taxes were not paid is not enough to constitute willful evasion.[12] In contrast, if the taxpayer has hidden income or assets or failed to file a return, the mere fact that simple non-payment of taxes is not a felony will not make the tax debt dischargeable in bankruptcy.[13] What does constitute willful evasion of tax as defined by Code §7201? According to the Ninth Circuit, filing a sham bankruptcy petition to release an IRS levy on wages falls into this category.[14]

The personal property of a Chapter 13 debtor is immune from administrative levies under Code §6334, but is not thereby exempt from federal tax liens imposed under §6321 for neglect or refusal to pay income tax after a demand has been made.[15]

Both federal and state taxes on income that the debtor earned or accrued pre-petition, but that were payable after the petition, are treated as "allowed unsecured claims" (with seventh priority in bankruptcy)—they do not qualify for first priority as administrative expenses.[16]

[¶4104.3] Statute of Limitations Questions

In early 1996, the U.S. Supreme Court denied the taxpayers a refund of over-withheld taxes because they did not file a return for the year in question. If no return is filed, there is no three-year lookback period to determine the earliest year for which a refund is available, and thus the default period of two years from the date of the mailing of the deficiency notice applies.[17]

Temporary and Proposed Regulations issued January 4, 1996 say that taxpayers need not pay in full when they request an automatic extension, but penalties and interest will still be due if the return proves to have a balance due when it is filed under the extension.[18]

The automatic stay does not apply to partners, guarantors, sureties, and insurers of the bankruptcy debtor,[19] but Code §6503(h), which suspends the statute of limitations during the taxpayer's bankruptcy, also suspends running of the statute of limitations against such derivatively liable parties, such as partners of a bankrupt partnership. Derivative parties who could take advantage of the statute of limitations when suit against the primary party is time-barred remain liable if the main suit can be revived.[20]

Several cases[21] permit the IRS to assert its priority claim in a Chapter 7 case, even if the assertion is untimely. In early 1995, the Sixth Circuit refused to extend this permission to Chapter 13 cases, finding that only timely-filed IRS claims can be allowed. The rationale is that Chapter 7 is a liquidating process, where creditors must wait for payment of claims, including late-filed claims. In contrast, the Chapter 13 debtor retains his or her assets and makes periodic payments to creditors.[22]

IRS' Form 872-A, the extension of time to assess tax, is a waiver of the statute of limitations, not a contract that terminates automatically 60 days after the taxpayer's bankruptcy filing.[23]

[¶4113] THE REFUND ROUTE

If the IRS seizes a third party's property to satisfy someone else's tax debt (e.g., if the property belongs to a creditor of a taxpayer who fails to pay payroll taxes), the third party is entitled to make both a refund claim and a wrongful levy claim. However, in a mid-1995 Ninth Circuit case, the plaintiff creditor failed to file the wrongful levy suit on time (the statute of limitations is nine months, which can be extended to 12 months). The request for release of levy must be sent to the IRS office that imposed the levy—not to the office where the third party pays its taxes.[24]

Webb v. U.S.[25] refuses equitable tolling of the §6511 statute of limitations. Thus, taxpayers whose financial adviser stole their money and compounded insult with injury by paying gift tax on this "gift" to himself with the taxpayers' money were unable to get a refund for gift tax paid more than two years before the filing of the refund claim. In contrast, the Ninth Circuit did allow equitable tolling (for mental incapacity) under §6511 in a case where a "senile" taxpayer sent the IRS a check for $7,000 instead of the appropriate $700.[26]

Although, in general, the IRS will comply with directions from a taxpayer, Code §6402(a) nonetheless gives the agency discretion to apply an overpayment to "any liability" of the taxpayer, including tax liability for a year other than that designated by the taxpayer.[27] If there are both underpayments and overpayments, each bearing a different interest rate, the two payments will only be netted if the IRS chooses to exercise its discretion under §6402(a) to credit the taxpayer's overpayment against the outstanding liability.[28]

[¶4119] TAX LIENS

In mid-1995, the Supreme Court decided that a party who makes a payment under protest of tax assessed against someone else (for the purpose of removing a tax lien from the property) can sue in federal District Court under 28 USC §1346(a)(1)—a civil action for the recovery of tax allegedly erroneously or illegally assessed or collected.[29] (The plaintiff was an ex-wife who received the family home in conjunction with a divorce; the lien covered all of the husband's property for taxes the wife was not liable on.)

The Supreme Court read the statute to give standing to any taxpayer, not merely the person against whom the tax was assessed (the IRS interpretation). As the Supreme Court pointed out, it is unlikely that the IRS will be assailed by hordes of volunteers who pay other people's taxes and then bedevil the IRS for removal of liens.

On a related issue, the Eighth Circuit decided that a house awarded entirely to a divorcing wife no longer belonged to the husband and thus could not be subject to IRS' §6321 lien on all his property.[30]

The Second Circuit permitted the IRS to levy on the bank accounts of a hospital's general partners when the hospital's payroll taxes went unpaid—even though the IRS did not provide written notice of seizure. The agency did send notice of levy which, when read in conjunction with the hospital's monthly bank statements, should have apprised the partners of the levy on the account.[31]

In 1996, the IRS announced that some parts of the Taxpayer Bill of Rights 2 initiative (which were included in the Revenue Reconciliation Act of 1995 that failed to pass) will nevertheless be implemented by the agency. For instance, the taxpayer ombudsman has the power to order the IRS to make an immediate hardship refund.

Effective April 1, 1996, taxpayers who are the target of proposed IRS liens, levies, or seizures will be issued copies of Publication 1660 explaining their appeal rights. The IRS can notify each spouse of collection activities against the other spouse (balancing a potential loss of privacy against protecting the rights of a possibly innocent spouse).[32]

ERISA contains an anti-alienation provision that generally prevents anticipation of a pension. However, a Sixth Circuit case from early 1996 permits garnishment of a vested plan interest to meet an IRS judgment. The anti-alienation provision contains language exempting federal tax levies and judgments, and the paramount federal interest in tax compliance means that the garnishment rules cannot be deemed arbitrary or capricious.[33]

— ENDNOTES —

1. Announcement 95-86, 1995-44 IRB 27.
2. *Johnson v. Sawyer*, 47 F.3d 716 (5th Cir. 3/16/95).
3. *Duncan v. C.I.R.*, 68 F.3d 315 (9th Cir. 10/12/95).
4. *Phillips v. IRS*, 64 LW 2445 (9th Cir. 1/10/96).
5. *Thomas v. C.I.R.*, 62 F.3d 97 (4th Cir. 8/14/95).
6. *Miller v. C.I.R.*, 65 F.3d 687 (9th Cir. 9/7/95).
7. *Stiteler*, T.C. Memo 1995-279 (6/21/95).
8. *Friedman v. C.I.R.*, 53 F.3d 523 (2nd Cir. 1995).
9. *U.S. v. Blackman*, 72 F.3d 1418 (9th Cir. 12/29/95).
10. 46 F.3d 1573 (Fed.Cir. 1/26/95).
11. *De Paolo v. U.S.*, 45 F.3d 373 (10th Cir. 1/9/95).
12. *Haas v. IRS*, 48 F.3d 1153 (11th Cir. 3/30/95).
13. *Bruner v. U.S.*, 55 F.3d 195 (5th Cir. 6/21/95).
14. *U.S. v. Huebner*, 48 F.3d 376 (9th Cir. 12/16/94).
15. *In re Voelker*, 42 F.3d 1050 (7th Cir. 12/12/94).
16. *Towers v. IRS*, 64 F.3d 1292 (9th Cir. 8/23/95) [federal]; *Missouri Dep't of Revenue v. L.J. O'Neill Shoe Co.*, 64 F.3d 1146 (8th Cir. 8/30/95) [state].
17. *Lundy v. C.I.R.*, #94-1785, 64 LW 4061 (S.Ct. 1/17/96), *reversing* 45 F.3d 856 (4th Cir. 1995).
18. IRS Announcement 96-5, 1996-4 IRB 99.
19. *National Tax Credit Partners v. Havlik*, 20 F.3d 705 (7th Cir. 1994).
20. *U.S. v. Wright*, 57 F.3d 561 (7th Cir. 6/14/95).
21. See, e.g., *In re Vecchio*, 20 F.3d 555 (2d Cir. 1994); *In re Pacific Atlantic Trading Co.*, 33 F.3d 1064 (9th Cir. 1994).
22. *U.S. v. Chavis*, 47 F.3d 818 (6th Cir. 2/23/95).

23. *Bilski v. C.I.R.*, 69 F.3d 64 (5th Cir. 11/20/95).

24. *WWSM Investors*, 75 AFTR2d ¶95-935 (9th Cir. 5/31/95).

25. 66 F.3d 691 (4th Cir. 10/2/95).

26. *Brockamp v. U.S.*, 67 F.3d 260 (9th Cir. 10/5/95).

27. *U.S. v. Ryan*, 64 F.3d 1516 (11th Cir. 9/26/95).

28. *Northern States Power Co. v. U.S.*, 64 LW 2430 (8th Cir. 1/2/96). Also see Rev.Proc. 95-17, 1995-1 C.B. 556, new uniform interest tables for overpayments and underpayments. The tables apply to calculations made after 12/31/94.

29. *U.S. v. Williams*, #94-395, 115 S.Ct. 1611, 131 L.Ed.2d 608 (Sup.Ct. 4/25/95).

30. *Thomson v. U.S.*, 66 F.3d 160 (8th Cir. 9/19/95).

31. *Kaggen v. IRS*, 57 F.3d 163 (2nd Cir. 11/29/95).

32. IRS Announcement 96-5, 1996-4 IRB 99.

33. *U.S. v. Sawaf*, 64 LW 2475 (6th Cir. 1/26/96).

— FOR FURTHER REFERENCE —

Brager, Dennis N., "IRS Guidelines for Installment Payment Agreements," 19 *Los Angeles Lawyer* 15 (March '96).

Donmayer, Ryan J., "IRS Issues: Private Collectors, Economic Reality, Ombudsman," 70 *Tax Notes* 501 (1/29/96).

Gardner, John C. and Susan L. Willey, "The Tax Practitioner's Guide to Circular 230," 26 *Tax Adviser* 711 (December '95).

Gideon, Kenneth W., "Use, Abuse, and Anti-Abuse," 73 *Taxes: The Tax Magazine* 637 (December '95).

Hahn, William W., "The Scope of Transferee Liability in Estate and Gift Tax Cases," 74 *Taxes: The Tax Magazine* 72 (January '96).

Johnson, Steve R., "Fog, Fairness and the Federal Fisc," 60 *Missouri L.Rev.* 839 (Fall '95).

Lynch, Michael, "Late Filing Penalties," 181 *J. of Accountancy* 29 (March '96).

Raby, William M. and Burgess J.W. Raby, "Proper Mailing of IRS Notices," 70 *Tax Notes* 995 (2/19/96).

Sheppard, Lee A., "Bankruptcy Tax Policy: How Far Should Equitable Subordination Go?" 69 *Tax Notes* 1317 (12/11/95).

Williford, Jerry S., "IRS' Real Estate Industry Handbooks for Examining Agents," 23 *J. of Real Estate Taxation* 208 (Spring '96).

TAX PLANNING

[¶4201] In mid-1995, the Supreme Court ruled that damages awarded under the Age Discrimination in Employment Act constitute taxable income, because they are not awarded for personal injury, nor are they sufficiently similar to tort damages to be excluded from income.[1]

Similarly, the Fifth Circuit decided that punitive damages received in a state-law malicious prosecution case are includible in gross income because they are imposed to punish the defendant rather than to make the plaintiff whole. Thus, they are not really damages for "personal injury."[2] Certiorari has been granted in a Tenth Circuit case including punitive damages ordered in a wrongful death case in income.[3]

On a related issue, the Tenth Circuit also decided that a statutory grant of prejudgment interest does not represent personal injury damages, and thus the interest must be included in taxable income.[4]

In P.L. 104-7, the Deduction for Health Insurance Costs of Self-Employed Individuals Act (4/11/95), Code §162(l)(1) has been amended to make the health insurance deduction permanent (for tax years beginning after 12/31/93). For taxable years beginning after 12/31/94, the deduction is increased from 25% to 30% of the amount paid by the self-employed to purchase their own health insurance.

The so-called "mailbox rule"—the rebuttable presumption that materials placed in a mailbox with proper address and stamp must have been delivered—has been held by the Sixth Circuit not to apply to regular mail sent to the IRS. In order to establish a date on which delivery can be presumed, the taxpayer must use registered mail.[5]

Defined-benefit plan actuaries are entitled to use conservative actuarial assumptions, thus requiring the corporation to contribute more to the plan but also increasing the tax deduction. In the Ninth Circuit's reading, actuaries have a greater duty to prevent plan underfunding (which could imperil payment of plan benefits) than to restrict the corporation's tax deduction.[6]

In 1995 and the early part of 1996, the IRS issued numerous rulings about electronic tax filing. It should be noted that anyone who must issue 250 or more W-2 forms is obligated to make the filing on magnetic media, unless a waiver for undue hardship is obtained. The IRS ruled on the correct method of filing various forms electronically (1040 series; 940, 941, 945) and via on-line services, as well as the requirements for developing substitutes for conventional paper tax forms and getting them approved for filing.[7]

[¶4204] TAX FEATURES OF PARTNERSHIP OPERATION

Final Regulations under §1.704-3 have been promulgated for allocating built-in gain and loss on property contributed to partnerships,[8] and anti-abuse regulations allow the IRS to recast transactions involving a partnership to prevent abusive tax planning.[9]

The Tenth Circuit permitted a law firm partner a §162 deduction for litigation costs (e.g., filing fees, travel expenses, fees of medical consultants) that the firm paid under its "gross fee" contingency arrangements with clients. Local bar rule (but not local statute) bars firms from paying (rather than merely advancing for future repayment) costs. The court said that unethical, but not illegal, expenses can qualify for a deduction.[10]

[¶4207] TAX FEATURES OF S CORPORATIONS

According to the Ninth Circuit, pass-through income received from an S Corporation does not constitute "net earnings from self-employment" that can be used to calculate a Keogh plan deduction.[11]

[¶4207.9] Built-In Gains

At the end of 1994, Final §1374 Regulations were promulgated for calculating the built-in gain when a C Corporation is converted to S Corporation status.[12]

[¶4211] LIMITED LIABILITY COMPANIES

In general, neither gain nor loss is recognized to the partners if a general partnership is converted to an LLC; a parallel is drawn between conversion to an LLC and conversion to a limited partnership, which is also generally a tax-free event.[13]

[¶4212] CUSHIONING PERSONAL AND BUSINESS LOSSES

It is no longer necessary to attach an information statement to the tax return to claim a loss on §1244 stock.[14]

The Third Circuit ruled out one attempt to cushion a loss. A corporation was fined $13.2 million because of inappropriate disposition of the toxic pesticide kepone. The corporation contributed $8 million to an environmental fund to reduce the environmental impact of the pesticide, with the result that the fine was reduced to $5 million. The Third Circuit denied a deduction, because §162(f) makes fines and penalties paid to the government non-deductible—and, by extension, amounts paid at the direction of the government are likewise nondeductible.[15]

Another unsuccessful attempt was parried by the Tax Court, when a lawyer who misappropriated client funds but made restitution before charges were filed attempted to treat the misappropriations as loans. Instead, he was required to report income for the year of the misappropriation, balanced by a miscellaneous itemized deduction, not used in calculating AMT, in the year of repayment.[16]

[¶4213] ACCOUNTING METHODS AND TAXABLE YEARS

Final Regulations have been issued under §1.446-1, permitting the IRS to impose a cut-off method when a taxpayer changes accounting methods.[17]

[¶4224] PLANNING FOR CAPITAL TRANSACTIONS

A mid-1995 Tax Court case compels capitalization of defense costs of a class action brought by minority shareholders alleging that a merger breached the board's fiduciary duty.[18]

Spare parts used to repair computers in compliance with service contracts were not inventory, because they were not held primarily for sale to customers. Therefore, according to the Federal Circuit, they could be treated as a depreciable capital asset.[19]

A professional musician's precious 17th century instrument, placed in service during the period 1980-1987, qualifies for ACRS depreciation under §168, whether or not it has a determinable useful life, and even if its value is actually increasing. Property is depreciable merely if it is subject to wear, tear, and exhaustion, even if it is not consumed within the foreseeable future.[20]

Printing costs and investment banking fees incurred in response to an initially hostile takeover attempt (later accepted by the target corporation) must be capitalized, according to the Tax Court.[21] The expenses are not currently deductible under §162 because they do not relate to production of current income or immediate corporate needs, and thus are not "ordinary and necessary." The Tax Court implied that a §165 loss deduction might be available for unsuccessful defensive measures, e.g., an unproductive search for a white knight, but not for measures resisting a transaction that was ultimately consummated.

[¶4227] SHIFTING INCOME IN THE FAMILY

For wages paid after 12/31/94, FICA and FUTA tax and income tax withholding can be done for "nannies" and other household employees on a calendar year rather than a quarterly basis, but W-2 forms must still be compiled and submitted to the employee and the IRS.[22]

— ENDNOTES —

1. *C.I.R. v. Schleier*, #94-500, 115 S.Ct. 2159 (Sup.Ct. 6/14/95).

2. *Estate of Moore v. C.I.R.*, 53 F.3d 712 (5th Cir. 6/2/95). Also see *Wesson v. U.S.*, 48 F.3d 894 (5th Cir. 3/30/95), *C.I.R. v. Miller*, 914 F.2d 586 (4th Cir. 1990), *Reese v. U.S.*, 24 F.3d 228 (Fed.Cir. 1994), and *Hawkins v. U.S.*, 30 F.3d 1077

(9th Cir. 1994), all of which include punitive damages in gross income. On the other hand, *Horton v. C.I.R.*, 33 F.3d 625 (6th Cir. 1994) excludes punitive damages from gross income, but the case involves Kentucky law, which deems punitive damages to be a hybrid between compensatory and punitive motivations. Amounts received in settlement of an ERISA class action against the ex-employer have been included in gross income, on the theory that they, too, are not damages for a tort-type personal injury: *Dotson v. U.S.*, 876 F.Supp. 911 (S.D.Tex. 2/15/95).

3. *O'Gilvie v. U.S.*, 66 F.3d 1550 (10th Cir. 9/19/95), *cert. granted* #95-955, -977, 116 S.Ct. 1316 (3/26/96).

4. *Brabson v. U.S.*, 64 LW 2461 (10th Cir. 1/11/96).

5. *Carroll v. C.I.R.*, 71 F.3d 1228 (6th Cir. 12/26/95).

6. *Citrus Valley Estates Inc. v. C.I.R.*, 49 F.3d 1410 (9th Cir. 3/8/95).

7. Rev.Proc. 95-49, 1995-50 IRB 5; Rev.Proc. 95-16, -17, -18, -20 1995-1 C.B. 525, 556, 657, 668; Rev.Proc. 96-18, 1996-4 IRB 73, Rev.Proc. 96-20, 1994-4 IRB 88.

8. T.D. 8585, 1995-1 C.B. 120 (12/27/94).

9. T.D. 8588, 1995-1 C.B. 109 (12/29/94).

10. *Boccardo v. C.I.R.*, 56 F.3d 1016 (9th Cir. 5/26/95).

11. *Durando v. U.S.*, 70 F.3d 548 (9th Cir. 11/6/95).

12. T.D. 8579, 1995-1 C.B. 170 (12/29/94).

13. Rev.Rul. 95-37, 1995-17 IRB 10.

14. T.D. 8594, 1995-1 C.B. 146 (4/27/95).

15. *Allied-Signal Inc. v. C.I.R.*, 1995 U.S.App. LEXIS 5130 (3rd Cir. 1995).

16. *James O'Hagan*, T.C. Memo 1995-409 (8/22/95).

17. T.D. 8608, 1995-36 IRB 10.

18. *Berry Petroleum Co.*, 104 T.C. No. 30 (5/22/95).

19. *Hewlett-Packard Co. v. U.S.*, 71 F.3d 398 (Fed.Cir. 12/7/95).

20. *Liddle v. C.I.R.*, 65 F.3d 329 (3rd Cir. 9/8/95).

21. *A.E. Staley Mfg. Co.*, 105 T.C. No. 14 (9/11/95).

22. Social Security Domestic Employment Reform Act of 1994, P.L. 103-387, as implemented by IRS Notice 95-18, 1995-1 C.B. 300.

— FOR FURTHER REFERENCE —

Barkin, Ilyse, "New Challenges to Use of the Plain Meaning Rule to Construe the IRC and Regs," 69 *Tax Notes* 1403 (12/11/95).

Botkin, Jeffrey, "A Sec. 179 Deduction Trap," 26 *Tax Adviser* 725 (December '95).

Davis, Richard O., "Interest Cap Rules for Flow-Through Entities and Related Parties," 83 *J. of Taxation* 380 (December '95).

Furchtgott-Roth, Diana, "Abuses of Income Distribution Tables in Tax Policy," 69 *Tax Notes* 1414 (12/11/95).

Harper, John, "Rollover of Gain on Sale of Principal Residence," 26 *Tax Adviser* 716 (December '95).

Kauttner, David J., "Taxable Compensation or Medical Reimbursement?" 27 *Tax Adviser* 13 (January '96).

Klein, Paul E., "Cash and Accrual Accounting: When Can the IRS Require a Change of Method?" 23 *J. of Real Estate Taxation* 161 (Winter '96).

Maynes, Todd F., "Getting Out the Vote: The Use of Voting Rights in Tax Planning," 73 *Taxes: The Tax Magazine* 813 (December '95).

Phelps, Mary Brooke, "Valuation of Closely Held Stock," 26 *Tax Adviser* 723 (December '95).

Sollee, William L. and Paul J. Schneider, "Final Regs. on Eligible Rollover Distributions from Qualified Plans," 84 *J. of Taxation* 54 (January '96).

Wallace, W. Kirk, "Final Treasury Regulations Regarding Publicly Traded Partnerships," 70 *Tax Notes* 211 (1/8/96).

Weitzner, Robert L. and Julian R. Sayre, "Small Business Tax Solutions," 180 *J. of Accountancy* 38 (December '95).

TRUSTS

[¶4301] Special rules are in place for the situation in which a U.S. citizen is survived by a non-citizen spouse. A Qualified Domestic Trust, or QDOT, can be used to minimize the extent to which tax treatment of non-citizen survivors is less favorable than that of citizen surviving spouses. Final Regulations governing QDOTs for decedents dying and gifts made after August 22, 1995 have been promulgated, as have Temporary Regulations to assure that Code §2056A QDOT estate tax actually gets collected.[1]

[¶4306] ESTATE AND GIFT TAXATION OF TRUSTS

The Sixth Circuit has joined the Fifth and Eighth Circuit in permitting a "wait and see" power that permits the executor to determine which property will be subject to the QTIP election at the time of the election itself. The IRS position is that property must satisfy the QTIP definition at the time of the first spouse's death; but the courts say that the election would degenerate into a mere formality if executors were not permitted to select the qualifying property at the time of the election.[2]

In a recent Seventh Circuit case, the wife was the beneficiary of two trusts—the Marital Trust and the Family Trust. Her share of the Family Trust was limited to 5% in any year, and only if the Marital Trust had already been exhausted. The court ruled that the wife had enough dominion to be construed to have a general power of appointment over both trusts. Thus, both trusts were included in her estate to some extent—but only 5% of the Family Trust was included in her estate.[3]

The Fifth Circuit allowed a QTIP, and criticized the Tax Court for including 100% of the proceeds of term life insurance, purchased with community funds, in the insured husband's gross estate. (The uninsured wife predeceased him.) Under Texas community property law, when the husband died, 50% of the proceeds belonged to his wife's residuary trust. The policy (payable to his estate) remained community property even though the husband renewed it after the wife's death; he did not create new, separate policies but only renewed the community property policy.[4]

The marital deduction was not available for trust assets going to the surviving spouse under a settlement agreement that resolved a dispute over the terms of the trust. The agreement gave the surviving spouse a life estate but no power of appointment. Furthermore, the surviving spouse's rights derived from the settlement, and not from a bona fide recognition of her spousal rights; nor did they pass from the decedent. All these factors determined the absence of a qualified terminable interest that would support the marital deduction.[5]

[¶4306.2]   Transfers Taking Effect at Death

Distributions made from a decedent's trust after his death, for completed gifts that are enforceable pre-mortem debts, constitute claims against the trust. As such, they cannot be deducted under §2053 as claims against the decedent's estate. Furthermore, the distributions were includible in the fair market value of the trust under §2038 because the distributions were mandatory, and therefore the decedent relinquished the power to revoke or amend the distributions within three years of death.[6]

— ENDNOTES —

1. T.D. 8612, 8613, 1995-38 IRB 7, 31.

2. *Estate of Spencer v. C.I.R.*, 43 F.3d 226 (6th Cir. 1/5/95); *Estate of Robertson v. Comm'r*, 15 F.3d 779 (8th Cir. 1994); *Estate of Clayton v. Comm'r*, 976 F.2d 1486 (5th Cir. 1992).

3. *Estate of Kurz v. C.I.R.*, 68 F.3d 1027 (7th Cir. 10/30/95).

4. *Estate of Cavenaugh*, 75 AFTR2d 2049 (5th Cir. 1995).

5. *Estate of Carpenter v. C.I.R.*, 52 F.3d 1266 (4th Cir. 1995).

6. *White v. U.S.*, 75 AFTR2d 95-767 (D.Mass. 1995).

— FOR FURTHER REFERENCE —

Horwich, Alan, "Bank Fiduciaries With Material Inside Information: Responsibilities and Risks," 113 *Banking Law J.* 4 (January '96).

Langbein, John H., "The Contractarian Basis of the Law of Trusts," 105 *Yale L.J.* 625 (December '95).

Lundy, Todd S., "Trust and Estate Lawyers: Use Cross-Selling to Your Advantage," 135 *Trusts & Estates* 26 (March '96).

Margolin, Stephen M. and Andrew M. Curtis, "The Flexible Irrevocable Trust," 50 *J.American Society of CLU & ChFC* 44 (January '96).

Schwab, Eileen Caulfield, "Requirements for QDOTs Liberalized in New Regulations," 23 *Estate Planning* 11 (January '96).

Shumaker, Roger L., "The World Wide Web is a Prime Resource for Trust Professionals," 134 *Trusts & Estates* 16 (December '95).

Steinkamp, John G., "Estate and Gift Taxation of Powers of Appointment Limited by Ascertainable Standards," 79 *Marquette L.Rev.* 195 (Fall '95).

Valente, Peter C. and Joann T. Palumbo, "Equitable Deviation from Terms of Trust Instrument," *N.Y.L.J.* 4/30/96 p. 3.

Zaritsky, Howard M., "IRS Loosens Rules on Gifts from Revocable Trusts," 23 *Estate Planning* 48 (January '96).

INDEX

Q

R

S